D1172718

SPLASH!

10,000 YEARS OF SWIMMING

SPLASH!

HOWARD MEANS

 hachette
BOOKS

New York

Hachette Books
Hachette Book Group
1290 Avenue of the Americas, New York, NY 10104
HachetteBooks.com
Twitter.com/HachetteBooks
Instagram.com/HachetteBooks

First Edition: June 2020

Published by Hachette Books, an imprint of Perseus Books, LLC,
a subsidiary of Hachette Book Group, Inc. The Hachette Books
name and logo is a trademark of the Hachette Book Group.

The Hachette Speakers Bureau provides a wide range of authors for speaking events.
To find out more, go to www.hachettespeakersbureau.com or call (866) 376-6591.

The publisher is not responsible for websites (or their
content) that are not owned by the publisher.

Unless otherwise noted, all photos and illustrations are in the public domain.

Print book interior design by Amy Quinn

Library of Congress Cataloging-in-Publication Data
Names: Means, Howard B., author.
Title: Splash!: 10,000 years of swimming / Howard Means.
Description: First edition. | New York : Hachette Books, [2020]
| Includes bibliographical references and index. |
Identifiers: LCCN 2019056316 | ISBN 9780306845666
(hardcover) | ISBN 9780306845642 (ebook)
Subjects: LCSH: Swimming--History. | Olympic
games (Ancient) | Olympics--History.
Classification: LCC GV836.4 .M43 2020 | DDC 797.2/1--dc23
LC record available at https://lccn.loc.gov/2019056316

ISBNs: 978-0-306-84566-6 (hardcover), 978-0-306-84564-2 (ebook)

Printed in the United States of America

LSC-C

10 9 8 7 6 5 4 3 2 1

In memoriam
Jonathan B. London

CONTENTS

Prologue: Once Upon a Time in Egypt . . . 1

1 Gods, Humans, and the Aquatic Ape 13

2 Swimming's Golden Age 27

3 First There Was Swimming; Then There Was None 39

4 Rediscovering a Lost Art 57

5 Swimming 2.0 73

6 A Frog in Every Tub 89

7 Diving in for Dollars and Pounds 107

8 Climb Every Mountain, Swim Every Sea 123

9 The Great Swimming Cover-Up 141

10 An Aussie Wrecking Ball Goes Rogue 157

11 Nylon, WWII, James Bond, and the G-String 171

12 Swimming Together, Swimming Alone 187

13 The Last Taboo 205

14 Growing Pains 223

15 The Fastest Swimmer Ever 239

16 Is Enough Ever Enough? 261

Epilogue: My Watery Life 285

Acknowledgments 293

Sources 295

Index 313

There is an essential rightness about swimming, as about all such flowing and, so to speak, *musical* activities. And then there is the wonder of buoyancy, of being suspended in this thick, transparent medium that supports and embraces us. One can move in water, play with it, in a way that has no analogue in the air. One can explore its dynamics, its flow, this way and that; one can move one's hands like propellers or direct them like little rudders; one can become a little hydroplane or submarine, investigating the physics of flow with one's own body. And, beyond this, there is all the symbolism of swimming—its imaginative resonances, its mythic potentials.

—Oliver Sacks

ONCE UPON A TIME IN EGYPT...

In the desert, you celebrate nothing but water.
—Michael Ondaatje

Swimming conjures many things: fierce competition, recreation, exercise, open water; a chance to cool off, show some skin, or sink below the surface and be all alone. Swimming is both a precise skill—see the Counsilman Center for the Science of Swimming at Indiana University—and a performance art. (Think water ballet and synchronized swimming.) It's wading, splashing, dunking, the dead man's float, Marco Polo, snorkeling, bodysurfing, a poolside or beachside or lakeside summer romance. The near weightlessness of swimming is the closest most of us will ever get to zero-gravity space travel. The terror of being submerged is the nearest some of us ever come to sheer hell.

Whatever swimming means to us individually, though, there's one thing it cannot do without: water. And therein lies a great irony because the most ancient representations of swimming ever found are eight-thousand-year-old pictographs on cave walls in what is now the driest spot on planet Earth.

But maybe that's not such a great irony after all because swimming, like any activity that dates back to the dawn of humankind, is also an index of change: of social mores, of fashion, of how we relate to nature, of religious teachings and superstitions, of sport and how we judge performance, and most notably in this case of climatological change. Which brings us back to the so-called Cave of the Swimmers at Wadi Sura in the Gilf Kebir, in the southwest corner of Egypt, not far from Libya and Sudan.*

The cave and its pictographs had long been known to Bedouin nomads, but they first came to the attention of the West in October 1933 thanks to the desert mapper and explorer László Almásy. The Hungarian-born Almásy was part of a small wave of adventurers who fanned out across the vast, unknown stretches of the eastern Sahara beginning in the late 1920s. In 1926, he motored the 1,350 miles from Cairo to Khartoum, among the earliest efforts to tame the Nile basin by automobile. That trip at least had the advantage of a river to follow, and river towns along the way. Three years later, Almásy ventured by car far more daringly across a long stretch of the Darb el Arbain, following the ancient caravan route from Selima in western Sudan to the southern Egyptian oasis at Karga.

The rugged Gilf Kebir plateau (its name translates as "Great Barrier") was slower to yield its secrets. The plateau is both massive—a sandstone outcropping the size of Puerto Rico, rising nearly a thousand feet above the desert floor—and massively remote. So far as is known, its existence was never mapped until early in the twentieth century when it was "discovered" by two of Egypt's most famous desert explorers: Ahmed Hassanein,

---

* To be exact, 23 degrees, 35 minutes, and 40.99 seconds north of the equator, and 25 degrees, 14 minutes, and 0.6 seconds east of the Prime Meridian.

who would later serve as chamberlain to King Farouk, and Prince Kamal el Dine Hussein, son of the Egyptian sultan Hussein Kamel.[*]

The western side of the plateau was particularly forbidding, unseen by European eyes until the early 1930s when Almásy and a twenty-three-year-old Englishman, Sir Robert Clayton-East-Clayton, the 9th Baronet of Marden, mounted a joint attack. Almásy would lead a fleet of automobiles across the desert, while Clayton handled reconnaissance overhead in his lightweight, single-engine de Havilland Gipsy Moth airplane. Flying low over the plateau, Clayton was able to pick out a promising, nearly hidden valley, but neither he nor Almásy on the ground below could find a way to ascend the abrupt plateau, and with fuel running low for both ground and air explorations, the party gave up and retreated to Cairo.

Robert Clayton would never complete the mission. He died of polio soon after returning to England. In the end, it was Almásy, Patrick Clayton (no relation to the Baronet), and several others who became the first Westerners to enter the valley and explore its caves—the first also to realize that they had stumbled upon a treasure trove of primitive ancient art. To Patrick Clayton goes credit for discovering the so-called Giraffe Rock, rich with paintings of the long-necked mammals. Other caves featured archers, cattle, and female figures. So plentiful were the figures that the site quickly became known as Wadi Sura—roughly, Valley (or Dry Riverbed) of the Pictures.

László Almásy, though, won the big prize, or at least the most inexplicable. In October 1933, he scrambled up some boulders, poked his head inside a previously unexplored cave fourteen meters by eight meters wide, and there, floating effortlessly on the rock wall, were multiple painted figures who gave every indication of being caught midstroke doing some highly relaxed version of the old-fashioned doggy paddle.

Almásy had found the Cave of the Swimmers, but the swimmers themselves posed far more questions than answers. The archers, the

---

[*] Hassanein was a multitalented man. He competed for Egypt in the épée and foil events in the 1920 and 1924 Olympics.

Eight-thousand-year-old pictographs found in the Cave of the Swimmers at Wadi Sura, in the southwest Egyptian desert. *(Roland Unger, altered to black & white)*

cattle, the female and other human figures were basically predictable. As daunting as the Sahara was, it was not uninhabited. Nomads had been crossing the sand for millennia. Ancient caravan routes like the one Almásy had traveled by car in 1929 were well established. Camels by the thousands, herded and wild, could still be found among the dunes and vast empty spaces.

But swimmers? Swimming implied more than ground moisture and sufficient rain to sustain grasses for grazing. Swimmers conjured up water in depth and quantity. The pictographs suggest that the bone-dry riverbeds that crisscrossed the Gilf plateau—Wadi Sura and nine others—had once fed lakes that had not only been swimmable but actually swum.

What did it all mean? László Almásy attempted to provide the answer in a little-read 1934 monograph, in Hungarian; subsequent research and archaeological evidence have backed Almásy in his broad details: The Sahara—the "Great Sand Sea" as it is often called—had been for the better part of many millennia a thoroughly inhabitable and very aquatic place. In some places, maybe in most, it appears to have been a very dangerous place to swim as well.

Recent excavations led by the National Geographic Society at the largest Stone Age graveyard ever found in the Sahara—at Gobero, in Niger's T'en'er'e Desert (the stark "desert within the desert")—revealed skeletal remains of crocodiles, hippos, and Nile perch. The hippos and perch particularly indicate a deep-water lake at the Gobero site: mature Nile perch, which can easily reach six feet and five hundred pounds, are not a fish made for shallow waters, or light fishing tackle either.

Skeletal evidence was also found of elephants, giraffes, hartebeests, warthogs, and pythons at the Gobero site. Similar fossil evidence can be found at Tassili n'Ajjer, the 72,000-square-kilometer plateau in southeast Algeria, where it meets Libya, Niger, and Mali. More important at Tassili are the fifteen thousand plus rock engravings and paintings that first came to Western attention in 1933, the same year Wadi Sura was discovered. Among them are a whole host of animals, including hippopotami, that have been absent from the area for thousands of years.

Wadi Sura hasn't received anything like the same well-funded archaeological attention that has been lavished on Tassili and especially Gobero. But it's on roughly the same latitude, and its pictographs suggest a similar, if less diverse, animal population and a hunter-gatherer human population that learned to take advantage of the water that nature had placed so generously at its doorstep.

Triangulating the evidence from all three sites and many, many others creates a fairly accurate timeline (that is, geological time—within, say, plus or minus a thousand years) of when this Green Sahara flourished.

What's known is that about twelve thousand years ago, the Earth, as it does every now and again, wobbled slightly in its orbit. That was enough to shift the seasonal monsoons we now associate with the Central African jungles slightly northward, bringing fresh rains to the previously parched Sahara. All across North Africa, lakes sprang up in long-dry indentations. The plentiful rains may have also reactivated river systems that date back to the Middle Miocene period, eleven to fifteen million years ago. One radar study posits a 300-kilometer drainage basin, beginning with three tributaries—one originating in the western Gilf Kebir, near Wadi Sura—and ending in the Mediterranean Sea.

Where water arises, fish and birds follow. Animals, too, including human ones. By ten thousand years ago, migrants had shown up in the previously desiccated Sahara in sufficient numbers to leave a discernible record behind them. That's when the towering Kiffian—sometimes six feet or taller—began settling into the Gobero site. Nile perch seem to have been plentiful. The Kiffian hunted them probably from reed boats, using bone-tipped harpoons.

For people accustomed to wild climatological extremes, this must have been a paradise, but not a permanent one. Circa eight thousand years ago, just about the time the swimmer-artists were hard at work at Wadi Sura, long history began to reassert itself. The monsoons once again went south. For a thousand years, the Sahara slowly reverted to its desiccated self, but then the climate gods intervened again. A fresh monsoon uptick, not as strong this time, not as much rain, regreened the desert for another two and a half millennia. Burial sites from this later period still show evidence of deep-water waders—an upper-arm bracelet carved from a hippo tusk, for example—but the fish skeletons that survived are smaller and suggest shallow water: tilapia instead of Nile perch.

And then? Maybe it was just the Earth wobbling yet again, or that plus the effects of grazing livestock and domesticated farming. But the monsoons retreated once more to Central Africa, perhaps for good. Rain in any quantity grew sparse, then all but vanished. The thin ground cover that remained offered little and finally no protection from the relentless sun. Desertification had a force multiplier. Dirt yielded to sand. The sand grew, encompassed, and overwhelmed virtually everything and everywhere, save for a few oases and deeply isolated valleys, and the swimmers on the cave wall at Wadi Sura—a lost tableau of the Green Sahara—entered into a kind of hibernation, not to be seen again by other than nomadic eyes for six thousand years or more.

The Cave of the Swimmers gained fame a quarter century ago because of Michael Ondaatje's novel *The English Patient,* and the subsequent movie of the same name, starring Ralph Fiennes.

Beautifully written, Ondaatje's novel is hard to grab hold of. Time and place seesaw back and forth. Truth is elusive; characters are sometimes intentionally amnesiac. One reviewer called the novel "a poetry of smoke and mirrors." It's every bit of that. László Almásy survives intact in Ondaatje's telling, at least as a person. He's the "English" patient, ironically enough, given his Hungarian roots. Robert Clayton-East-Clayton becomes Geoffrey Clifton. (The blue blood remains, but the baronetcy is gone.) Dorothea, Clayton's new wife in the real world, is transformed in this fictional one into Katharine Clifton, Almásy's lover. (There's irony here, as well. By all accounts, Almásy was gay.)

The timeline has been pushed forward to embrace World War II. Suicide, violent death, hideous wounds sometimes seem to be everywhere. Treachery, too. Clifton fronts as a freelancing aerial photographer but is secretly mapping the desert for British intelligence. Almásy ultimately betrays British secrets to the Germans, as he did in real life.

For the greatest part, the story is set in the near-ruins of an Italian villa, but the Gilf Kebir, the surrounding desert, and the cave and its swimmers are always there in the background. Director Anthony Minghella opens the movie with an unknown hand—Katharine's, we later learn—brush-stroking renderings of the suspended figures on the cave wall and segues from there to an aerial sweep of the surrounding desert, sand wave upon sand wave. He closes it in much the same way. Almásy carries the dead Katharine out of the Cave of the Swimmers and then flies her body over the Great Sand Sea and into the horror that awaits him, before the camera makes a final shift back to now-liberated Italy.

In his novel, Ondaatje also keeps returning to the cave and to the Sahara more broadly. When Almásy falls to earth burning from his plane, the Bedouins make a "boat of sticks" to transport him. They keep him alive because "I had information like a sea in me"—maps of the seafloor they traveled. "These were water people," he writes still later. "Even today caravans look like a river." As with the sea, nothing in the desert is strapped down or permanent. Dunes disappear. Like waves, they are pushed across the desert surface and vanish. People disappear, too—drowned as completely in sand as they might be in water. Maybe most important: "In the desert, you celebrate nothing but water." Exactly what the Cave of the Swimmers ultimately does.

Between the 1992 book (which won the prestigious Booker Prize), the 1996 movie (nine Academy Awards, including Best Picture and Best Director), and the sheer exoticness of the site, Wadi Sura would seem to have been ripe for a tourist invasion, and indeed there has been some tourism and attendant desecration of the cave paintings such as by, for example, splashing water on the cave wall to sharpen the contrast for photographs or chipping off pieces of paintings for take-home souvenirs.

But tourism remains the exception at Wadi Sura, and for good reasons. For starters, there is no infrastructure within hundreds of miles of the Gilf Kebir. Such expeditions as there are commonly leave from Cairo, head to the oasis at Bahariya and then on to the White Desert for a first night of camping. From there, it's a week of hard driving via Land Rovers or their equivalent across the desert, to the Ammonite Scarp, rich in tiny sea fossils (another reminder of the Sahara's ancient wet past), then deep into remote landscapes, and finally—a punishing week or so into

Looking out the mouth of the Cave of the Swimmers. Wadi Sura is the driest spot on Earth. *(Carlos de la Fuente, altered to black & white)*

the trip—through the Aqaba Pass and on to the Gilf Kebir and to Wadi Sura. If you get there at all.

One adventure travel outfit that includes Wadi Sura on its itinerary warns at the outset that given "the realities of travel across the Gilf Kebir . . . it is not possible to guarantee the tour will pan out exactly as described." Sandstorms, mechanical problems, shifting terrains are commonplace. National authorities restrict and open access as the political climate shifts in nearby Libya and Sudan. Since 2010, every expedition must also be accompanied by a police vehicle and armed police officer. "This is a journey of a lifetime," the warning continues, "for the true desert lover prepared to tolerate some discomfort in order to see places only a few Westerners have ever visited."

Another guidebook is more specific about the potential "discomfort": "Don't even think of going with less than three 4WD vehicles, or without a GPS set and satellite phone." Even then, the book cautions, "sand gets into every crevice of your body, there's no water to spare for washing, and you start to stink—like everybody else in the vehicle." Little wonder that in the film version of *The English Patient*, the "Wadi Sura" scenes were actually shot in Tunisia.

For its part, the British Foreign Service as late as spring 2019 was warning "against all but essential travel" to anywhere remotely near to the very far-flung Gilf Kebir. All of which probably explains why seventy years passed before a second major rock art site became known in the Wadi Sura valley, the so-called Cave of the Beasts, with at least fifteen hundred representations of animals and humans on its mute stone walls, including more swimmers painted in a style similar to those discovered by László Almásy.

And then there's Wadi Sura itself. While many places claim to be the driest spot in the world, this totemic home of primitive swimming art really does seem to take the prize, especially if you measure by the aridity index—a ratio of the evaporation power of the solar energy that hits a specific location to the rainfall actually received there. In the case of Wadi Sura, that ratio is 200. Put another way, the sun is capable of evaporating two hundred times the local precipitation, which is annually negligible or nonexistent. At the Cave of the Swimmers, water doesn't have a chance in hell.

The Swimmers themselves, those depicted on the cave walls, dealt with no such discomforts. The planet hadn't yet rewobbled on its axis, condemning a huge swath of North Africa to desert. For all they can imagine, the water will be out there waiting for them every day to come until the end of time.

No one can say exactly what the swimmers are swimming through. Nor are scholars unanimously convinced they are swimming at all. In a 2009 article for *Anthropologie,* Jiri Svoboda contends the figures are more likely floating in thin air—perhaps because they are in an altered state of consciousness or more likely because they have been literally thrown in the air by unseen humans below them as part of an ancient African ritual dance. Douglas Coulson, founder of TARA (Trust for African Rock Art), also posits that the seemingly floating bodies are a "visual metaphor" for the artist's (or artists') out-of-body experience, maybe induced through hallucinogens or via the kind of rhythmic clapping and chanting Coulson has witnessed among other African desert people.

Other scholars have suggested that the swimmers are actually negotiating a region called Nun, a primordial ocean that the dead must pass through on their way to a beneficent afterlife and where the evil dead are culled for special tortures. As evidence, the authors cite the presence of similar beastlike figures in the paintings found at both sites, in 1933 at the Cave of the Swimmers and in 2003 at the Cave of the Beasts.

Maybe, then, this really is a case of afterlife hell; Christians didn't invent purgatory. The beasts are many times larger than the swimmers and undeniably scary, but if those monsters are culling the evil, why is there so little panic among the swimmers? The ones on the wall at Wadi Sura look like they could keep going all day.

Besides, anyone deeply familiar with the doggy paddle knows it when she sees it: the feet, the hands, the position of the head are unmistakable.

Those representations of swimmers could have been modeled at the Brookside pool in Lancaster, Pennsylvania; the Crozet Community Park pool in rural Virginia; and other venues where I lifeguarded and taught swimming to boys and girls—and men and women—who had no idea how to otherwise move through the water.

Who knows? Eight-thousand-year-old mysteries are not easily solved. The key point is—dead or alive, heading for the afterlife or just beating the midday sun, or maybe just plain stoned—the swimmers are actually *swimming,* feet stretched behind them or legs bent at the knee as if getting ready for a new kick, arms reaching out in front. What's more, even if these are tableaus of tripping, not swimming, the artist or artists responsible still had a frame of ready reference for portraying it, another near-gravity-free experience that didn't require hallucinogens or frantic dancing to enjoy.

Wheeled vehicles were still four millennia in the future, hieroglyphs almost five thousand years away. But in an area that is now so like the barren surface of Mars that NASA has used it for landing simulations, swimming was common enough that prehistoric artists enshrined it on walls that have preserved the record for at least eight thousand years.

1

GODS, HUMANS, AND THE AQUATIC APE

Over 380 million years ago, the basic form of our limbs was already in place, albeit in fish which swam through the Devonian sea.
—Brian Switek

Creationists and evolutionists agree on at least one thing: life began with water.

In the opening lines of the Book of Genesis, God creates an Earth without form and void, an Earth on which darkness is upon the face of the deep. Then in verse 2, less than thirty words into the six-hundred-thousand-word Old Testament, God's Spirit moves upon the water, and the fine work of creation begins. God separates light from darkness. He divides the waters under the firmament from those above it—the oceans from Heaven. Dry land appears, vegetation, the sun and the moon, creatures of the deep, fowl of every kind, and beasts as well, four-legged ones and creeping things. Then on Day Six, God creates his masterwork—humankind in his own image—and on the Seventh Day he rests.

Evolution gets us to the same place but takes four billion-plus years longer. The one-cell creatures of that first, all-encompassing deep grow to two cells, eight cells, complicated fish with gills capable of taking oxygen out of H_2O, and on from there. Eventually, air breathers struggle ashore, get a foothold on the land, and finally half a million years or so ago, *Homo sapiens*—our long-distant ancestors—begin to leave their first footprints.

Either way, in creationism's fast lane or along the scenic route of evolution, water is central to the story. It's where life first formed, and maybe where life as far we can imagine it will end. (See Kevin Costner's *Waterworld*, Steven Spielberg's *A.I.*, global warming, and more.) Even today, we humans are aquatic mammals until virtually the moment of our birth. Our first breath out of the womb can't be that different from the one taken by the first proto-us who stumbled or more likely finned themselves ashore—pure surprise!

Although we are eons to the hundredth power removed from those first fish that crawled or flopped or pushed themselves out of the sea, we still bear some striking anatomical resemblances to them and their immediate ancestors. The fish genus known as *Tinirau* dates back at least 375 million years. *Tinirau* never left the ocean, but in an evolutionary sense, it clearly was preparing to. Instead of the sort of fins any fisherman would recognize—fans of thin bones, often spikey at the tip—*Tinirau*'s four fins were each attached to its body by a single bone, just as our arms are attached to our bodies by the humerus and our legs by the femur. Today's "walking catfish" of South Florida are closer to chunky snakes— they wriggle their way forward. The *Tinirau* heralded the dawn of tetrapods—four-footed creatures, just like us before standing up caught on.

As Brian Switek wrote back in 2012 for Wired.com, "Over 380 million years ago, the basic form of our limbs was already in place, albeit in fish which swam through the Devonian sea." Something to think about!

The fish–human comparisons don't end there. Swimming also remains deeply encoded in our biology. Full or even partial submersion triggers a whole suite of involuntary responses that would seem far more helpful to animals that lived in the water than to those that walk on dry land.

Spend an hour up to your head in water heated to 32 degrees Centigrade (almost 90 degrees Fahrenheit), and your heart rate will drop on average by 15 percent, and systolic and diastolic blood pressure by 11 and 12 percent, respectively. Knock the temperature down 10 percent or more (toward the range that competitive swimmers prefer) and the benefits in cardiopulmonary efficiency are greater still. A study in the *International Journal of Circumpolar Health* found that "winter swimming" (and remember, we're talking "circumpolar" here) reduces tension, fatigue, and negativity while boosting vigor and relieving pain from multiple conditions including rheumatism, fibromyalgia, and asthma. No wonder whales often seem more at peace with themselves than we humans do.

One more piece of evidence reinforces that there's something genetically aquatic about us humans: the mammalian diving reflex. Plunge into cold water, and three things happen automatically:

- Your heart rate slows by up to 30 percent, or 50 percent or more in trained individuals. (The triggers here are the trigeminal facial nerves, which run on either side of the nose, and the vagus nerve, which connects brain, heart, lungs, and digestive tract.)
- As that happens, muscle contractions in blood vessel walls reduce blood flow to the extremities, preserving blood (and critically the oxygen it carries) for the core organs—your brain and heart.
- Continue descending below the surface, and you trigger a third phenomenon: blood plasma and water fill your chest cavity to protect the critical organs there—lungs and heart—from the increased external water pressure.

Granted, other than pearl hunters, maybe Navy SEALs, and so-called free divers, no part of this reflex is broadly useful for humans.*
The water has to be 70 degrees Fahrenheit or colder to trigger the diving reflex, an uncomfortable temperature for most of us. What's more, humans simply aren't made to swim with the ease, strength, or power of the mammals most dependent on the diving reflex—whales, seals, otters, porpoises, and the like. But that such a reflex exists at all surely suggests our watery past.

One variant of the reflex provides an important safeguard for human newborns. Submerge an infant up to the age of about six months in water, and his or her windpipe automatically closes to keep water out of the lungs—the secret behind "water-baby" classes and the like taught at so many YMCAs.

And then there's sound. Out of the water, sounds travels through air to our inner ear, where it is detected and sent to the brain for translation. But as Helen Czerski points out in a fascinating "Everyday Physics" piece for the *Wall Street Journal,* below the water line, the outer ear is blocked by water. Instead, sound waves reach the inner ear through what's known as "bone conduction"—that is, by traveling through the jaw bone and skull. One result is that we hear high-pitched sounds and sharp ones like tapping and clicking—exactly the kind of "language" that whales, porpoises, and other large aquatic mammals use—far better underwater than we do above. Maybe our underwater ears were made to hear them, and we just forgot what all those sounds mean.

Combine the embedded human water responses described above with Darwin's theory of evolution, and it can be tempting to arrive at the

---

* No artificial breathing aids are allowed in free diving, but the variants in what is permissible—monofins, sleds and weights to quicken descent, and so forth—are so great that it's hard to name a gold standard of achievement. Austrian Herbert Nitsch is among the giants of the sport. In 2012, he free-dove to a depth of 831 feet. At that depth, the pressure on his body was 360 pounds per square inch, more than ten times the pressure in a fully inflated automobile tire. Such feats would be impossible without the mammalian diving reflex.

Up until about age six months, an infant's wind-pipe automatically closes underwater, an indication perhaps of our aquatic heritage. *(Affebook, altered to black & white)*

aquatic ape theory. Back in 1960, British biologist Sir Alister Hardy posited that humans first began to differentiate themselves from other apes when they climbed down from the trees and set up house beside the sea and other large bodies of water. Academically, that was a big leap. Conventional wisdom held that those first proto-humans set out as hunter-gatherers across the grasslands rather than heading for the beach. But, at another level, Hardy's theory was nothing more than common sense.

Mastering rivers, deltas, and coastal waters would have extended the range of those first human-apes, broadened their diet to include the roots and tubers of water lilies and the like, and critically forced them into an upright stance so they could wade through the water with their heads held high and hands free to forage. Adding swimming and diving to the skill set—not just entering the water but also, in a sense, conquering it—would have yielded even greater rewards: access to protein- and omega-3-rich food sources such as fish, shellfish, and kelp—a banquet less subject to seasonal variations than nuts or berries or migrating land animals.

From that premise, other ape–human differentiations appear to fall more or less naturally in place. Proto-humans began to shed their fur, replacing it with subcutaneous fat, both to keep themselves warm when foraging in colder waters and icy weather and to protect their young. Just as their windpipes naturally close when submerged—and for the same reason: air trapped in their lungs—newborn humans naturally float. No other ape-descended newborn can claim that.

Grasslands or wetlands? Big-game savannah hunters or waterside foragers? That's basically where the controversy stood in 1972 when Elaine Morgan tossed a feminist grenade into the mix with her book *The Descent of Woman*. Morgan had no problem with Alister Hardy's theory—in fact, she thoroughly embraced it—but Hardy hadn't pursued his own logic deeply enough. The grasslands theory had always favored men. They were the strong ones. They led the hunt and developed big brains to coordinate the kill. The women followed along, cooked the meat, serviced the hunters, had their babies, and on life went, killing and rutting.

Hardy's aquatic ape opened up for Elaine Morgan a whole new world of reasoning. If women weren't leading the water foraging in those proto-human societies, why did they develop thicker layers of subcutaneous fat than men? And why is it that, even today, the only sport in which women are clearly superior to men is long-distance (as in, *very* long distance) open-water swimming? Michael Phelps might have a chest full of Olympic gold medals, but Lynne Cox has swum the Bering Strait between Alaska and Russia, in water that averaged 43 degrees Fahrenheit. Which is the greater accomplishment? Well, it depends on what you set out to do.

Alister Hardy's aquatic ape theory—and Elaine Morgan's feminist take on it—still struggles for traction in the academic world, but swimming's role in evolution seems beyond dispute. At the simplest level, a high comfort level with water might be a key discriminator between which strains of early hominids survived the massive climate shifts of prehistory and which didn't. Seas rose. Oceans flooded. A bolt of lightning could turn hundreds of miles of sere grasslands into a raging wall of flame. At such tipping points, those who didn't fear water could take to the sea in rafts in search of more hospitable living circumstances, while those who feared water stayed put and perished.

By the eighteenth century BCE, when Hammurabi put together his famous code of laws, swimming had become in an odd way a key element of an entire judicial system. Hammurabi's code is an astoundingly thorough document. For adultery alone, it makes nine distinctions and provides as many separate legal remedies, many of them more women-centered than Hester Prynne encountered in Salem, Massachusetts, in the late seventeenth century CE. Three of the strictures, though, do seem both primitive and punitive:

- If a wife of a man be taken in lying with another man, they shall bind them and throw them into the water.
- If the finger have been pointed at the wife of a man because of another man, and she have not been taken in lying with another man, for her husband's sake she shall throw herself into the river.
- If that woman do not protect her body and enter into another house, they shall call that woman to account and they shall throw her into the water.

Even in these cases, though, swimming provides an out. In the first instance, a repentant husband is allowed to jump into the water and rescue his accused wife. In the second and third, where the woman is unbound, her fate is presumably up to the river gods. If she's innocent, they will rescue her. If not, goodbye. On the other hand, if the accused already knows some rudimentary swimming skills, why not fake it and let the gods take credit?

An even more dramatic example of swimming's utility four thousand years ago can be found in the second of Hammurabi's 282 laws:

If anyone bring an accusation against a man and the accused go to the river and leap into the river, if he sink in the river his accuser shall take possession of his house. But if the river proves that accused is not guilty and he escapes unhurt, then he who hath brought the allegation shall be put to death, while he who leaped into the river shall take possession of the house that belonged to his accuser.

As Alan Isles and John Pearn write in their essay "Swimming and Survival: Two Lessons from History": "In the greatest city of the world in its time, it was more important to be able to swim than to be honest." Given such a watery system of litigation and justice, one suspects the Euphrates was filled after dark with homeowners—and would-be homeowners and maybe even tempted women—working secretly on their strokes.

SWIMMING EXISTS ONLY BY INFERENCE IN HAMMURABI'S CODE. THERE seems to have been no word for it: you knew swimming when you saw it. Leap forward five hundred years, though, to the reign of Akhenaten—about 1360 BCE, during the Eighteenth Dynasty of ancient Egypt—and swimmers have moved into high-end household art. Carved cosmetic spoons from that epoch often feature a swimming motif: a young woman, stretched out on the water with her head held high and, in her extended arms, a shallow, lidded saucer to hold whatever cosmetic might be desired.

One such swimmer-girl spoon from Akhenaten's reign has the figure's tightly crimped hair piled high on her head to keep it dry. Another, carved from alabaster with slate trimmings, shows a swimming girl being towed by a pet gazelle whose back is indented in a spoon shape. This from thirteen centuries *before* the Christian era. Jump forward another five hundred years, and swimming has broken through art and entered the language—or rather multiple tongues.

While the Bible is stingy on specific references to swimming, Isaiah 25:10–11 provides a clear example of its ubiquity: "The Moabites shall be trodden down in their place as straw is trodden down in a dung

Nine centuries before the Christian era, Assyrian warriors were using inflated animal skins to surprise their enemies. *(BibleLandPictures .com/Alamy Stock Photo)*

pit. Though they spread out their hands in the midst of it, as swimmers spread out their hands to swim, their pride will be laid low despite the struggle of their hands."

Obscure? Yes, also somewhat scatological and definitely anti-Moabite. But focus on origins. This is from the first third of the Book of Isaiah, generally credited to the prophet Isaiah himself, from the eighth century BCE, and swimming is apparently a familiar enough activity that the prophet Isaiah can throw it around as a commonplace simile.*

From almost exactly the same time frame comes a far less obscure proverb from the Chinese Book of Odes, advising people confronting a body of water to "row across if it is deep and swim across when it is shallow."

Swimming's toehold by the seventh and eighth centuries BCE was more than linguistic. Etruscan tombs from 600 BCE and earlier depict swimmers. Huge carved reliefs taken from the palace of the Assyrian

---

* Moab, a mountainous kingdom in what is now Jordan, got off to a bad start. Its patriarch was a drunken Lot, who committed incest with his oldest daughter after she had lost her fiancé when Sodom and Gomorrah were laid low. At least in the Bible, the Moabites never recovered.

king Ashurnasirpal II, who ruled from 883 to 859 BCE, show warriors in full battle gear swimming a river, some in pursuit, others to escape their pursuers as arrows rain down from above, not unlike a cowboy-and-Indian B movie of yore.

Just as common as the swimming warriors in those reliefs are what might be thought of as water-wing warriors—soldiers who are using flotation devices, probably inflated goatskins, judging by their size, and seemingly keeping pace with the action. Reliefs from a century and a half closer to our time, taken from a palace at Nineveh, show Assyrians using floats in peacetime: swimming while lying prone on the inflated goatskin, somewhat like paddling oneself on a surfboard, and fishing midriver sitting astride the float.

In a 1942 essay for the *Journal of the Royal Anthropological Institute of Great Britain and Ireland*, James Hornell cites multiple examples of this kind of semi-swimming from the deep vault of history. During Julius Caesar's Spanish campaign in 49 BCE, foraging parties were bedeviled by Lusitanians who used inflated bladders to cross the River Segre and harass them. "These men," Caesar wrote afterward, "could readily swim across the river because it is the custom of all these people not to join their armies without bladders."

On the lighter side, a scene found on a gateway of the Buddhist temple at Sanchi, in India, depicts men using inflated bladders and logs to stay afloat as they frolic in a lotus tank. Such evidence leads Hornell to speculate that using floats was the gateway to swimming itself:

> It is doubtful if early man became acquainted with the art of swimming prior to the utilization or invention of some form of buoyant appliance capable of supporting his body when he ventured beyond his depth in river or lake.

Floating while holding onto, say, a log led to kicking to propel and direct the log in still waters, which led to straddling the log while lying down and using the arms to propel and direct the log even more effectively, which led to finally abandoning the log (or rolling off it) and . . . voilà, swimming! Maybe so, but swimmers in the Cave of the Swimmers from five millennia before those Assyrian reliefs were carved are doing just fine without a single flotation device in sight.

Neither the Bible nor the Chinese Book of Odes makes reference to the one thing that any swimmer in those early years of recorded history would likely have most feared about water: not the current or the waves or the eddies—that would have been sweating the small stuff—but the demon forces therein.

Born of water, dependent on it, surrounded by it either near (islands, isthmuses, etc.) or far (continents), humankind perhaps inevitably enshrouded water in myth and filled it with gods and demigods. And the gods sometimes went out of their way to make swimming as difficult and danger fraught as possible.

Hindu mythology tells us that the ocean god Varuna can be both vengeful and gracious, but his angry moments are more common and definitely more memorable, especially for those who have sworn falsely. The ancient Maori never went to sea without making offerings to Tangaroa, their jealous god of the sea, who did constant battle with Tane, ruler of the forests. The God of the Judeo-Christian Bible kindly parts the Red Sea for the fleeing Israelites, then closes it ruthlessly on the Pharaoh's army, with calamitous results. The same God nearly scours the Earth of sin with a deluge that rages forty days and nights.

The *Epic of Gilgamesh,* one of the world's oldest known literary works—written in Sumerian, of Mesopotamian origins, sometime between eleven and sixteen centuries before Christ—tells an eerily similar story about the gods voting to destroy humankind and how one of them, the God of Wisdom, alerted a Noah-like figure to construct a huge ark in which he, his family, and the seed of every living thing might ride out the destruction and restore life to the planet once the waters receded.

In fact, flood myths and angry gods are so prevalent across cultures and around the world in the millennia before the birth of Christ that it's half amazing any living thing was left on Earth to greet the Christian savior. The story of Manu and Matsya, which first appears in India circa 700 BCE, tells of the god Matsya—Lord Vishnu incarnated as a fish—who warns the human Manu of an impending flood and tells him to gather up all the grains of the world in a boat. The mythological great flood that the Incans call Una Pachakuti was launched deep in prehistory by the Creator Varicocha to slay all the people around Lake Titicaca save for the two who would then populate the rest of the world.

Not to be outdone, ancient Greek mythology tells us that an aggrieved Zeus used yet another great flood to kill all the inhabitants of Earth save the requisite two: Deucalion, son of Prometheus, and Pyrrha. Likewise, in the ten-year War of the Titans, the monstrous Hecatoncheires—"hundred-handed" ones, not to mention their fifty heads—let loose ferocious earthquakes and tsunamis that precious few manage to survive.

As befits a maritime people, Greek mythology is rich with seafaring adventures that sometimes seem to presage the violent-action drama of the *Grand Theft Auto* video game franchise. In the greatest of the Greek tales, Homer's *Odyssey,* Odysseus survives ten years of every peril imaginable—most notably, the sea god Poseidon's wrath—to reclaim his throne at Ithaca and slay his wife's many suitors. But the very fact that Odysseus survives at all (and in human form, no less) makes him virtually an outlier when it comes to aquatic encounters with the many deities of ancient Greece.

In a 2009 study, Stathis Avramidis of the Leeds Metropolitan University scoured a database of forty thousand names mentioned in ancient and mythological Greek literature for any evidence of drowning or near-drowning incidents. In all, he came up with thirty-seven names of which twenty-one were mythological accounts. Of those twenty-one, several were accidental or self-imposed deaths. Icarus flew too close to the sun and plunged into the sea when his wings melted. Mistakenly thinking that his son had been killed by the Minotaur, Aegeus jumped to his death in the sea that was later named for him: the Aegean.

Far more often, though—seventeen of the twenty-one mythical drownings and near-drownings—a god or a demigod is somehow involved.

When Ceyx and Alcyone anger the gods by jokingly calling themselves Zeus and Hera, Zeus slays Ceyx with a thunderbolt while he's at sea; then when Alcyone sees her lover's body wash up on the shore, she throws herself into the sea. Only when she, too, is dead do the gods take pity and turn them both into kingfishers.*

And so it goes. Narcissus overadmires his own watery reflection, falls into a lake, apparently has no idea how to save himself (even though, as we will see in the next chapter, Greeks were generally excellent swimmers), but instead of drowning gets transformed into the flower that we know today by his name. Voutis would have drowned as well after he was lured into the sea by the song of the Sirens, but Aphrodite rescued him at the last minute, less from mercy than to make him her lover.

Virtually all ancient cultures recognized in one way or another the same four elements: earth, air, fire, and water. They're the mixing bowl of life—impossible to ignore. But in all of them the greatest tests are often reserved for the last of those elements: water. Think of the Christian doctrine alone. Jesus's miracles in the New Testament are many, but none is more compelling than when he performs the one act we all know cannot be done by mere mortals: walking on water, the one element in which we can never live fully again. Or can we?

Wasn't that the true lure of Guillermo del Toro's *The Shape of Water*, the 2017 Oscar winner for Best Picture? That we can breach the border? That, like Sally Hawkins's Eliza Esposito, we have a choice between the two mediums? That, with just a little nudge from magic realism, neck scars can become gills? Those of us who have spent a lifetime swimming up and down pools, across lakes, and along ocean shorelines

---

* In honor of the star-crossed couple, the genus *Ceyx*, part of the river kingfisher family, is named for him, while the tree kingfisher family, *Halcyonidae*, is named for her. Immortality of a sort.

probably dream more often than we should that such things can happen. But water forgives our infirmities, physical and otherwise. It frees us to dream. Swimming is an equal playing field.

One could even argue that swimming makes us whole: we humans are, after all, 70 percent water, nearly identical to the percentage of the Earth's surface that is ocean: 71 percent. Rather than fight that dualism and natural affinity, the Greeks and Romans at the height of their civilizations embraced it in ways we can still distantly witness.

2

SWIMMING'S GOLDEN AGE

A man is not learned until he can read, write, and swim.

—Plato

For swimmers and swimming, the classical period truly was the golden age, not just among Greeks and Romans but also across a wide sweep of the world. In his well-regarded *Letters on Egypt,* Claude-Étienne Savary notes Egyptians of the time—men, women, and children—were almost to a person remarkably able and graceful in the water. At the height of the Armenian kingdom in the first century BCE, royals and aristocrats trained their male offspring in the "manly sports": boxing, wrestling, and swimming. Within the same time frame, the Japanese were having organized swim races.

The Greeks of antiquity took their swimming just as seriously, but for them, swimming was elevated to a civic virtue. Plato's famous maxim, above, was honored in practice as well as in word. "Swimming," one commentator tells us, "was a material part of youthful education among the

Greeks." Even Aristotle ventured advice on the subject: saltwater was better than fresh for swimming, and the colder, the better.

The Romans treasured swimming, too, and built municipal baths in part for the purpose as well as for hygiene, other forms of exercise, and the sheer pleasure of a good soak. For them, Plato's words were turned into an insult, a dis: "The man can neither swim nor read!" Like Aristotle, the Roman poet Horace weighed in with aquatic council: "Let those who are in need of deep sleep, anointed swim thrice across the Tiber." Like many leading Romans, Cato the Elder was at pains to teach his son to swim.

The story of Hero and Leander, lovers who lived on either side of the Hellespont, was part of the cultural fabric of both Greece and Rome, and it's an open-water romance through and through. Nightly, the priestess Hero would light a lamp in her lonely tower at Sestos. And nightly, Leander would brave the narrows from Abydos, guided by Hero's beacon, to be with her . . . until the wintry night when howling winds extinguished Hero's lamp; Leander, unguided, succumbed to the storm-tossed sea; and Hero leapt from her tower to join her lover, in death if not in life.

As Frances Norwood noted in a 1950 article for *Phoenix*, the journal of the Classical Association of Canada, the story was so commonplace that when Virgil referred to it in the first century BCE, he didn't even bother to mention the lovers' names. Everyone would have known.

Not surprisingly, given such broad and varied support, the secular pantheons of both cultures are filled with swimmer-heroes. Predictably, too, swimming's first utility for both the Greeks and the Romans was as a military art, and its first aquatic heroes were born of combat.

In 480 BCE, during the great naval clash in the Straits of Salamis between the Persian fleet of Xerxes and an alliance of Greek city-states, the celebrated Macedonian diver and swimming teacher Scyllis first hired himself out to the Persians to recover treasure lost when several of their ships went down in a storm. Then, when Xerxes tried to detain him, Scyllis leapt overboard and swam underwater to Artemisium—a distance of eighty *stadia*, about ten miles, perhaps using a reed as a snorkel and hopefully taking advantage of currents and the tides—to warn the Greek fleet of the Persian king's plans.

That's from Herodotus's account, written within a half century of the events he describes. The second-century CE Greek geographer Pausanias also credits Scyllis and his daughter (and fellow swimming teacher) Cyana with starting the whole mess when they dove beneath the Persian ships as a storm bore down and cut their anchor lines. Regardless of which version of the event is more accurate, the greatly outnumbered Greek fleet prevailed, and for their heroism Scyllis and Cyana both had statues consecrated at the Temple at Delphi. Centuries later, Nero was so taken with Cyana's likeness that he had her statue brought back to Rome for his own enjoyment.*

Even with the use of a reed snorkel, Scyllis's ten-mile underwater swim might stretch credulity—Herodotus, for one, suspects he took a boat. But in a 1934 essay for the *Classical Journal,* Brown University classicist H. N. Couch cites two other "undoubtedly historical" examples of swimming lending the winning edge in battle. In 425 BCE, for example, when a Spartan army found itself besieged by Athenians on the toxic-sounding island of Sphacteria, volunteers supplied the Spartans with food by swimming underwater dragging behind them skins stuffed with poppy seeds mixed with honey and pounded linseed.

Still more impressive and also well documented is the role swimming played in the Athenian naval attack on Syracuse, an ancient city on the southeast coast of Sicily, in 415–413 BCE. Forewarned that the Greeks were coming, the locals drove piles into the Mediterranean floor at the front of the harbor to protect their fleet and to prevent the Greeks from landing. When they arrived, the Greeks set about pulling out the visible pilings that were exposed on top with a mechanical device brought along

---

* The very fact that Scyllis and Cyana come down to us through the millennia as "swimming teachers" says volumes about the activity's central role in classical life.

for that purpose. But the underwater pilings that threatened to gut the hull of a ship were left to divers, who sawed them off for extra pay.

"This was an exceedingly difficult task," Couch writes, "as anyone can testify who has attempted to saw through a wet log under the most favorable conditions. . . . Such skill in the water would be so generally found only among a people who were regularly taught as children to swim."[*]

As much as swimming benefited the Athenian and Spartan militaries, an absence of any talent or capacity for swimming frequently proved fatal to Greece's enemies. About the famous Battle of Salamis that propelled Scyllis and Cyana to stardom, Herodotus writes, "The loss of the Greeks was but small. As they were expert in swimming, they, whose ships were destroyed, and who did not perish by the sword, made their escape to Salamis. Great numbers of the Barbarians, from their ignorance of this art, were drowned." And Salamis is but one of many examples cited by Herodotus and others. When their fleet was shipwrecked off Mount Athos, Persians by the hundreds died, not from the storm but from their inability to swim even the relatively short distance to shore. During the Peloponnesian War, the Thracians (from the Balkans) were driven by the Thebans into the Euripus Strait, along Greece's central eastern coast, but most were unable to swim to their fleet, which was waiting not far offshore, just out of arrow range.

In his essay, H. N. Couch wonders why the Greeks should have been so good at swimming and their enemies so bad. The climate of Greece is not all that different from that of the Balkans, just to the north, he writes. Modern Iran is more southerly, but with plenty of coast along the Red and Caspian Seas. The best answer Couch can come up with is an issue that dogs swimming to this day: attitudes toward public nudity.

---

[*] Although the swimmers performed well, it should be noted that the Sicilian expedition did not go swimmingly for the Athenians on the whole. For his part, Professor Couch sounds as though he might have actually tried to hand-saw through sodden wood, a miserable task.

According to Thucydides, an Athenian historian and general, the Greeks had only recently begun to practice their sports in the raw. Until then, they had swum encumbered by loincloths at the very least. Plato says much the same. Earlier Greeks thought it improper for a man to be seen in the altogether. Plutarch tells the story of Agesilaus, who had his Asiatic prisoners stripped naked at Ephesus both to humiliate them and to let their pasty white bodies be an object lesson to his fellow Greeks to let the sun shine in. The Greeks apparently listened to Agesilaus, while the barbarians continued to dress modestly, cover their manhood, and drown wholesale when the opportunity presented itself.*

Nonmilitary evidence of the liberated Greek view of swimming and nudity is offered by the magnificent Tomb of the Diver, found at Paestum, south of the Amalfi Coast, in what is now the Campania region of Italy but which was then part of Magna Graecia (Greater Greece). Dating back to 470 BCE, the tomb is composed of five limestone slabs. Frescoes on the interior depict a gathering of what are presumably the dead man's friends, including two amorous male lovers, a boy piping in new guests, and two other men seemingly playing a betting game that involves tossing wine dregs from a cup.

All that's rare enough—tomb paintings of that time almost never depicted human figures. The real prize, though, is the underside of the top slab, the one the deceased was facing: a beautifully executed fresco roughly three feet by seven feet of a naked young man diving off what looks to be a tower or a wall into the waves. Perhaps it's a younger version of the person who occupied the tomb. Perhaps there's an allegory here: the dead man diving into the afterlife. But whatever the provenance and intent, veiled or otherwise, the artist was no stranger to water sports. The diver is in the final stages of a front dive, layout position, at least three meters up—degree of difficulty 1.6—and he gives every indication

---

* Agesilaus's treatment of his Asiatic prisoners calls to mind the treatment of Muslim prisoners at Abu Ghraib, Guantanamo, and elsewhere by US interrogators during the post-9/11 War on Terror. Stripping and exposing the prisoners was part of the process of breaking them psychologically.

The interior of the Tomb of the Diver, circa 470 BCE, discovered at Paestum in the Campania region of Italy. *(Courtesy of author)*

of being about to enter the water with barely a ripple and for no purpose other than the sheer joy of doing so.

Turns out, you didn't have to have bloody combat in mind to enjoy a high dive and a good swim in the buff, and, of course, you still don't. Something about the small seas that surround Greece and Italy—the Aegean, the Adriatic, the Tyrrhenian and Ligurian and Ionian—almost compels a naked plunge.

I remember watching a young woman walk out of the walled city of Dubrovnik, on the Croatian coast, at lunchtime, strip naked on a large rounded rock not far above the Adriatic, and dive in. After ten minutes or so, she climbed out, had her lunch on the rock while the sun dried her, then pulled her clothes back on and headed back into town, presumably to whatever work she was taking a break from. *Heaven*, I thought, as my wife and I similarly sundried ourselves on the dock of an island park a few hundred yards offshore. *Sheer heaven.*

The Romans were not Greeks Redux. They had less interest in the humanities and the arts than the Greeks. They never produced philosophers to match Socrates, Plato, or Aristotle; playwrights the equal of Aeschylus or Sophocles or Euripides; epic poetry on a level with *The Iliad* and *The Odyssey*.

The Romans were a practical people. They reasoned. They conquered. And they engineered. To the Romans, at least in the early stages of the empire, the Greeks seriously overdid things when it came to sports. All that practice! All that exercise! Why bother when you could build a beautiful coliseum and let others do blood battle for your amusement? Why swim for exercise or pleasure when you could fill a huge outdoor arena with water, as Titus did in 80 CE to celebrate the opening of the Flavian Amphitheater, and stage mock naval battles for the public's amusement?

And all that Greek nudity—what was that about?

Early attitudes eventually eased and even reversed as the Roman Empire matured, and swimming helped bring the two worldviews together. Both cultures put a high premium on the military value of swimming. Vegetius, in his influential treatise *De Re Militari,* written early in the fifth century CE, recommends that the entire Roman army be trained in swimming.

Like the Greeks, the Romans seem to have been gender- and status-neutral in anointing their swimming heroes. The Republic was still forming when the Etruscan king Porsinna laid siege to Rome. Fearing an assassination attempt—Livy, one of the three great Roman historians, tells this story—Porsinna agrees to withdraw his siege, but only if Rome delivers to the Etruscan camp across the Tiber River a cluster of young women and men as hostages.

This Rome does, and the group includes Cloelia, a virgin who refuses to buy in to the plan. As the sun sets, Cloelia deceives her guard, gathers all the female hostages, and rushes them to the river, where they dive in and swim for the Roman side—"amid a hail of enemy spears," Livy tells us. Cloelia brings up the rear. But the story doesn't end here.

Porsinna is outraged, at first, and ready to renew the siege, but he quickly comes to admire Cloelia's courage. He sends word that he will continue to withdraw if—but only if—Cloelia is returned to him, not as a prisoner but as an honored member of his court. The Romans comply, too, with this demand, sending Cloelia to Porsinna's stronghold at Clusium, located roughly in the center of current-day Tuscany, but here the tale hits a fork in the road.

The standard ending (Livy's) has Porsinna continuing to praise Cloelia and granting her half of the males she was originally taken hostage with. In this account, she chooses the youngest of them, as they were the most likely to be injured or killed in warfare. A rogue version of the story has Cloelia swimming home to Rome, some hundred miles down the Tiber—a passage with some daunting geology to negotiate.

What's known for sure is that Cloelia was so highly regarded that at the top of the Via Sacra in Rome a statue of her was erected—an equestrian one, alas, with her rigid upon horseback, not midstroke crossing the river that brought her such fame.

AT THE OTHER END OF THE ROMAN SWIMMING PANTHEON IS JULIUS CAESAR himself. The famed emperor was much celebrated in his own lifetime for his swimming feats, especially when he led his legions into battle in 47 BCE against Ptolemy's forces in the Egyptian port of Alexandria.

Near-mythical claims have attached over the centuries to the emperor's aquatic heroism that day. For sure, Caesar's troops were buckling under Ptolemy's land and sea assault when he leapt into the water and swam from vessel to vessel in his naval force. Some accounts have him holding his famous *Gallic Commentaries* high and dry with one hand as he proceeded. Others have him clenching a jacket of mail in his teeth, most likely a *lorica hamate,* the chainmail vest commonly worn by Roman soldiers that would have tipped the scales at about nine pounds. Suetonius, another Roman historian who wrote during the early Imperial era and who is the initial source of the *lorica hamate* part of the story, tells us that Caesar's total swim that day covered about three hundred meters—no small feat with nine pounds of metal clamped between his teeth and arrows flying this way and that. The most adoring versions have the emperor single-handedly turning the course of the battle with his bravery.

The *Commentary on the Alexandrian War*—supposedly penned by Caesar himself, but far more likely ghostwritten by Hirtius, who wasn't there—goes light on both the detail and the heroics. In this version, Caesar leaps into the water only because the battle is going poorly and his own ship is so packed with his retreating army that it can't set sail. Once in the water, the commander in chief did swim "to the ships that lay at some distance. Hence dispatching boats to succor his men, he, by that means, preserved a small number." Certainly, there's bravery there, and admirable swimming. But the gesture was nowhere near as successful as Caesar's hagiographers sometimes suggest: as many as eight hundred Roman soldiers, sailors, and rowers were lost in the action, and afterward, Ptolemy was far from finished.

Like the best times of those of us who swam competitively, the past is subject to exaggeration. But seventeen centuries later, William Shakespeare was clearly well enough aware of Caesar's aquatic propensities that he added swimming to the many other gripes with which "lean and hungry" Cassius filled poor Brutus's ear. In this instance, "the troubled Tiber was chafing with her shores" when Caesar challenged Cassius to a race, and off they went, as Cassius tells it:

> *The torrent roar'd, and we did buffet it*
> *With lusty sinews, throwing it aside*
> *And stemming it with hearts of controversy;*
> *But ere we could arrive the point proposed,*
> *Caesar cried "Help me, Cassius, or I sink!"*

Cassius did, and heroically so, according to him, but he seems to have regretted doing so ever after: "This man / Is now become a god, and Cassius is / A wretched creature and must bend his body, / If Caesar carelessly but nod on him."

In any event, this is from Act 3, Scene 2 of the Bard's famous tragedy *Julius Caesar*: Assassination to follow!

One final issue to settle here: History tells us that the Greeks and Romans were swimming fools, and Shakespeare assures us that these two specific Romans swam with "lusty sinews," but with what stroke did they buffet the roaring torrent? Was it anything like swimming today?

Shakespeare almost certainly had no frame of reference with which to answer that question. Swimming was all but unknown in the England of Shakespeare's time. But the answer, it turns out, is: yes, Cassius and Caesar were likely swimming a distinctly modern stroke. And for that we have, among other sources, the late H. A. Sanders of the University of Michigan to thank.

In a 1925 article for the *Classical Journal,* Sanders takes it as a given that the Greeks and Romans loved to swim and excelled at it. The written evidence is too strong to contend otherwise. As to *what* they swam, the record is thinner, but still compelling. There's the Greek vase in the Louvre, for example, that "shows a woman swimming with alternate strokes of the hands and apparently striking the feet downward somewhat after the manner of the 'crawl stroke,'" Sanders writes. "Certainly the feet are raised to a possible position for such a downward motion." But that's only the beginning.

In "The Love Elegies," the classical Roman poet Sextus Propertius writes of the beautiful Cynthia who, with "alternate hands," moved through the "easily yielding water." In his *Metamorphosis,* Ovid describes swimming with "alternate stroke through the transparent flood." Skip ahead to near the end of the Roman Empire, and the imperial poet

A coin from the late second century, depicting Leander swimming the Hellespont to be with his beloved Hero. His last swim did not go well for either party.

Rutilius Claudius Manatianus mentions a swimmer using alternate arms to cut through the waves.

I would offer one additional piece of evidence: At least four coins from the second and third centuries CE—three from Troas in modern Turkey, and one from Thrace on the Greek side of the Dardanelles—depict Hero in her tower and Leander trying to reach her, and in all of them, Leander has one arm reaching in front, about to begin his stroke, and the other trailing behind, completing its passage through the water.

H. A. Sander's conclusion applies only to the more modern of the two great Mediterranean civilizations, but it seems equally applicable to ancient Greece as well: "Not only did the Romans use the alternate stroke in swimming, but they used that form of it in which the hands came out of the water at every stroke. It seems clear that their style of swimming was the one which we call native swimming and find most speedy and effective today."

We will get to the "native swimming" part in a few chapters. For now, suffice it to note that Sextus Propertius, Ovid, Rutilius Claudius Manatianus, the ancient coin artists of Troas and Thrace, and H. D. Sanders are all describing a style of swimming that would die with the Roman Empire and not be seen again in Europe for well over a thousand years.

3

FIRST THERE WAS SWIMMING; THEN THERE WAS NONE

> The surest way to discover such as practice witchcraft
> is by their swimming upon the water.
> —Richard Boulton

For the Romans, swimming was more than a civic virtue, although it was certainly that too. Swimming drove architecture. It established cities. It was a cultural determinant. Elsewhere in barbaric Europe, as the Romans thought of it, darkness reigned. Even the rich and powerful—maybe most of all the rich and powerful—shut themselves in, previewing the Dark Ages to come. The Romans, by contrast, opened themselves up: to the sun, to communal activities and common governance, maybe most of all to water. Resort sites boomed at lakes and along the coastline. Municipal baths built upon the glory that had been Greece enshrined the grandeur that was now Rome.

The Romans worshipped at many altars, but they glorified water and all its uses: water was the empire's genius—the aqueducts that carried it, the fountains that displayed and dispensed it; the baths for soaking and cleaning, the pools for exercising and lollygagging, even the latrines that carried waste away, formed the core of urban leisure. And when the end came for the empire toward the end of the fifth century, the fountains, the baths, the pools, along with almost everything else that carried or contained water, were among the first of the Roman marvels to sink into disuse.

Two sites tell the story.

A letter from Pliny the Younger to the historian Tacitus provides a firsthand description of the events of August 24, in the year 79 CE, and of the morning that followed in the shadow of Mount Vesuvius:

> At the seventh hour, my mother indicated to [my father, Pliny the Elder] a cloud, unusual both in size and appearance. . . .
>
> The cloud, whose likeness and form indicated nothing less than a pine tree, was rising up. . . .
>
> Meanwhile, broad flames and tall fires were blazing forth in many places from Mount Vesuvius, the splendor and clearness of which were heightened by the darkness of the night. . . .
>
> Not long after, the cloud descended upon the land and covered the sea. . . .
>
> The fire remained at a distance, again darkness, and again ash thick and heavy. Arising, we kept shaking it off lest in some way we be engulfed and even crushed by the weight. . . .
>
> Soon a true daylight. Even the sun shone. . . . Now to our anxious eyes, everything appeared changed and covered by a deep layer of cinders, as if by snow.

It wouldn't end there. What Pliny the Younger was describing, of course, was Day One of the three-day eruption of Mount Vesuvius, a cataclysm that deposited a pall of ash and stones up to eight feet deep at a radius as far as twenty-five kilometers from the center of the volcano. By the time the ash and rock had stopped falling, several thousand people were dead, and two thriving provincial towns had basically disappeared: Herculaneum and Pompeii. Or, maybe more accurately, the towns became frozen in time. And so Pompeii remains still—a ghostly expression of the absolute centrality of water to Roman life at the height of the empire.

The Aqua Augusta, constructed between 30 and 20 BCE under the reign of Caesar Augustus, was one of the engineering marvels of the ancient world. Almost ninety miles long, the aqueduct carried water from the springs of Serino, high up Monte Terminio in the Picentini range, through underground tunnels, across ravines and chasms, and around the back of Mount Vesuvius to nine towns around the Bay of Naples, to multiple villas of the Roman rich, and to the *Piscina Mirablis*—the vast cistern dug out of rock that supplied drinking water to the imperial naval base at Misenum. But its first stop was the town closest to Vesuvius: Pompeii.

The aqueduct fed Pompeii's fountains and filled its baths. Walking the streets of that sprawling ruin today, it's easy to imagine the town as a vacation destination bubbling with spas, overflowing with water features and inviting guesthouses. One remarkably well-preserved garden—at the villa of Julia Felix, near the Palestra—is planned around an elongated fishpond crossed by three small arched walkways. Not far away, at the villa of Loreius Tiburtinus, a narrow canal, also fish filled, bisected the entire length of a vast garden adorned with fountains and statues.

Other villas took their water features inside and complemented them with beautifully frescoed walls, which have been preserved today in the National Archaeological Museum in Naples. Old money sometimes screams out from the vestiges of Pompeii the same way it screams out from America's oldest seaside resorts, places like Newport, Rhode Island, where American oligarchs used to take to the sea in private splendor. But unlike Newport in its glory days, Pompeii was first and foremost a port, a commercial center, a marketplace.

In a 1980 article for the *Classical Outlook,* Robert I. Curtis tallies at least thirty bakeries within the town walls. Vineyards, he writes, dotted the surrounding countryside. The clothing industry was a major employer. The village bustled with shops and vending stalls. Buying and selling were Pompeiians' main activities. As with so much of the empire, profit seems to have been on everyone's mind. Curtis cites mottos designed into the mosaic floors in three of the town's partially standing homes. One reads (in Latin): "Profit is a delight." Another: "Hail profit!" A third advises: "Acquire a profit!" Pompeii would have driven Karl Marx nuts!

The Forum, inevitably, was the town center, as it was throughout the empire—large enough (at 125 by 514 feet) to contain all of Pompeii's population, paved with travertine, and for pedestrians only. The Basilica, home to the city's law courts; temples to household gods, Jupiter, and Apollo; municipal offices; imposing commercial buildings; a large covered market known as the Macellum; statues to Augustus's sister Octavia and other notables—all lined the perimeter of the Forum, many of them fronted by two-story porticos.

Even today, the lost grandeur of the Forum can be almost overwhelming. But study the street plan of Pompeii, imagining yourself a resident there in the decades before it was reduced to ruins, and you get the strong sense that its waterworks formed the town's soul. At the time of its destruction, Pompeii had four public baths within its walls, and a fifth just outside them. Virtually everyone who could went to one or another of them daily, beginning around noon, and these were magnificent, all-purpose building complexes.

The Stabian Baths, the oldest, dates back to the fourth century BCE, but most of the construction was finished three centuries later. The entrance led patrons directly into the palaestra, an exercise yard, and, to the east, an area with an open-air pool roughly ten yards by eight yards, and four feet deep, about the size of a modern motel pool. Staring into it, I found myself thinking of all the motel pools I've tried to make do for a morning swim before heading off to an interview or to do research or just to poke around some unknown place. For the record, it takes 165 lengths in a ten-yard pool to swim a metric mile: 164 turns in all.

Did anyone do that regularly in the Stabian pool? I have no idea, but I had no trouble imagining that on the day before Vesuvius erupted, it might have been used much as modern-day motel pools are: a few dog-tired seniors gabbing at one end, some swimmers stroking toward the other end, and in the middle a gaggle of indefatigable kids lost in a noisy game of Marcus Antonius. (Marco Polo, before there was a Marco Polo to name it after.)

"Marcus?"

"Antonius!"

"Marcus?"

"Antonius!"

Etcetera . . . while the mountain next door stewed in its own juices.

Nor did I have trouble imagining the onslaught of sounds that the Stoic philosopher Seneca complained about, emanating from the baths he lived above in Rome: the grunting weightlifter out in the palaestra, the *slap-slap* of a slave-masseuse, "the enthusiast who plunges into the swimming-tank with unconscionable noise and splashing."

A pool, after all, is a pool the world around and across time.

This one at the Stabian Baths was flanked by two rooms with shallow basins so exercisers could wash themselves off before plunging in. ("Please shower before entering pool.") Across the palaestra were separate bathing facilities for men and women, each with a tepidarium, calidarium, and frigidarium—for lukewarm, hot, and cold soaking, respectively, done in that order—and separate dressing rooms.

The newer baths—Central, Forum, and Sarno—put the ritz on a bit more. Central was still under construction, part of the rebuilding after the 62 CE earthquake that perhaps should have warned Pompeiians the end might be nigh. Unlike some of the older baths, Central was flooded with light inside. It also had a laconicum, basically a sweat lodge or sauna, hotter even than the calidarium. Still to be built were its own swimming pool, to match that of the Stabian Baths, and accompanying gymnasium.

Large shops sat near the entrance along with a mini-factory for dyeing fabric and the posh villa of M. Lucretius, the Priest of Mars.

The Forum Baths—not to be confused with the Forum Latrines, although they too benefited from Pompeii's lush water supply—were mostly for out-of-towners, visitors to the Forum for business and ceremonial purposes. As such, they were both the smallest of the city's baths and the most elegant, with a marble tub for bathing, colonnades along three sides and handsome arches on the fourth, and a frigidarium that suggests a Renaissance baptistery.

The Sarno Baths barely exist at all anymore, but surviving evidence shows that Sarno was multilevel, with luxury apartments featuring private entrances to the baths. The Suburban Baths, just beyond the city walls, was undergoing repairs from the 62 CE earthquake when Vesuvius buried it in ash and stone, but it seems to have been closer than any of the others to a true resort, constructed on a man-made terrace facing the sea and richly adorned with brightly colored frescoes.[*]

And then there was the large palaestra out by the amphitheater—exercise stripped down to its basics but on the grand scale: a vast square 150 yards by 140, far larger than a modern football field, surrounded on three sides by a portico, and near its middle a large pool with a sloping bottom, a place where it's almost impossible *not* to imagine doing lap after lap. No frigidarium here. No laconicum either, and no changing rooms. This palaestra was purpose-driven—for sweating, for swimming, for competitions, and for the annual exhibitions put on by the *collegium iuvenum*, Pompeii's equivalent of a municipal sports organization.

Pompeii's baths weren't slap-dash constructions, architectural afterthoughts. They had heft, style, and design. They sat at main intersections or, in the case of the Suburban Baths, just outside a main gate for a good reason: the baths were of the essence of life in the Roman Empire, inseparable from the ebb and flow of commerce, the rhythm of daily life.

---

[*] As Robert Curtis points out, the Bay of Naples has receded over the last two millennia. Ancient Pompeii was much closer to the coast than the ruins and modern Pompei are today.

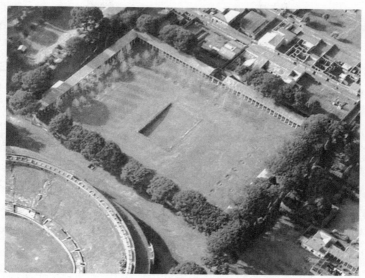

The Great Palaestra at the ruins of Pompeii—larger by far than a football field, with an oversized, sloping swimming pool at its center. The overflow from the pool was used to flush the latrines. *(Google Earth)*

At terrible cost, Vesuvius preserved at least the carapace of that world. Perhaps the best known of all Rome's far-flung baths—the Aquae Sulis, in what is now the city of Bath in England—suggests what might have happened to Pompeii's pride if Vesuvius had remained dormant.

When the Roman legions landed in Britain in 43 CE, they encountered people still living in the Iron Age. Europe was forever away across the English Channel. Contact with anything approaching outside civilizations was all but unknown. This "New World" of the Old World was begging for improvement, and that, after all, is what the Romans did best.

First, they built their military road, the Fosse Way. Then, when the military road happened upon someplace strategically important, or already settled, or maybe just bursting with potential, they stopped, had a look around, and if the stars all seemed in alignment, they started building.

Thus was it so at what we now know as Bath, in Somerset, in the English southwest. The military road crossed the River Avon. Nearby was a very large and very hot natural spring dedicated to a Celtic goddess of healing named Sulis. The site, as future exploration would show, was Britain's *only* thermal springs, but no one knew that then. Still, hot springs could not be ignored. They presaged formal public baths, *thermae,* as the Romans called them, and the daily volume of the spring—343,000 gallons—encouraged the Romans to think big. What's more, the revered Sulis was close enough to one of Rome's own goddesses, Minerva, to be her sibling if not twin sister. Never ones to pass up a chance to assimilate a conquered people and undoubtedly missing the comforts of home, the Romans started constructing what became the baths at Bath about 60 CE, two decades before Pompeii was destroyed. And they kept building and adding on to the bath complex for at least another two centuries.

First, they had to stabilize the ground around the spring—no challenge for this ace construction crew. Then came a temple dedicated to Sulis Minerva, a four-columned building in the classical mode set on a pediment so it loomed over the surrounding colonnaded courtyard. This was followed by the Great Bath—24 by 9 meters, lined with forty-five sheets of lead and fed by lead pipes and lead-lined channels. A little over five feet deep, the pool was filled with water naturally heated and made buoyant like the Dead Sea by its high iron salts content. Alcoves for seating and casual conversation surrounded the Great Bath, and the whole was covered (as of the second century CE) by a ceramic vaulted ceiling 145 feet overhead.[*]

Finally, there were the lesser buildings: the East and West Baths, with heated rooms and plunge pools; a laconicum—whatever it took to make Aquae Sulis the complete pagan spa package, Pompeii boiled down to its watery essence and multiply branded. Pilgrims came to worship at the temple. The lame and halt arrived to take the healing waters as they had been doing since Anglo-Saxon days. (According to one source,

---

[*] The restored Great Bath is still watertight, but not open for swimming. The same water, though, is now fed to a rooftop pool across the street. On the brisk, rainy early May day I climbed down the ladder to get in—there was no room to dive or jump—the pool was full to the gills and enormously refreshing.

The Great Bath at the restored Roman spa at Bath, in England. *(Courtesy of author)*

the site had been known to pre-Romans as Acemannesceastre, "Aching Man's City.") Soldiers and others came to do what the Romans themselves had long been doing—relax, chill out, renew, restore, refresh. The soldiers might well have tossed lap swimming into the mix: the Great Bath was only a meter shy of an official short-course competition pool today, and swimming was an essential part of Roman military training.

Hadrian gummed up the works in the second century CE when he decreed that mixed bathing was no longer acceptable across the empire, but still business boomed. Bath grew even as the Roman Empire itself shrunk in its ability to defend its perimeter. And then reality settled in. As the fourth century drew to a close, invaders from Ireland and northern Europe began sacking the wealthy villas beyond Aquae Sulis's walls. Travel dried up under the onslaught and, with it, customers for the baths.

By 410, the Romans had essentially pulled out of Britain. The last century of the empire had begun. Locals tried to keep the baths going, but crime plagued the city. In 440, a young girl's head was found in an oven on what is now Abbeygate Street, just a few blocks south of the Baths—a bad omen. At roughly the same time, the Avon—whose banks were no longer maintained by the Romans—experienced a series of disastrous floods that spewed black mud all through the baths.

In relatively short order, the roof of the Grand Bath collapsed into the stagnant and muddy water below, and the Temple of Sulis was reduced to rubble. That debris, in turn, seems to have been used to help fill in and pave over large parts of the bath complex. Carbon dating is still incomplete, but there's a good chance that in less than three decades after the last Roman legions departed, the Aquae Sulis was unrecognizable as what it had so long been—a shining light of colonization. Eventually, even the memory of its golden days faded from historical memory. Not until 1727, when workmen uncovered a gilt bronze head of Minerva while trenching the main street for a sewer, did the good people of Bath realize what a treasure lay buried beneath their feet.

As Aquae Sulis was sagging into oblivion, the Middle Ages began. At least in Europe, swimming slipped into the dark for a full millennium.

What happened to swimming? Five observations:

- The breakdown of civil authority and the attendant collapse of infrastructure. By the end of the first century CE, Rome's water system was supplying the empire's capital with more water than New York City enjoyed near the end of the twentieth century. But pools, baths, lead pipes, lead-lined channels, furnaces for heating the water, aqueducts to bring it in from the countryside—they don't maintain themselves. They need attention. Finally, no one was left to keep them going. And the invaders, it seemed, couldn't be bothered.
- Rising insularity. Swimming and bathing in Greece and Rome had been a communal activity, but as city-states and fiefdoms replaced Europe's long-time *uber*-power, community waned. The rich and royal disappeared inside their castles. The Catholic Church went

to ground in its monasteries. Not only was there no place to swim; there was no one to swim with. The old camper's maxim—"Always Swim with a Buddy"—goes to deeper issues as well, or used to.

- Prudery played a role. The medieval church was far more obsessed with avoiding sin and punishing evil than with doing good works and emulating the Christ of the New Testament. The Greeks had swum naked; the Romans, too—and for good reason. Wet clothes are a hindrance. But what better place for Satan to lurk than in the literal fleshpots of public baths?*

- Sanitation. This was another underside of the fall of Rome and the collapse of infrastructure. The empire's pools and baths were far from sanitary by modern standards: warm water—whether naturally warm or heated—is a breeding ground for bacteria of all sorts. Open wounds soaked in such a medium can easily turn gangrenous. But Roman engineering also carried away the bacteria-and-feces-ridden waters that urban populations of necessity produce. That largely ceased when the empire ceased. Even if you wanted to go for a swim in medieval Europe—and retained some vestigial sense of how to stay afloat—where would you dare go, especially given the wave of plagues that swept Europe in the mid-fourteenth century? Credit for the Black Death goes to rats—or more specifically to the Oriental fleas that lived on rats—but blame is as likely to fall on the Continent's diseased waterways and crumbling, or crumbled, infrastructure. And with a hundred million or more dead after the plagues retreated, there was neither the means nor the manpower nor the willpower to recover.**

- Imagination gets a star turn, as well. One of the lesser-heralded geniuses of the Greeks and Romans was to temper the water demons—their angry, avenging gods and demigods. Herodotus

---

* Three centuries after the Middle Ages had died and the Enlightenment had been born, Victorian England was still trying to resolve this conundrum, without great success.
** The Black Death trailed off after 1351. Two full centuries would pass before Europe returned to the same population level.

recounts Scyllis's feats in the Battle of Salamis without ever once dragging Poseidon or his minions into the story other than as occasional literary embellishment. Livy does the same with Cloelia. No demigod parts the waters for her or her virgin band; they cross the Tiber all on their own, bravely or terrified, with spears flying at their backs. The same holds for the various accounts of Caesar's swim at the Battle of Alexandria. The details may veer toward disbelief in some accounts, but the story is all about Caesar, not the divinities that buoyed him up or the demons that tried to sink him.[*]

As my five-year-old granddaughter likes to say, "I did it all by myself!" But as the comfort and security of a bureaucratic empire faded and the cultural memory of swimming disappeared into the mists of time, the demons came roaring back. Water was once again to be feared. Submersion risked being grabbed by the heels by who knows what . . . never to rise to the surface again.

All that is too simplistic, of course. The Middle Ages didn't send swimming globally into eclipse. Beyond the reach of the Holy Roman Empire and its ecclesiastical henchmen, swimming seems to have survived just fine.

Sixteen-hundred-year-old wall paintings in the Buddhist caves at Kizil, along the Silk Road in Xinjiang Province, China, show men swimming merrily along. Paintings from the Mogao Caves, in Gansu Province—dating from about 600 CE—depict swimmers, who might seem to be floating in thin air if ducks were not happily paddling along beside them. Elsewhere in the Mogao Caves, from about a century later, battle scenes, with swimmers racing down a river to escape mounted warriors, adorn the walls.

---

[*] In his book *Early British Swimming*, Nicholas Orme suggests a sixth possible reason. Medieval commentaries on the passage from Isaiah 25 cited earlier—the one about Moabites being trodden down in a dung pit even though they spread their hands like swimmers—often equated swimming with the fate of the damned.

One Chinese account from the twelfth century tells of an annual event along the Qiantang River, famous for its tidal bore. "Far in the horizon, the tide will approach swiftly. . . . Then hundreds of excellent swimmers will dash against the formidable and mighty tide like arrows, with colorful flags in hand." After the dash was over, wealthy nobles and businessmen showered the swimmers with gold and silver.

A mid-seventeenth-century mural in the Potala Palace in Lhasa, Tibet, shows another swimming race, this one to honor the investiture of the fifth Dalai Lama, born in 1617. Everyone looks to be having a jolly good time—diving, swimming, somehow capering on top of the water. One monk sitting in a lotus position seems incapable of sinking.

An illustrated Persian manuscript from four centuries earlier depicts Alexander the Great and his men watching lithe naked girls with hair falling down below their knees as they swim and cavort at the water's edge. Sunshine, the tactile thrill of water, the joy of the exposed human form—how could Europeans have forgotten all this?

There were, of course, pockets of resistance. The seagoing Vikings are said to have taught their children to swim at an early age. Like Samurai and Roman soldiers, medieval knights in Europe were expected to be excellent swimmers. Swimming was one of the virtues incumbent upon knighthood. But in reality, water seems to have scared the bejesus out of most of them. In Chrétien de Troyes's *Lancelot*, the title character is so unmanned by a "wicked-looking stream"—"as swift and raging, as black and turgid, as fierce and terrible as if it were the devil's stream"— that he chooses instead to cross the water on a "sword bridge," as sharp as a scythe, with perhaps two lions or tigers chained to a tree on the far side.

Among the European ruling classes, swimming retained some status for several centuries after the fall of Rome. Charlemagne (742–814 CE), for one, was known to be an ardent swimmer. According to his contemporary and biographer Einhard, the Holy Roman Emperor favored the natural warm springs at Aachen (also known as Aix-la-Chapelle) in what is now the extreme west of Germany. Charlemagne, Einhard writes, "often practiced swimming, in which he was such an adept that none could surpass him." Eventually, Charlemagne would build a palace at the site and pass his later years in the warm springs surrounded by his sons, other nobles and friends, and "now and then a troop of his retinue or body guard, so that a hundred or more persons sometimes bathed with him."

Charlemagne's aquatic crowdsourcing, though, was the exception, not the rule. Most scholars believe that, at least by the time of the Norman Conquest, the aristocracy had lost all interest in swimming. Among aristocrats, one medieval author declares, swimming was almost never learned, though "it is possible that some boys mastered it, though never girls."

And those who did swim were deemed bizarre. England's Edward II was known to enjoy "frolics in the water"—but "frolics" might be the giveaway. In 1315, he took a swimming holiday with a group that one chronicler called "his silly company of swimmers."* Shakespeare catches some of that same spirit in *Henry VIII* when Cardinal Wolsey rues that he has waded into matters far beyond his depth "like wanton boys that swim on bladders."

In a 1999 piece for the *Journal of the Society of Architectural Historians,* Jill Caskey argues that the Middle Ages were not "a thousand years without a bath," as the old joke holds. During the thirteenth century, architecturally sophisticated baths were built at Amalfi, Ravello, and Pontone, along the Campania coast in the southwest of Italy. A similar bath was constructed at roughly the same time at the inland hill town of Caserta Vecchia. A century earlier at Bath in England, a new structure known as the King's Bath was raised out of the ruins of the Aquae Sulis.

People did wash. Warm water, plunging, floating, and soaking still had their lure. But all this hardly amounts to a revival of the Roman habits of communal bathing and swimming. The Caserta Vecchia bath was

---

* That Edward II was a miserable, feckless king, eventually forced to abdicate and murdered, could not have helped swimming's reputation in medieval England.

part of the castle complex that dominates the hill town. The King's Bath was far from public; it sat within a monastery that had claimed the space around the old Sacred Spring where Anglo-Saxons had once worshipped. Also against such exceptions have to be placed the darker uses to which water was put in medieval times—the beautifully named "Grace of Wapping," for example.

A form of capital punishment reserved for pirates, the "Grace" began with the partial strangulation of the convicted, followed by wrapping them in chains and placing them in the River Thames at Wapping in Central London, where they were submerged by three tides before being pulled out again and disposed.

Witches and water were another often fatal combination during much of the Middle Ages and well into the Renaissance. From at least the fifteenth century on, accused witches were subject to a process known as "swimming a witch." A 1613 pamphlet published in London and entitled *Witches Apprehended, Examined, and Executed* described how the "swimming" had been applied the previous year to two Bedford women— Mother Sutton and her daughter, who stood accused of, among the other crimes, murdering the son of a Master Enger.

First came the preliminary trial in which the two women were stripped to their underclothes, then tied up with arms crossed and thrown into a deep nearby mill pond. Both had a rope tied around their middle so they could be rescued if they sank to the bottom, but in this instance, both floated, which confirmed not their innocence, as one might expect, but their probable guilt. That led to a second trial much the same as the previous one, but this time with the women bound more traditionally: left thumb tied to right toe, right thumb to left toe. Again the Suttons mother and daughter were unfortunate enough to float, not sink. A more formal trial on witchcraft charges followed, but the outcome was basically preordained—as was their subsequent execution.

Imagine witnessing that and ever considering swimming again: floating = guilty. Yikes! But two decades into the eighteenth century, Richard Boulton—Oxford graduate, medical writer, and generally a learned man of his enlightened time—was still defending the practice on strictly theological grounds. The following is from Boulton's *Compleat History of Magick, Sorcery, and Witchcraft*, published in 1722: "The surest way to discover such as practice [witchcraft], besides their evil lives and conversations is first, by their mark, which is insensible, and secondly, by their swimming upon the water, God having ordained, that such as had cast off water by baptism, should not be received into water, but swim upon it."

The Middle Ages did have its swimming heroes—amazing heroes, worthy of the DC Comics pantheon of the greatest heroes ever, right up there with Superman, Batman, Wonder Woman, and Aquaman, although never in *Aquaman* (to my recollection, and I had a subscription for years) was there anything like the ocean outing that Beowulf and his childhood friend Breca undertook.

That story gets told in the great Anglo-Saxon epic *Beowulf*, written sometime between the eighth and eleventh centuries and a doozy of a tale. For five days and nights, mostly for the sheer joy of swimming, Beowulf and Breca "stake their lives far at sea," wearing mail armor and hauling heavy swords "to guard us against the whales," until "churning waves and chillest water" divide them. And thus Beowulf must ultimately face alone maybe the ultimate monster the deep has ever spawned: Grendel's mother.

Perhaps Beowulf is the model for other swimming heroes of his time. Maybe he is simply another expression of the impulse to make heroic an activity that had come to seem so far beyond the capacity of mortal men. That's an open question. But as Peter A. Jorgensen shows in a 1978 article for *Folklore*, *Beowulf* in its time had plenty of company.

In the Icelandic *Halfdanar* saga, the title character, Halfdan, and his foe, Aki—both dressed in armor, both also carrying heavy swords—swim up a storm before Halfdan gets the upper hand and holds Aki underwater from morning until midafternoon. Even that is not enough to kill Aki, but it does discourage him from further battle. So it goes in saga after saga from the later Middle Ages: heroes galore, epic swimming feats, breath-holding that beggars the imagination. All in all, this was a golden age for aquatic derring-do.

Except it's all imaginary. The less people knew about how to swim, the more they heard tales of swimming as it could never be. By the time the tales crested and the Middle Ages began to break open on the shores of the Renaissance, most Europeans had lost even the most basic knowledge of how to propel themselves through the water, or survive submersion in it.

4

REDISCOVERING A LOST ART

There is an exercise, which is right profitable in extreme danger of wars, but because . . . it hath not been of long time much used, especially among noblemen, perchance some readers will little esteem it, I mean swimming.

—Sir Thomas Elyot

A tale of two poets, a myth, and of course swimming . . .

The two poets, separated by almost a thousand years, are Musaeus and Christopher Marlowe. Of Musaeus, almost nothing is known for sure. He seems to have been a Greek schoolmaster who likely lived in Alexandria, at the mouth of the Nile, in the last half of the fifth century CE, about the time the Roman Empire was expiring.

Of Christopher (or "Kit") Marlowe, a great deal is known, but not everything. Born in Canterbury, England, in 1564, the same year as Shakespeare, Marlowe was a bright comet streaking across the Elizabethan literary skies, the leading tragedian of his day. *Edward the Second* and *The Tragical History of Doctor Faustus* made Marlowe famous.

Shakespeare labored in *his* shadow until Marlowe was stabbed to death in 1593, at age twenty-nine, not long after being arrested for writing a manuscript that was alleged to contain "vile heretical concepts." The nature of those "concepts" has never been determined, or whether they were connected to his murder, but suspicion runs high.

The myth that connects the two poets was mentioned earlier: the story of Hero and Leander, the hapless lovers separated by the stormy Hellespont and united finally in death when Leander drowns trying to reach his beloved and Hero throws herself in the sea, grieving his death. Musaeus survives in memory today only through the 342 lines of poetry in which he recounts the ancient myth of Hero and Leander. Marlowe survives for many reasons, among them his own treatment of the same myth, but the two men's poetic takes on the same subject could not be more different when it comes to swimming.

Musaeus was a swimmer himself, and not just in mild waters. You can hear and feel it in his poetry. Here he is describing Leander setting off on his fatal swim:

> *. . . in that dark watch of night*
> *When winds are fiercest, flinging at the sea*
> *The deadliest javelins of their armory.*
> *Leandar, all impetuous for his bride,*
> *Started to breast the swollen surge and ride*
> *The storm-foot horse of the unmastered main*
> *That carried him helpless, a rider without rein.*
> *Wave curled on wave; the sea and heavenly vault*
> *Were mixed, and all the winds in savage assault*
> *Shrieked as they fought—the West Wind with the East,*
> *South with the terrible North; nor ever ceased*
> *The thunder of the unforgiving surge.*

Reading Musaeus for the first time, I thought of the time my friend John and I drove half the night through eastern Pennsylvania and across

New Jersey. A storm had been lashing Ocean City, kicking up what looked on the television like monster waves, at least by East Coast standards. We wanted to body surf them at first light. Twenty minutes or more of swimming through pounding surf brought us out to where the biggest waves were breaking, nearly to the end of the fishing pier not far down the beach. The rides back into shore were so long and powerful that we could roll on our sides to breathe and fall right back into the wave: an "unmastered main," as Musaeus put it, that carried us "helpless, riders without rein." This was the fall of 1961—we were sixteen, on the high school swimming team, stupid beyond belief.

A millennium after Musaeus, Marlowe sat down to the same basic storyboard and came up with a completely different treatment:

> Leander, being up, began to swim
> And, looking back, saw Neptune follow him,
> Whereat aghast, the poor soul 'gan to cry
> "O, let me visit Hero ere I die!"
> The god put Helle's bracelet on his arm,
> And swore the sea should never do him harm.
> He clapped his plump cheeks, with his tresses played
> And, smiling wantonly, his love bewrayed.
> He watched his arms and, as they opened wide
> At every stroke, betwixt them would he slide
> And steal a kiss, and then run out and dance,
> And, as he turned, cast many a lustful glance,
> And threw him gaudy toys to please his eye,
> And dive into the water, and pry
> Upon his breast, his thighs, and every limb,
> And up again, and close beside him swim,
> And talk of love.

The poetry is first-rate—nicely rounded couplets, flawless iambic pentameter. Neptune is clearly besotted by the plump-cheeked Leander.

Anything goes in this seductive aquacade, but what about the sea—the swimming part of the famous swimmer myth? What's that motion Marlowe describes where Leander's "arms are opened wide at every stroke"—so wide that Neptune can slide inside and "steal a kiss"? Breaststroke, perhaps, but where are the "swollen surges" of Musaeus's "unmastered main." This is a dark and stormy night, after all, not a becalmed and glassy sea.

As the classicist Douglas Bush once asked, "Why, in [Marlowe's] long account of Leander's swim, there is such a lack of feeling for the sea. Though the passage has its beautiful bits, the general impression is of Leander gliding over waves of mythological tapestry."[*]

The answer to all these questions is almost certainly the simplest one available. Christopher Marlowe might have been the greatest tragedian of his time, but this was England in the last half of the sixteenth century. Odds are strong that Marlowe had never submerged himself in the ocean, that he would have had absolutely no idea how to stay afloat or move forward if he had, that indeed he had never seen anyone even attempt to swim.

That an entire realm of human activity should have virtually disappeared across an entire continent for the better part of a thousand years seems bizarre at best. That this should have happened on the British Isles seems almost inexplicable. Isles are, by definition, surrounded by water. They foster a maritime people. Ships sink. Able swimmers at least have a chance of reaching land, and in the case of these isles, it's a generally welcoming shore, indented by coves and ringed here and there by sandy beaches. And that's not to mention innumerable freshwater lakes, smooth-flowing rivers, cooling ponds for hot summer days, and on and on.

Why deny yourself such pleasures? Why not turn survival odds in your favor? Yet the England of Marlowe and Shakespeare's time was just

---

[*] To which Michael West adds, in a 1984 article for *Renaissance Quarterly,* "Does the passage reflect first-hand experience of swimming on Marlowe's part or fantasies of being groped in a bathhouse?"

as much a swimming backwater as was any European country, maybe even more so. Few people knew how to swim or had any easy way to learn. Medical opinion often fought against the practice. Educators thought physical training of any sort was mostly a waste of time. Even the few who advocated for sports in school seemed to save most of their reservations for swimming: Richard Mulcaster, for example.

As the head of the Merchant Taylors' School in London—then the largest school in England—Mulcaster had clout, and in his 1581 book *Positions*, he used it to go all in for teaching boys to play sports, including swimming. But as Michael West points out in a 1973 article for *Renaissance Quarterly*, Mulcaster undercuts his enthusiasm for water sports at nearly every turn. True enough, swimming could help with headaches. It cleared up stuffy sinuses and improved one's sense of smell, but swimming could also be physically threatening if "rotten and corrupt vapors enter the pores of the body." What's more, "all swimming must needs be ill for the head, considering the continual exhalation which ascends still from the water," whatever precisely that means.

With friends like Mulcaster, swimming needed no enemies. The times, though, were slowly changing, and first credit for that, at least in England, goes to a book that preceded Mulcaster's by half a century: Sir Thomas Elyot's 1531 work, *The Boke Named the Governour*.

Born around 1490, Elyot was a scholar and diplomat—so well regarded at court that Henry VIII dispatched him to Rome to try to convince Charles V, the Holy Roman Emperor, to approve Henry's divorce from Catherine of Aragon. We know how that worked out, but Elyot was also interested in improving governance generally. His book was meant for the English ruling class—royals, aristocrats, and the rare commoner who might ascend to a high governmental post—to remind them of the manly virtues, high character, and sound practices of the ancient Greeks and Romans.

As the author writes near the beginning, "In the first [book] shall be comprehended the best form of education or bringing up of noble children from their nativity in such manner as they may be found worthy and so able to be governors of a public weal." That's a broad mandate and a big task, and swimming—nearly as long lost as the ancient cultures Elyot is trying to revive—is part of his argument.

"There is an exercise, which is right profitable in extreme danger of wars," Elyot writes, "but because there seemeth to be some peril in the learning thereof, and also it hath not been of long time much used, especially among noblemen, perchance some readers will little esteem it, I mean swimming."

That Elyot steps into his subject so gingerly says volumes about the low esteem to which swimming had sunk by the sixteenth century—as if it were the sport that dare not speak its name. But Elyot doesn't shrink from the cause. He goes on to cite numerous instances when the ability to swim turned the course of battle and perhaps even bent history. Among them:

- Horatius Cocles, who during the Etruscan siege of Rome, single-handedly defended the Tiber River bridge against a horde of invaders, then when hope seemed gone, ordered the bridge destroyed and tumbled into the water with his foes. Unable to swim, the Etruscans perished, while Horatius, though fully armored and sorely wounded, was able to swim ashore, having "saved the city of Rome from perpetual servitude."[*]
- Sertorius, who during a Roman campaign in France, first put the enemy to rout, then wounded and with his horse dead, leapt with his shield and sword "into the river of Rhone, which is wonderfully swift, and swimming against the stream, came to company, not without great wondering of all his enemies, who stood and beheld him."
- Also a naval battle during the first Roman war with the Carthaginians during which the vanquished enemy fleet would have gladly set

---

[*] This is the same siege of Rome that yielded the swimmer-heroine Cloelia, profiled in Chapter 2.

sails and fled except for the many young Romans who "threw themselves into [the] sea, and swimming unto the ships, enforced their enemies to strike on land, and there assaulted them so roughly, that the captain of the Romans, called Lucretius, might easily take them."

Alexander the Great gets a cameo in Elyot's accounting as well, a scene from the Indian subcontinent. Stymied by the Indus River during his campaign against King Porus, Alexander laments, "O how most unhappy am I of all others, that have not 'ere this time learned to swim!"—then overcoming his fear, throws his shield into the water, climbs on it, and uses it as a raft to reach the other shore, an example quickly followed by his abashed troops.

Even horses get a turn. They, too, need to be trained to swim, Elyot cautions, "that by such usage they should more aptly and boldly pass over great rivers, and be more able to resist, or cut the waves, and be not afraid of great storms. For it hath been often times seen, that by the good swimming of horses, many men have been saved."

Finally, in this relatively short section on swimming, Elyot dares to address Henry VIII himself to remind His Majesty "what great advantage is in the feat of swimming, since no King, be he never so powerful or perfect in the experience of wars, may assure himself from the necessities, which fortune soweth among men that be mortal." Actually, that's a pretty bold statement, given this particular Tudor's general penchant for executing those who dared to step out of line.

As popular as Eloyt's book was—it was republished in 1537, 1544, and 1546—it did not automatically launch a new Golden Age of Swimming, or even do much to tamp down the sport's naysayers. But Elyot did crack open the door for other advocates and enthusiasts to follow, or maybe he simply caught the front end of a wave that was ready to break over the British Isles and Europe.

Seven years after *The Governour* first appeared, Nicholas Wynman— a Swiss-born language professor at the University of Ingolstadt in

Bavaria—published the first known book to be devoted solely to swimming: *Colymbetes*. The text is in Latin, but the title comes from the Greek word for a swimmer or diver, doubly appropriate since the Greeks were ardent swimmers and because the book, in the classical mode, is in the form of an extended dialogue between two characters, one taking the part of Wynman himself.

Wynman was an early and able swimmer, an exception to his time and place. He learned as a thirteen-year-old watching other boys cavort in the hot springs close to his home, and in his part of the dialogue, he offers basic stroke advice and discourses on river swimming versus swimming in ponds and the sea. Like Elyot, he also provides multiple examples of heroic Roman swimmers and reminds his German audience of the praise lavished on their ancient swimming talent by Herodotus and Tacitus, among others.

But as Nicholas Orme notes in *Early British Swimming*, *Colymbetes* is more an extended ode to the sport—"'a merry dialogue and pleasant reading,' as the title page describes it"—than a systematic effort to teach swimming or water safety, or to involve the public in its practice, and in any event, Wynman and his book appeared and disappeared without much of a splash, having done little to increase swimming's stature.

Forty years after Thomas Elyot called swimmers to arms, and a little over three decades after Nicholas Wynman joined the fight, the vice chancellor of the University of Cambridge banned students altogether from swimming in the nearby River Cam, upon penalty of two days of flogging, probably for good reason. Few of them had any notion of how to deal with the water, and these being university students, one guesses adult beverages played a leading role in their decision to try, too often with fatal results.

Within twenty years, though, Cambridge had also given us (or more accurately spit out) the man who would become swimming's first great modern advocate—Everard Digby, author of the first book to devote its entirety to reintroducing the Renaissance world to water and providing readers with the tools, knowledge, and "practical" advice to use this reclaimed medium: *De Arte Natandi* (in English, *The Art of Swimming*).

Everard Digby is an unlikely hero. Opinionated, brash, headstrong, combative—he often seems to have been a cannonball looking for a diving board to jump off. Simultaneously, he was a scholar of some stature; a senior fellow of St. John's College, Cambridge; and rector of several churches in the general vicinity of his college.

By 1587, when *The Art of Swimming* was first published, Digby was nearing forty years old and playing with fire—suspected of being a Catholic sympathizer within a college solidly Protestant at the highest administrative levels. William Whitaker, the reigning master of St. John's, was a prominent Puritan. Henry Alvey, the college steward, had cast his lot with the Puritan movement, too. Even worse, Digby made no attempt to find common ground with either man. In 1587, Whitaker and Alvey struck back, with all the fury that academic squabbles can sometime muster.

First came trumped-up charges from Alvey that Digby had been dilatory in paying the steward for his share of the "commons"—meals for the fellows and scholars who attended St. John's. Nonsense, Digby replied; Alvey had failed to call at his chambers to collect the payment. Balderdash, retorted Alvey: That was the old custom; the new one was for the fellows to show up at the steward's door with their money. Very shortly, both men had their heels dug in, and the situation so deteriorated from there that the board of visitors had to be called in, powerful alumni were moved to write letters, and Whitaker himself filed twenty-two additional charges against what was by now his and Alvey's mortal enemy. Among them (and I'm indebted here to Nicholas Orme):

- Digby was "vehemently suspect, upon good presumptions, to be of corrupt religion."
- He kept company in Cambridge with known Catholics.

- He had gone fishing with a casting net when he should have been in chapel.
- He was accustomed "to blow a horn often in the college in the day time and halloo after it."
- He had shouted in public (in Latin, of course) that the college president was a bad logician and had beaten his hands on the table as he did so.
- And, last of the twenty-two, he had had the impudence to sit in Whitaker's place at table, while the master was away.

(This really does sound like faculty politics, doesn't it?)

A high council was held, with the first major decision going Digby's way, but that one was overturned in 1588, in Whitaker and Avery's favor, and this second decision was the keeper. As seems almost inevitable from day one, Everard Digby was stripped of his status as a senior fellow, shown to the gate, and forced to find his place in history not through his commentaries on Renaissance theologians but as the godfather of modern swimming. Luckily for him.

In his introduction to the abridged English-language version of *De Arte Natandi,* published in 1595, translator Christopher Middleton lauds Everard Digby as the equivalent of Virgil for the tillage of the earth; Vegetius for the military profession; Hippocrates and Galen for medicine; Justinian for the law; Aristotle, Euclid, and others for the liberal sciences; Pomponius Mela for cosmography; and Mercator for the globes of the world.

That seems more than a little exaggerated for a thin book—115 pages in Middleton's shortened and simplified version, including 40 pages of woodcuts—that makes some wild claims about swimming and more than a few bizarre recommendations on how to go about it. Nicholas Orme seems more on the money when he praises Everard Digby for his methodical descriptions and especially his lasting influence: "The history of swimming forms only one small rivulet beside the great river of European history in general, but Digby is the greatest fish in the sixteenth century and one of the greatest before the nineteenth."

In the opening pages, Digby himself makes a compelling claim to his book's value and to the seriousness of swimming generally:

> If medicine be worthy of commendations, in respect of the nature in purging poisoned humors, drying away contagious diseases, and by this means adding longer date unto the life of man, well then may this Art of Swimming come within the number of other Sciences, which preserve the precious life of man, amidst the furious billows of the lawless waters, where neither riches nor friends, neither birth nor kin, neither liberal Sciences or other Arts, only itself excepted, can rid him from the danger of death, but it is also a necessary thing for every man to use, even in the pleasantest and securest time of his life especially: as the fittest thing to purge the skin from all external pollutions or uncleanliness whatsoever, as sweat and such like, as also it helps to temper the extreme heat of the body in the burning time of year.[*]

Still, there are all the oddities to deal with. Digby's claim, for instance, that man "above all fouls [*sic*] of the air, fishes of the sea, beasts of the earth, or other creatures whatsoever excels in [swimming]." Excel over fish? Really? Absolutely, according to the author:

> The fishes in the sea, whose continual life is spent in the water, in them does no man deny swimming to be [the] only gift which nature has bestowed upon them, and shall we think it artificial in a man, which in [water] does by so many degrees excel them, as diving down to the bottoms of the deepest waters and fetching from thence whatsoever is there sunk down, transporting things to and from at his please, sitting, tumbling, leaping, walking, and at his ease performing many fine feats

---

[*] The language here and following is from Middleton's abridged English translation (1595) of Digby's book although I've modernized spellings and occasionally rearranged sentences and substituted words for ease of reading and understanding.

in the water that far exceeds the natural gifts bestowed on fishes? Nay, so fit is the constitution of man's body that anyone who thoroughly considers it cannot but accord with me in this: that a man of all creatures under the circumference of heaven naturally excels in swimming.

How about the fact that humans are far more likely than fish—or dogs, deer, horses, squirrels, etc.—to drown in this medium of water in which they so excel over all other living things? Digby is on top of that as well, and selling his book and promoting its mission at the same time. The reason is simple: Men "have not had some practice in swimming heretofore. When by any sinister occasion they fall into the water, the discreet use of their senses is taken away by a sudden fear, and so laboring disorderly in the water, they pull themselves down under the water by the indirect moving of their bodies, and so are drowned, which to avoid I leave it to every man's consideration how necessary a thing this art of swimming is."

Point made, but from a modern perspective, reading *The Art of Swimming* is like traveling via time machine to some distant, primitive epoch in history when cave dwellers still had no word for "wet." Digby truly starts *de novo*—as if his audience has just encountered for the very first time one of Earth's four essential elements.

The best time for swimming in England, he tells his readers, is May through August when the sun shines brightest and the water is most temperate. Beware the chill north winds. Don't swim in rain, which can hurt the body and limit vision. Watch out for river banks with thick grass, which can hide snakes and poisonous toads. Look for clear running water, not stagnant ponds covered with slime, and so on.

Is it possible people didn't know or at least intuit these things in 1587? Apparently so.

And then there are the forty woodcuts, which are both handsomely executed and collectively more than a little bizarre. Woodcut 3, for example, advises one who can already swim to enter the water by "laying his hands on his neck and forcibly running to the bank where declining his head downwards and turning round over with his heels, he may light into the water upon his back"—sort of a back half-sommersault that ends with a back belly flop. Why?

Or, alternatively, in woodcut 4, you can just do a sideways dive, either left or right. Again, why?

Woodcut 6 gets to the "first degree of swimming," which looks a lot like a leisurely doggy paddle. Number 7 moves on to "'swimming upon the back'—a gift which [Nature] has denied even to the watery inhabitants of the sea. No fish, no fowl, no other creature whatsoever that hath any living or being, either in the depth of the sea or surface of the water, swims upon his back, only man excepted." Tell it to the whales. Alert the seals and otters.

And so it goes. There are illustrated instructions for swimming on your back by pulling your legs out and in; for swimming on your stomach by joining your palms together, "the thumbs right upward," and pulling

Two woodcuts from Everard Digby's 1587 guide *De Arte Natandi*, or *The Art of Swimming*. Left, an example of Digby's ornamental swimming. At right, he offers advice on how to pare one's toenails while floating merrily along. *(British Library)*

the hands into the breast and then forward again without parting them"; for a sidestroke that looks a lot like a modern sidestroke; for treading water and "turning like a roach"; for swimming on the stomach and the back while holding one foot behind your back with the opposite hand, to ease "cramps and other infirmities"; for "play[ing] above the water with one foot" (really!); for paring toenails while lying on your back in the water (more really! and why?); for showing four parts of your body above the water at once; and last, woodcut 40, for swimming like a dolphin, which is always a blast.

But in a way, all that is petty on my part. Maybe the ultimate gift of Everard Digby's book—and the reason, conscious or otherwise, for its many oddities—is that, after a thousand years of darkness, he promised that swimming could be fun again. You could take swimming seriously. In fact, you should. But you could also goof off in the water once you got the hang of it: roll over, fall sideways into a pond, even do that weird half flip Digby starts the woodcuts with. Whooie!

One more note on Everard Digby: he and his swimming book might well have influenced one of the early masterpieces of English literature, Edmund Spenser's *The Faerie Queene*. In a *Renaissance Quarterly* article titled "Spenser, Everard Digby, and the Renaissance Art of Swimming," Michael West notes that, whereas Spenser avoids any mention of swimming through the first four books of *The Faerie Queene*, in Book V he suddenly springs a somewhat strained scene in which two knights fall off a booby-trapped bridge into a river and proceed to do battle.

The villain, Pollente, "well knew" swimming, Spenser tells us, and "to fight in water great advantage had." Artegall, the hero-knight, was no landlubber either. He, too, "in swimming skillful was, / And durst the depth of any water sound. / So ought each knight, the use of peril has, / In swimming be expert, through water's force to pass."

In short, it was on the face of things an even match, but not quite. Though "both were skilled in that experiment . . . Artegall was better breathed beside." Thus, when Pollente tires and breaks for shore, the better-conditioned Artegall swims him down and beheads him—a swim to the death, as it were, and one more reason why competitive swimmers shouldn't quit on their sprint drills.

But why the sudden shift to swimming and aquatic combat? Well, West writes, when Spenser returned to England in 1589, to shepherd the first three books of *The Faerie Queene* through publication, he quite likely would have noticed Digby's *De Arte Natandi* for sale in the London bookstalls, and seeing who had written it, Spenser might well have purchased a copy because he had arrived at Cambridge just two years behind Digby; because Digby had remained on as student, lecturer, and eventually fellow at the university for the next two decades, until given the unceremonial boot; and because, as we saw earlier, Digby was apparently a hard person to ignore.

That's not much of a stretch, but the real clincher might be the fact that, like his contemporary Christopher Marlowe, Spenser's swimming passage lacks any real feel for the activity. It's action learned from a book, not experienced firsthand, in the sinew and bones, which might explain why Spenser has his two knights do battle and swim about without even bothering to shed their armor. And by 1589, Digby's book was the eight-hundred-pound tuna of swimming literature.

Finally, it needs noting that although Digby's book was even more popular than Elyot's *The Boke Named the Governour*, it, too, was not a complete game changer. A quarter of a century after its publication, when Henry Frederick, the Prince of Wales, died after a few days of sickness, royal physicians "bemoaned his enthusiasm for swimming in the river after a full meal or walking in a moonlit rain."

Swimming was remerging, but in a narrow band. Its broader acceptance was still more than a century away.

5

SWIMMING 2.0

Learn fairly to swim, as I wish all men were taught to do in
their youth; they would, on many occurrences, be the safer
for having that skill, and on many more the happier.

—Benjamin Franklin

The revival of swimming in the Western world owes much to three
very different men: Benjamin Franklin, Richard Russell, and George
Gordon, aka Lord Byron. Edgar Allan Poe would like to be recognized,
too, but Poe gets ahead of the story.

In a ghostly way, Everard Digby continued as the go-to source for
swimming through all of the seventeenth century. Not only was his *De
Arte Natandi* frequently reprinted, especially in Middleton's shortened
English translation, but also his book was heavily borrowed from by the
few writers who dared to tackle the subject in his wake.

William Percey in his 1658 work *The Compleat Swimmer* opens with
a look back at the author's youth, especially the near-drowning incident

"which danger wrought in me such an earnest desire to learn to swim that I seldom did forbear the exercise a day, till I was become a perfect swimmer." Perfect? Nothing at this remove is known about Percey, but he seems to have been rich in self-confidence.

In his front-of-the-book discussion, Percey also expresses something Everard Digby probably never would have dreamed of: teaching women as well as men to swim as perfectly as he did. But as Nicholas Orme notes, when Percey gets down to work, "the form and content of [his] treatise is entirely based on Digby," with no acknowledgment of the debt and no effort to include women in the discussion.

Almost four decades later, in 1696, the century coughed up a second, more famous treatise on swimming, Melchisédech Thévenot's *L'Art de Nager*—the French version of Digby's *De Arte Natandi* of a century-plus earlier. Born about 1620, Thévenot worked for the French crown in Genoa briefly in his twenties and in Rome for several years in his thirties; wrote four travel books drawing on accounts of voyagers to distant points in the world; eventually became keeper of the royal library of Louis XIV; and died near Paris in 1692, four years before his book was published posthumously. He was, in short, a man of parts.

Like William Percey, Thévenot makes some original observations in his preface, including the then radical assertion that "the Indians and Negroes surpass all other men in the art of swimming and diving." (As we will see in the next chapter, they did—far surpassed them in fact.) Unlike Percey, Thévenot also at least makes reference to Digby's book and to Nicholas Wynman's, as well, but—again citing Nicholas Orme—"the acknowledgement to Digby is a large understatement since his book . . . is based upon [*De Arte Natandi*] almost entirely," even to the point of having an engraver basically rework most of Digby's woodcuts in a more contemporary style.

Plagiarized as his book was, Thévenot—and through him, Everard Digby—did have one important reader who marked, learned, and inwardly digested seemingly every word the Frenchman wrote: Benjamin Franklin.

In a 1771 letter to his son, sixty-five-year-old Franklin described his early life in Boston and his youthful attraction to the sea and swimming. Franklin's formal education, such as it was, ended at age ten when he joined his father in the candle-making business, work that brought him no pleasure. "I dislik'd the Trade and had a strong Inclination for the Sea; but my Father declar'd against it; however, living near the Water, I was much in and about it, learnt early to swim well, and to manage Boats, and when in a Boat or Canoe with other Boys I was commonly allow'd to govern, especially in any case of Difficulty."

A decade later, in his very early twenties, Franklin found work at Watts's Printinghouse, in London. There, a fellow employee named Wygate expressed a desire to learn how to swim. Turns out, Wygate had asked just the right person:

> I taught him, and a Friend of his, to swim, at twice going into the River [Thames], and they soon became good Swimmers. They introduc'd me to some Gentlemen from the Country who went to Chelsea by Water to see the College and Don Saltero's Curiosities. In our Return, at the Request of the Company, whose Curiosity Wygate had excited, I stript and leapt into the River, and swam from near Chelsea to Blackfryars, performing on the Way many Feats of Activity both upon and under Water, that surpriz'd and pleas'd those to whom they were Novelties. I had from a Child been ever delighted with this Exercise, had studied and practis'd all Thevenot's Motions and Positions, added some of my own, aiming at the graceful and easy, as well as the Useful. All these I took this Occasion of exhibiting to the Company, and was much flatter'd by their Admiration.

The thought of the future diplomat, beloved polymath, and Founding Father of his nation buck-naked in the Thames, performing Digby's "roach turn," showing all four body parts at once (*which ones?*), and swimming facedown holding one foot behind his back with his opposite hand while he covered the roughly three miles from Chelsea to Blackfriars is almost too much to contemplate.

Word of Franklin's escapades in the Thames must have spread far and wide through London because he soon found himself the object of great interest. Sir William Wyndham, a well-known Tory politician who had earlier served as Secretary of War and Chancellor of the Exchequer, asked Franklin to tutor his two sons in swimming and proposed to pay him handsomely. Franklin had to turn down the offer—the sons couldn't come to London immediately, and Franklin was planning to return home—but he was tempted nonetheless.

"From this Incident I thought it likely, that if I were to remain in England and open a Swimming School, I might get a good deal of Money. And it struck me so strongly, that had the Overture been sooner made me, probably I should not so soon have returned to America."

Think of how *that* might have changed the history of the United States, and of swimming.

Swimming was, in a sense, a perfect medium for Benjamin Franklin. It satisfied his youthful need for vigorous activity. As Edmund S. Morgan writes in his 2002 biography of Franklin, we think of him today as the plump, seemingly sedentary man captured by portraitists once he was famous on two continents. But the Franklin who dove into the Thames and swam to Blackfriars, the one who would sometimes have himself lowered overboard for a swim when his ship was becalmed in still waters, that Franklin was bursting with raw energy.

Swimming also gave Franklin a medium to tinker within. He experimented with hand and foot paddles of his own device, close enough to the training implements used today to be their primitive ancestors.

At the other end of the broad spectrum of his interests, swimming—along with fire brigades, mutual insurance companies, public libraries, postal services, and other examples—was also part and parcel of Franklin's almost endless attempts at bettering the people and society around him. In his "Proposals Relating to the Education of Youth in Pennsylvania," published in Philadelphia in 1749, Franklin first regrets that "Youth of this Province . . . have no Academy in which they might receive the Accomplishments of a regular education"; then he goes on to enumerate his five essential qualities for such an institution:

- That a house be provided for the academy in or close to Philadelphia, "not far from a River, having a Garden, Orchard, Meadow, and Field or two."
- That such house be furnished with a library with "Maps of all Countries, Globes, some mathematical Instruments, an Apparatus for experiments in Natural philosophy, and for Mechanics; Prints, of all Kinds, Prospects, Buildings, Machines, &c."
- That the academy rector be "a Man of good Understanding; good Morals, diligent and patient, learn'd in the Languages and Sciences, and a correct pure Speaker and Writer of the English Tongue."
- "That the boarding Scholars diet together, plainly, temperately, and frugally."
- And that to keep the students "in Health, and to strengthen and render active their Bodies, they be frequently, exercis'd in Running, Leaping, Wrestling, and Swimming, &c."

Maybe most important for him, swimming and water fed his boundless curiosity. Franklin didn't merely live in the world. He explored it endlessly and stopped to examine in detail whatever sufficiently arrested his attention. Examples are dotted all through his papers. In a 1761 letter, he expounded on his theory of "imbibing" and "discharging" pores. The imbibing ones, he writes, explains why even if he enters the water thirsty, he never is for long, but they explain more phenomena than that:

These imbibing Pores, however, are very fine, perhaps fine enough in filtring to separate Salt from Water; for tho' I have been soak'd by swimming, when a Boy, several Hours in the Day for several Days successively in Saltwater, I never found my Blood and Juices salted by that means, so as to make me thirsty or feel a salt Taste in my Mouth: And it is remarkable that the Flesh of Sea Fish, tho' bred in Salt Water, is not salt. Hence I imagine, that if People at Sea, distress'd by Thirst when their fresh Water is unfortunately spent, would make Bathing-Tubs of their empty Water Casks, and filling them with Sea Water, sit in them an Hour or two each Day, they might be greatly reliev'd.

Okay, even Franklin was wrong occasionally.

In another letter, this one written in 1773 to his friend and fellow Declaration of Independence signer Dr. Benjamin Rush, Franklin uses swimming to illustrate that colds are caused not by coldness or dampness, as was commonly assumed, but by "too *full Living* with too *little Exercise.*" Along the way, he also offers evidence of just how frequently and long he swam when the weather was willing.

"Travelling in our severe Winters, I have suffered Cold sometimes to an Extremity only short of Freezing, but this did not make me catch Cold. And for Moisture, I have been in the River every Evening two or three Hours for a Fortnight together, when one would suppose I might imbibe enough of it to take Cold if Humidity could give it; but no such Effect followed: Boys never get Cold by Swimming."

Two to three hours every evening for two weeks running? What was he training for?

In yet another letter, this one dated 1784, Franklin posits a lifesaving tip for swim-savvy mariners who have lost their ship but not yet their hope or minds: "A man who can swim, may be aided in a long traverse by his handkerchief formed into a kite, by two cross sticks extending to the four corners; which being raised in the air, when the wind is fair and fresh, will tow him along while lying on his back." Somehow it's hard to imagine anyone other than Benjamin Franklin really trying that.

In a 1762 letter to Oliver Neave, Franklin notes that when two stones are struck smartly together under water, "the stroke may be heard at a greater distance by an ear also placed under water in the same river, than it can be heard through the air"—as much as a mile distant, quite possibly more. Why? That sometimes seems to be the biggest word in Benjamin Franklin's vocabulary.*

Franklin's most thorough statement of advice on how and why to learn to swim—delivered in another letter to Neave—is light-years removed from anything Everard Digby or his many imitators and/or plagiarizers ever committed to paper. Science, curiosity, the commonweal, endless observation and reading, and extensive personal experience all flow together to produce a document that might still provide a solid basis for a Red Cross introductory water-safety course.

Franklin being Franklin, he begins with some deeply practical advice. To overcome your fear of the water, he suggests to Neave, confront it head-on. Wade into the river at the bottom of your garden, at a place where the water deepens gradually, until you are up to your breast. Next, turn back toward shore, toss an egg in front of you and let it sink to the bottom in someplace still deep enough that you can't simply reach down and grab it without submerging yourself. Finally, keeping your eyes open, dive for the egg, thrash for it, do whatever you have to do to grab that egg and bring it back to the surface—and note as you do how very hard it is to actually sink in the water!

Pages later, after expounding at length on the seven principles of flotation, Franklin concludes with an exhortation meant for Neave but still broadly applicable.

> Learn fairly to swim, as I wish all men were taught to do in their youth; they would, on many occurrences, be the safer for having that skill, and on many more the happier, as freer from painful apprehensions of danger, to say nothing of the enjoyment in so delightful and wholesome an exercise. Soldiers particularly should, methinks, all be taught to swim; it might be of frequent use either in surprising an enemy, or saving themselves. And if I had now boys to educate, I should prefer

---

* Actually, the answer can be found in Chapter 1: bone conduction.

those schools (other things being equal) where an opportunity was af-
forded for acquiring so advantageous an art, which once learnt is never
forgotten.

I've not been able to find evidence that Richard Russell could swim at
all, or even cared to, but if Franklin brought reason and enthusiasm to the
broad public acceptance of swimming, Richard Russell somewhat inad-
vertently provided the activity with critical infrastructure.

Russell was born in Lewes, in the south of England, in November
1687. His father and grandfather were both surgeons and apothecaries,
and young Richard followed the family calling, initially as an apprentice
to his father. After achieving financial independence—he married rich—
Russell gave up his apprenticeship and decamped for the University of
Leiden, in the Netherlands, to study under Herman Boerhaave, often
thought of as the father of the modern teaching hospital. In 1724, by now
closing in on forty years old, Russell received his doctorate of medicine
and returned to England to practice.

Russell's thesis at Leiden was on epilepsy in children, but his abiding
interest seems to have been in the medicinal properties of seawater, both
taken internally and while bathing in the ocean. Finally, in 1750, at age
sixty-three and after twenty-five years of experimentation, Russell published his masterwork on the subject, *De tabe glandulari, sive de usu aquae
marinae in morbis glandularum dissertatio,* or *A Dissertation Concerning the
Use of Sea Water in Diseases of the Glands, Etc.*

Russell's long title masks a fairly simple premise: the very qualities
that historically have made the oceans frightening for so many people—crashing waves, storm-tossed seas, evil currents—also serve to
make ocean water an invaluable health resource. As Russell puts it in his
preface:

That great Body of Water therefore, which we call the Sea, and which
is roiled with such Violence by Tempests round the World, passing over

all the Submarine Plants, Fish, Salts, Minerals, and in short, whatsoever else is found betwixt Shore and Shore, must probably wash off some parts of the whole, and be impregnated, or saturated with the Transpiration, if I may so term it, of all the Bodies it passes over: the finest Parts of which are perpetually flying off in Steams, and attempting to escape to the outward Air, till they are entangled by the Sea, and made Part of its Composition. Whilst the Salts also are every Moment imparting some of their Substances to enrich it, and keep it from Putrefaction.

In his preface, Russell expounds on what he terms the four characteristics of seawater—saltiness, bitterness, nitrosity, and unctuosity—and then moves on to explaining how each of these qualities is effective in various ways in "subduing Diseases of the Glands." We don't need to go there other than to note that modern alternative medicine literature also shows some enthusiasm for seawater, but only from the ocean depths, two hundred meters and farther below the surface. However, the renal specialist I consulted opined that voluntarily ingesting any amount of seawater from any depth risked kidney and liver failure and altered mental states, endangered those with marginal heart function, and was crazier than ingesting two horned toads. Maybe glands and organs were stronger in 1750.

Whatever its ultimate medical value, Russell's book did catch a swell compounded of a rising interest in swimming, the first hints of seaside resorts on the Channel coast of England, and the burgeoning faith in science and medicine that accompanied the Age of Reason. So popular was his dissertation and such a sensation was Russell himself that he was elected a fellow of the Royal Society in 1752, by which time the first edition of his book—in Latin, like the title—was sold out. Unauthorized English translations appeared in London that same year and in Dublin the following year, driving Russell to translate his own work into his native tongue. The last London edition, the fifth, was published in 1769, ten years after Russell's death. But Russell's impact didn't die with him.

In his book, Russell had taken particular note of the high medicinal quality of the seawater near the coastal town of Brightelmston, ten miles or so from his childhood home at Lewes. In 1753, he built a house there, by the water, large enough for patients to board while they took Russell's cures and sufficiently grand that the brother of George III, the Duke of Cumberland, rented it for decades during the summer season after Russell was gone. The Duke was still renting in 1783 when his nephew—the Prince of Wales—visited him, fell in love with the coast, and kept returning to the town for another forty years, as Prince Regent and toward the end as George IV. Thus did sleepy Brightelmston metamorphose into the fashionable (and strategically renamed) resort we know today as Brighton.

Other resorts prospered as well. A statue of George III stands in Weymouth, the coastal town he came to favor for his royal holidays. Ramsgate, Margate, Southend, Scarborough—they all became so synonymous with upper-class summers that Jane Austen used an aspiring seaside resort as the principal setting for her unfinished novel *Sanditon*, suspended shortly before her death in 1817.

Mind you, this vacationing rarely involved swimming per se. Russell's regimen didn't allow for frivolity—no capering in the water à la Digby's guidelines. Women might wade into the ocean for a minute or two, rarely longer, lest the water become excessive and unhealthy. For men, too, a seaside venture in the late eighteenth century was more likely to involve standing in the waves than lying upon them or plunging into them. Looking at the literature, one gets the sense that diving under the waves at the turn of that century was only slightly more reassuring than, say, bungee jumping today.

But Benjamin Franklin helped turn swimming from a vague art into an exact science. Richard Russell pointed his fellow countrymen toward the sea. What was still missing was a genuine hero—someone to get everyone to dive in and start stroking toward some near or distant shore. Enter George Gordon, Lord Byron, with his usual flair for attention.

The Founding Fathers of swimming in the English-speaking world: Benjamin Franklin [left], Dr. Richard Russell [right], and [bottom], George Gordon, aka Lord Byron, recovering from his swim across the Hellespont.

Byron's family history is dotted with water disasters. Both his maternal great-grandfather and grandfather were officially listed as drowning victims, although as Vybarr Cregan-Reid cautions in a 2004 article for *Critical Survey*, there's more than a little reason to suspect that suicide was the actual cause in both instances. Byron's great-grandfather, for example, presumably drowned in the dead of night, in a mostly frozen river—a more-than-odd time for a bracing swim. Prevailing law also held that in the event of suicide, all property of the victim would go to the Crown, and in the case of Byron's mother's family, that was considerable property—somewhere in the £30,000 range toward the end of the eighteenth century, about £4.3 million in today's money.[*]

Whether the young Lord Byron was taught to swim as protection against the supposed ill fortune of his forebears or he took to the sport because he was born with a clubfoot and water was a playing field that ignored his disability is an open question. Both seem likely. But take to swimming Byron definitely did. And loudly.

Byron was only twenty-two in late April 1810 when he and a companion, Lieutenant Eckenhead, made their first attempt at crossing the Hellespont, in a reprise of Leander's last, doomed swim—although in the opposite direction. That effort didn't take. The swimmers miscalculated the current and were about to be swept through the Dardanelles out into open sea when they called it quits. A week later, on May 3, they went back to work, this time successfully. Swimming breaststroke all the way, Byron covered the distance in an hour and ten minutes. (Eckenhead beat him by five minutes, a fact largely lost to history.) And then, Byron being Byron, he began to tout his conquest.[**]

Back on shore, he fired off letter after letter alerting the world to his accomplishment. "This morning I swam from Sestos to Abydos, the immediate distance is not above a mile but the current renders it hazardous," he wrote to his friend Henry Drury, on May 3, perhaps still wet from the swim. Similar letters to other friends followed on May 5, May 23, and June 23. There were also three letters to his mother between May 18 and June 28. In one of those, he wrote, "I plume myself on this achievement

---

[*] The fortune wouldn't last. Byron's father, "Mad Jack," ran through his wife's money like fat through a goose, as the saying goes. Happily, Byron inherited his uncle's sizable estate at age ten and became the 6th Baron Byron of Rochdale.

[**] Vybarr Cregan-Reid suggests that Byron's "disability" might have actually aided his swimming: "The shortened Achilles tendon might make some aspect of his swimming stroke easier. It may facilitate the wide side-facing kick of the breast stroke, which is the most important part of the action as it is responsible for propelling the body forwards through the water in preparation for the hands to support the body as the legs are brought back to begin the stroke again."

more than I could possibly do any kind of glory, political, poetical, or rhetorical."

He enshrined the swim in verse, as well, twice. The first was shortly after the swim was completed, in a lighthearted poem titled, unsurprisingly, "Written After Swimming from Sestos to Abydos." Sample: "In the genial month of May, / My dripping limbs I faintly stretch, / And think I've done a feat today." Then, nine years later, 1819, in perhaps his best-known work, the mock-epic *Don Juan*, Byron used the swim as benchmark praise for his hero's swimming talents: "He could, perhaps, have passed the Hellespont, / As once (a feat on which ourselves we prided) Leander, / Mr. Eckenhead, and I did." By then, Byron was the most famous poet of the Romantic movement, a hero throughout Europe, really the first modern celebrity, and swimming did much to continue stoking the fires of his fame.[*]

In Venice, where he lived from 1816 to 1819 in the Mocenigo Palace on the Grand Canal—with fourteen servants, two monkeys, a fox, and two mastiffs—Byron once stroked four hours against the tide from the Lido to the Rialto Bridge, bracketing his swim at either end with lovemaking.[**]

On another Venetian occasion, Byron gladly rose to the moment when "an Italian who knew no more of swimming than a camel" challenged him to a race.

> Not wishing that any foreigner at least should beat me at my own arms,
> I consented to engage in the contest. Alexander Scott proposed to be of
> the party, and we started from Lido. Our land-lubber was very soon in
> the rear, and Scott saw him make for a Gondola. He rested himself first

[*] Sir William Allan, a leading Scottish artist of the day, would further immortalize the feat with his 1831 painting, *Lord Byron in a Turkish Fisherman's House After Swimming Across the Hellespont*, but by then Byron had been dead seven years. (See page 83 for painting.)

[**] The swim was well attended; the lovemaking private but widely circulated. Indeed, Byron might well have spread the story himself. Women often seem to have been interchangeable parts of his self-mythologizing.

against one, and then against another, and gave in before we got half way to St. Mark's Place. We saw no more of him, but continued our course through the Grand Canal, landing at my palace-stairs.

Somehow "landing at my palace-stairs" captures the essence of Byron's swimming career. No wonder he was not only the most famous poet of the Romantic movement but also its most famous swimmer. He put the whimsy into waves, the cutthroat into competition, and did it all with a joy that was infectious and a self-promotion that seems relentless at this remove. In fact, I thought immediately of Byron when I came across this reference to another famous swimmer in a 2008 article by Willard Spiegelman for the *American Scholar:* "According to Mark Spitz, swimming is perfect for narcissists. Like the mind, the body is self-absorbed. Spitz calls swimming the only sport that puts a competitor on a pedestal (i.e., the racing block) even before he begins, where he 'is introduced and applauded. He hasn't even done anything. Instant recognition. That's so much of what an athlete wants.'" Maybe a poet, too.

George Gordon, Lord Byron, would have loved "selfies"—that's a given—and probably Twitter, too. But another renowned poet and author of the era deserves a mention here, and he wasn't much impressed by Byron's swimming prowess.

In this 1843 letter to a friend, Edgar Allan Poe compares his own swimming feats with Byron's much-lauded swim across the Hellespont and looks forward to goals not yet attained. The swim Poe refers to took place when he was fifteen, in 1824, on the James River near Richmond, Virginia, beginning at its "falls," roughly where current-day I-95 crosses the river, and continuing east toward the Tidewater and the Atlantic Ocean beyond it:

There can be no comparison between them. Any swimmer "in the falls" in my days, would have swum the Hellespont, and thought nothing of the matter. I swam from Ludlam's wharf to Warwick, (six miles,) in a hot June sun, against one of the strongest tides ever known in the river. It would have been a feat comparatively easy to swim twenty miles in still water. I would not think much of attempting to swim the British Channel from Dover to Calais.

Poe would be dead almost a quarter of a century before anyone actually did that, but the stroke that first conquered the English Channel was already being perfected in some of best loos in London when Poe swam his way from Ludlam's wharf to Warwick.

6

A FROG IN EVERY TUB

The hands are useless for propelling the body through the
water; that office is reserved for the feet alone.
—John Leahy

Benjamin Franklin, Dr. Russell, and Lord Byron did their part to revive swimming in the Old World. Interest had been piqued. (Who
didn't want to be Byron, except maybe for the clubfoot?) Infrastructure
was flourishing, and not only seaside. London had had an outdoor pool
since the mid-eighteenth century—the vast (170 feet by 108 feet) private Peerless Pool, a former duck pond that had been fitted with a gravel
bottom, embanked sides, and all manner of other luxuries. At an annual cost of almost $300 in current dollars, the Peerless Pool was mostly
for peers of the realm and their wannabes, but opportunity was ripening
more broadly, too: the Industrial Revolution would soon spawn both a
middle class and leisure time. Ever in search of a trend, the publishing
world took note as well.

In 1832, the *Penny* magazine reprinted Franklin's letter to Oliver Neave, the one in which Franklin suggests his egg exercise. For Englishmen and women, this might well have been the most practical swimming advice they had ever seen in print. The year 1834 saw the publication of Donald Walker's *British Manly Exercises,* with twenty-six illustrations of swimming taking up thirteen full pages. So popular was Walker's book that a second edition appeared within two weeks. Ultimately, the book would appear in eleven editions, released over more than half a century. In all of them, Byron's conquest of the Hellespont was lauded as swimming's "ultra accomplishment," that beyond which there was no other.[*]

Like swimming itself in these formative years of the sport's rebirth on the Continent and in England, Walker's book is an odd combination. Franklin's infinitely practical letter to Oliver Neave is included in multiple editions. But then again, so is mention of the "Bernardi Method of Upright Swimming," first brought to light in a two-volume treatise on swimming published in Naples in 1794 and written by Oronzio de' Bernardi. Bernardi argues that because humans walk upright, the most natural way for them to swim is upright as well. Basically, this means treading water and advancing forward by shooting the arms out together, then pulling back forcefully against the water—an upright breaststroke without the kick, one that also maximizes water resistance.

Over the years and through various translations into multiple languages, elaborate claims attached themselves to Bernardi's method, the most remarkable being that a swimmer could cover three miles an hour using it. That is, roughly twenty minutes a mile—a remarkable claim given that as late as the 1932 Olympics, the first and second place finishers in the 1,500-meter freestyle, Kusuo Kitamura of Japan and America's Buster Crabbe, finished just on either side of twenty minutes.

Just as remarkable, swimming scholars were still debating whether the sport was best done horizontally or vertically as late as 1867, when the

[*] The eleventh edition, published in 1886, reprints the "ultra accomplishment" praise for Byron even though Matthew Webb had swum the English Channel eleven years earlier. Enough already!

Australian swimming champion Charles Steedman finally put the matter to bed by citing the humble seahorse: "There is but one well known exception to the rule that fishes retain a horizontal position when swimming. It is the Hippocampus, or sea-horse, which swims vertically or in an upright position. But as it is probably the slowest of all fishes in its progress, it serves to strengthen the argument in favour of horizontal swimming."

Serves to *strengthen* the argument? How could there ever have been a question? And remember, this was only a century and a half ago. Greek and Roman swimmers from antiquity time-traveling into the Bernardi controversy might have thought they'd landed among a people with Stone Age reasoning powers. One suspects that Bernardi himself vertical-swam in his imagination only. Five minutes in the water would have put his method to rout.

In between *Penny* magazine's 1832 homage to Ben Franklin and Donald Walker's 1834 runaway swimming best seller came a thin, thirty-page booklet titled *Twelve Maxims,* published in 1833 and written by William Clark under the pen name Ebenezer Cullchickweed. As other authors had before him, Clark/Cullchickweed laments that three decades into the nineteenth century, most would-be English swimmers had no idea how to actually swim in any effective way.

"Swimming is not encouraged—it is vehemently interdicted to our boys, and the consequence is, that no people on the face of the earth, approximate to great waters, are so impotent in the liquid element as the English."

There was, however, a solution: frogs.

Swimming's "schools are our ponds, our brooks, our canals or river, and our seas," Clark writes. "Its greatest professor is the frog—a creature which for ages past has taught the human tyro gratis. He may be found, on summer evenings, gravely disporting himself in the dewy meadows that skirt the banks of the Cam and Isis, and if gently entreated by the young gentlemen of the universities would favour them with a demonstration in a punchbowl."

Mind you, by 1833 the idea of swimmers imitating frogs was hardly new. Nicholas Wynman, in his 1538 swimming guide, suggests studying how frogs kick with their hind legs. In one of his many stroke variations, Everard Digby (or his translator, more accurately) has readers "drawing up your legs and extending them straight again"—close enough to the modern breaststroke kick to count.

Early English satirists had also been giving "frog swimming" a good working over for more than a century. Ralph Thomas's charming 1904 bibliography of swimming-related books includes a scene from Thomas Shadwell's 1676 comedy *The Virtuoso* in which a Lord Nicholas Gimcrack is receiving swimming instruction when two callers, Longvil and Bruce, appear and ask to see him.

Lady Gimcrack: The truth on't is, he's learning to swim.
       Longvil: Is there any Water hereabouts, Madam?
      L. Gim: He does not learn to swim in the Water, Sir.
        Bruce: Not in the Water, Madam! How then?
      L. Gim: In his Laboratory, a spacious Room, where all his In-
              struments and fine Knacks are.
      Longvil: How is this possible?

        . . .

      L. Gim: He has a Frog in a Bowl of Water, ty'd with a pack-
              thred by the loins; which pack-thred Sir Nicholas
              holds in his teeth, lying upon his belly on a Table;
              and as the Frog strikes, he strikes; and his Swim-
              ming Master stands by, to tell him when he does well
              or ill.

Later, we get to see Lord Gimcrack at his labors, attended by his swimming master and a Sir Formal, who is being either a complete toady or deeply ironic when he gushes to His Lordship: "In earnest this is very fine: I doubt not, Sir, but in a short space of time, you will arrive at the

Breaststroke anyone? Harnessed in a
German machine from the late 1800s, a
boy looks particularly frog-like as he gets
ready to strike out with arms and legs.

curiosity, in this watery Science, that not a frog breathing will exceed
you."*

That said, frogs were a perfectly logical starting point for a culture
trying to reacquaint itself with an activity that had lain mostly dormant
for over a thousand years and had left so little instructional material behind. Dogs—one of Digby's go-to examples in *De Arte Natandi*—had
proved poor models for human swimming. Horses—big dogs when it
comes to water locomotion—hadn't done any better. Both had four legs.
Frogs, like humans, had both legs and arms (sort of), and they were demonstrably well adapted for water.

Why not capture and tether them to a tub or a basin as per Lord
Gimcrack and his swim instructor, or toss them into a handy punch bowl

---

* I vote for deeply ironic. Sir Formal's little speech reminds me of Franz Kafka's short
story "A Report to an Academy" in which an ape captured in Africa explains how he
managed to transition from performing in a circus to becoming a respected member of
society. By employing multiple tutors and leaping from room to room, the ape explains,
"I attained the average education of a European."

as per Ebenezer Cullchickweed and his *Twelve Maxims*. And having gone to that trouble, why not study their motions and convince yourself that the frog stroke (with its tiny human-like arms) and the frog kick (with its bigger human-like legs) were the perfect model for reentering such a daunting medium as water? What became quickly known as breaststroke (because the hands are drawn into the breast on recovery) just made sense.

By 1833, larger cultural forces were also working in the frogs'—and swimming's—favor. Romantic poets like William Wordsworth were celebrating nature, the great outdoors. Simultaneously, Charles Darwin was almost halfway through his 1831 expedition aboard the HMS *Beagle*. Darwin returned in 1836 a science rock star and brought with him a new legitimacy and immediacy for the natural world. Humans, it turned out, had much to learn from frogs and other creeping, crawling, and hopping things. Nearly a quarter century later, Darwin and Alfred Russell Wallace would even imply that we might have descended together with these other creatures from one common primordial link.

As Christopher Love shows in *A Social History of Swimming in England, 1800–1918*, urban betterment movements—improved sanitation, and bathing and recreational opportunities for England's increasingly crowded cities—played a role, too. In 1828, the municipally funded St. George's Baths in Liverpool opened as England's first indoor public pool. A privately funded pool opened in York nine years later, by which time the National Swimming Society was holding meets in six outdoor swimming pools in and around London. In 1839 and again in 1840, the Society even sponsored essay contests and awarded medals for the best writing about the sport. An 1843 swimming gala at the Holborn Baths included races for youths younger than sixteen, another for adults, and a "fancy swimming" competition—shades of Everard Digby and Ben Franklin!

The 1846 Baths and Washing-Houses Act concerned itself primarily with the urban poor and hygiene issues—clean bodies and clothes for those with little access to the means for either—but it also made provisions for the regulation of open-air pools. The act, however, did not necessarily democratize swimming itself. Many of the "baths" in and around London featured multiple pools. One might be set aside for women. The others allowed for first-class, second-class, sometimes even third-class swimming "experiences," at progressively cheaper admission costs.

At Lambeth Baths, for example, the first-class pool featured a fountain at its center. Not so, the second-class one. The same general principle applied to pools at Islington, Marylebone, Paddington, and St. Pancras in London and to pools in Manchester and elsewhere across the country, a practice that continued into the twentieth century. A 1906 handbook on constructing baths recommended that the first-class pool be 100 feet by 40 feet; the second-class one, 75 feet by 35 feet; and the women's pool, 60 feet by 30 feet.

Before water filtration became generally available after World War I, the only way to clean a pool was to drain it. Where only one pool was available, the freshness of the water might determine which swimming days were first-class, second-class, or lower. Presumably, this had the practical advantage of turning the pool over to its poorest, least-washed patrons just before the oldest water was swapped for new.

By 1870, London had enough pools to justify a survey by one R. E. Dudgeon. His summary: The pools were almost uniformly too small to do much swimming at all. "When any considerable number of bathers are in the water, then there is hardly room for the swimmers, who are consequently continually butting against, or kicking, or even scratching one another in a manner anything but favorable for the preservation of good temper." Any lap swimmer who has had to share a lane with a swimmer incapable of staying on his or her side of the lane line will sympathize immediately.

Dudgeon found only two pools in London sufficiently long enough for a swimmer to get much exercise between the ends: one 20 yards by 8 yards, the other 19 by 8. As a preteen winter YMCA swimmer in Pennsylvania in the 1950s, I competed in a long parade of chlorine-choked 20-yard pools. They place a high premium on turns.

For wide-open swimming spaces, no turns at all, just strokes straight ahead, there were always the rivers—the Severn, the Thames, the Trent, the Great Ouse, the River Wye, the Avon and the Cam, and on and on—the Serpentine, the four-thousand-foot-long recreational lake in Hyde Park; or the surrounding seas. But wherever swimmers chose to gather, it was almost certain they would all be swimming the same stroke.

Meanwhile, an alternative to breaststroke was hiding in plain view, waiting to be discovered. What's more, the stroke was executed in a remarkably consistent manner over large stretches of the rest of the world.

In a 2006 article for the *Journal of American History*, Kevin Dawson documents multiple testimonies over a wide swath of time of the swimming prowess of Africans. In the late 1500s, a Flemish traveler, Pieter de Marees, wrote that Gold Coast Africans "can swim very fast, generally easily outdoing people of our nation in swimming and diving." Likewise, in 1606, a Dutch merchant recorded that the Africans at Gorée Island, a slave-trade nexus off the coast of Dakar, on the Senegalese coast, were "extraordinarily strong swimmers." In both instances, the Africans were using what we would today call "crawl," or more commonly "freestyle."[*]

In the late seventeenth century, a commercial agent named Jean Barbot specifically compared the crawl stroke used by Africans of Elmina, another slaving stronghold in present-day Ghana, to the breaststroke then beginning to appear sporadically in Europe. "The Blacks of Mina out-do all others at the coast in dexterity of swimming, throwing one [arm] after another forward, as if they were paddling, and not extending their arms equally, and striking with them both together, as Europeans do." Nor was it just the men who excelled at the sport. Pieter de Marees noted that many of the women in West Africa were able swimmers as well.

Dawson's research even suggests that Africans took up surfing on their own, without Polynesian influence and when Southern California was still a sparsely populated Mexican colony. Visiting Ghana in 1834,

---

[*] "Freestyle" means any stroke can be swum, but for practical purposes, that stroke is almost invariably the fastest one—what's known as the "crawl," short for "Australian crawl."

James Edward Alexander wrote that "from the beach . . . might be seen boys swimming into the sea, with light boards under their stomachs. They waited for a surf; and came rolling like a cloud on top of it."

Maybe that's early boogie-boarding, not surfing, but still.

As with Africa, so with far stretches of the newly explored Pacific. European observers marveled at the swimming ability of the indigenous peoples, while the natives frolicked in the water, just had fun, and probably wondered why these strange visitors didn't join in.

During his 1519–1521 attempt to circumnavigate the globe, Ferdinand Magellan noted the swimming skills of Micronesian Islanders, specifically their use of an alternate, overarm stroke. Similarly, during his 1785–1786 exploration of the Pacific islands, the intrepid French explorer Jean-François de Galaup, the Count de Lapérouse, recorded that the inhabitants of Easter Island also used the overarm stroke and were remarkable swimmers.[*]

The New World was no different from the almost unknown one. In 1739, William Byrd II—a leading colonial Virginia planter; the founder of Richmond; a legislator, author, and lord of Westover, a grand estate that still stands on the north bank of the James River—described a Native American stroke as reaching out "not with both hands together but alternately one after another, whereby they are able to swim both further and faster than we do."

A century further along, George Catlin, the nonpareil Native American portraitist, wrote that "the art of swimming is known to all the American Indians; and perhaps no people on earth have taken more pains to learn it, nor any who turn it to better account."

Catlin goes on to describe swimming as practiced among the Mandans, a North Dakota tribe he painted and studied at length, specifically comparing their technique to the breaststroke:

---

[*] Lapérouse's observation was included in expedition notes left behind when he sailed from Australia in 1786, headed eventually back to France. He and his crew were never heard from again.

The Indian, instead of parting his hands simultaneously under the chin, and making the stroke outward in a horizontal direction . . . throws his body alternately upon the left and the right side, raising one arm entirely above the water and reaching as far forward as he can, to dip it, whilst his whole weight and force are spent upon the one that is passing under him, like a paddle propelling him along. Whilst this arm is making a half circle, and is being raised out of the water behind him, the opposite arm is describing a similar arch in the air over his head, to be dipped in the water as far as he can reach before him with the hand turned under, forming a sort of bucket, to act most effectively as it passes in its turn underneath him.

By this bold and powerful mode of swimming, which may want the grace they would wish to see, I am quite sure, from the experience I had had, that much of the fatigue and strain upon the breast and spine are avoided, and that a man will preserve his strength and his breath much longer in this alternate and rolling motion than he can in the usual mode of swimming in the polished world.

Later in Volume 1 of his *North American Indians,* Catlin describes another encounter with the Mandans and swimming, this time involving teenage girls. He and two companions are first placed in a "bull boat"—buffalo skin stretched across a willow-bough frame—then launched into a stream by a young woman who takes hold of the boat with one hand and seems to effortlessly swim it with the other out to midstream, where, Catlin writes:

We were soon surrounded by a dozen or more beautiful girls, from twelve to fifteen and eighteen years of age, who were at that time bathing on the opposite shore.

They all swam in a bold and graceful manner, and as confidently as so many otters or beavers; and gathering around us, with their long black hair floating about on the water, whilst their faces were glowing with jokes and fun, which they were cracking about us and which we could not understand.

Sounds like paradise, doesn't it? No wonder Catlin's 1836–1837 portraits of the Mandans and other northern tribes encamped along the Upper Missouri River and its tributaries are often considered his best work—and done just in time, as events turned out. When Catlin first visited the Mandan in 1836, their population stood at about sixteen hundred. In 1838, the year he returned East with his portraits, a smallpox epidemic savaged the tribe, paring their numbers by more than 90 percent to an estimated 125 survivors.

George Catlin's first volume of his notes and letters was published in 1841. Three years later, on April 21, 1844, the "polished world," as Catlin called it, got a chance to witness this bizarre overarm stroke in person when two visiting Ojibway—Tobacco and Flying Gull—were invited to take part in a race staged at the Holborn Baths in London. The London *Times* picks up the story from there:

"At a signal, the Indians jumped in to the Bath, and on a pistol being discharged, they struck out and swam to the other end (a distance of 130 feet), in less than half a minute. The *Flying Gull* was the victor by seven feet. They then swam back to the starting-place, where *Flying Gull* (so named from his remarkable skill in the water) was a second time the conqueror."

Flying Gull's time—the rough equivalent (given the sketchy details) of about thirty-one seconds for a 50-yard race—would hardly be respectable for lower-age-group swimming today, but this was 1844, and the results seemed indisputable: the old swimming stroke of the New World was clearly superior to the new swimming stroke of the Old World. However, as the *Times* went on to explain to its readers, speed in this instance was attained at an unacceptable cost in decorum: "Their style of swimming is totally un-European. They lash the water violently with their arms, like the sails of a windmill, and beat downwards with their feet, blowing with force, and performing grotesque antics."

True, Flying Gull and Tobacco "dived from one end of the Bath to the other with the rapidity of an arrow," but . . . *really*! Besides, in a subsequent match-up with Mr. Kenworthy, whom the *Times* described as "one of the best swimmers in England," the local hero beat the "Red Indians . . . with the greatest of ease." In the end—and somehow this feels predictable—the polished world both lost and won.[*]

An 1866 compilation of articles from *London Society* magazine nicely captures the state of swimming in England as America was recovering from its four-year Civil War. The hero of the sport is Harry Gurr, a five-foot-three-and-a-half nineteen-year-old who got his start in life shining shoes outside the public baths and washing-houses at St. Giles and St. George's at Endell Street. Allowed inside to take a bath every evening in return for picking up towels, Gurr showed an early aptitude for the water, was tutored by an assistant at the baths, and finally became the protégé of a young university man and soon had won the Two Miles Champion Cup and what sounds like a wagonload of other awards.

Although it is to be "regretted that the position of Champion Swimmer of Great Britain has no great height in society," the author of the piece writes, perhaps with a not quite straight face, "when stripped and in good condition, which is generally the case, [Gurr] presents a most sturdy appearance, especially about the shoulders and chest"—which is to say that his diminutive height notwithstanding, Gurr was built pretty much like a champion swimmer of today.

As for the strokes commonly employed, they are four in number, the magazine tells its readers:

- "Side swimming," what we know as sidestroke, which is "capital for work against the tide but is principally used to gain speed" and is "doubtless as old as Adam. . . . Sidestroke favors your long, thin man."

---

[*] Besting upstart foreigners seems to be a sub-theme in the London *Times* swimming coverage of the era. A year later, on May 1, 1845, the newspaper reported on another match-up at the Holborn Baths, this one between local swimmers and a high-caste Brahmin who had been sent to London to study medicine at London University. The Brahmin "swam his heats beautifully," the *Times* wrote, but in vain. Messrs. Turner and Styles took the medals.

- Backstroke, which is wonderful for resting in the ocean but useless for "locomotion."
- "Overhand," or crawl, the "most exhausting" stroke, to be used "where rapidity is needed for a short distance, as, for instance, at the end of a swimming race." Overhand is preferred by those "relatively stronger in the upper limbs than in the lower."
- And the "chest stroke," or breaststroke, which favors "your round, stout-limbed fellow" and "is, and will always be, the most popular. . . . A good swimmer never tires at this, and while it is a most graceful stroke, it is better performed, as a rule, than all the other strokes put together."

John Leahy could not have agreed more. In his lengthy 1875 compendium of notes titled *The Art of Swimming in the Eton Style,* the ex-Army sergeant and swimming teacher at the famous college—or preparatory school, in American terms—still wouldn't hear of the overarm stroke, or anything like it. "The hands are useless for propelling the body through the water," he writes at the outset; "that office is reserved for the feet alone, which are shaped to the very best observation for this purpose." Thus, for example, he writes later: "You may see a gentleman, who does next to nothing all the year round, beat at swimming a hard working man—a man who toils with his arms more than the generality of men, and yet the gentleman will beat him in swimming, for the legs and feet of one are as used to toil and to bear the weight of the body as the other."

Like so many of these early guides to swimming, Leahy's *Eton Style* is a smorgasbord of disparate elements: a guide to manliness, a how-to manual peppered with some useful advice and a boatload of misinformation, an exhortation to swim and a celebration of the sport itself, and random odd musings all overlaid—as one might expect of a swimming "professor" at such a high-brow school—with jingoism and occasional raw snobbery.

Leahy flaunts his own credentials and manhood near the front of the book. He was stationed with the 78th Highlanders at what was then the

British naval stronghold at Aden, at the bottom of the Arabian peninsula, when one early morning he noticed a ship lying some distance out in the Red Sea and decided to swim for it, the sea's famous sharks be damned. This he does, leaving at six a.m. sharp. When he arrives at the ship and is hauled aboard, he first asks the captain for the exact time (6:45) and then how far it is to the ten-gun shore battery where he began. About two and a half miles, the captain replies.

"Then, said I, I have swam 2½ miles in three-quarters of an hour."

Really? Eighteen minutes a mile? And breaststroke all the way? Unless Leahy was swimming with a powerful tide, the claim is ludicrous on its face, just as are the mile times claimed for Bernardi's upright swimmer.

Leahy's dictum that the head must always be kept a minimum of four inches out of the water while doing the breaststroke seems over-the-top, too—an unnecessary strain on the neck and back—although given the water quality of the Thames or the Serpentine in 1875, this one might be excusable.* His insistence that, in swimming, the hands and arms are of minor importance compared to the legs and feet seems less forgivable. Are the poor arms to be used for nothing? Apparently so.

The book does contain some practical advice—how to resuscitate the "apparently dead," for example, and some ringing calls to the sport. "Swimming," he writes, "is the most necessary accomplishment of almost all out-door sports and pastimes; and every man or boy in the kingdom ought to learn to overcome his dread of the water, and even delight in it." Agreed.

He also has some harsh words for older boys who like to "duck" the younger ones who are just learning to swim: "I cannot speak in too strong terms of this evil practice. . . . Any boy who indulges in this practice should be told of this whenever he does it; he forgets that he belongs to the most plucky race in the world, a race unworthy of such ignominious tyranny."

---

* The 1866 *London Society* compilation cited earlier tells us that swimming champ Harry Gurr became violently ill after taking in some water while racing in the Serpentine, as did the three men who competed in an eight-mile race on the Thames.

To give Leahy a bit of credit, he does sport a quasi-feminist streak. He argues that girls should be taught to swim between ages seven and thirteen—but for questionable reasons: "It is very seldom that a woman would have more than fifty or sixty yards to swim to shore if capsized. If she knew anything about swimming she would not be in one-fiftieth the danger which a woman who was quite ignorant of the art would incur. Even the being accustomed to the shock of suddenly entering cold water might save her life, as not unfrequently a shock to the nerves would prove fatal to a woman." Early mansplaining.

Just to add to the general condescending tone, Leahy notes near the end that though everyone needs to learn swimming, the aristocracy is most in need, for "in travelling over fresh and salt water they are exposed to more dangers than the poorer classes, who, even if they wish to travel, have not the means to do so." The fortunate poor!

Thus, Great Britain continued mostly to breaststroke away.

American swimmers seem to have been less wedded to the breast-stroke than their late-nineteenth-century British counterparts, but no less condescending toward "primitive" swimming. "Wonderful tales are often told of the aquatic feats performed by the South Sea Islanders or by the Hawaiians, until one almost becomes convinced that the art of swimming is carried to perfection among them," begins an 1890 book review of *How to Swim*, by Captain Davis Dalton, Chief Inspector of the United States Volunteer Life Saving Corps.

Not so, though; the reviewer continues: "It at once becomes obvious that civilized man, by the practice of certain rules and by the application of higher intelligence, can acquire a greater mastery over water than the native of the tropics, who has only experience as his teacher. But, as in all contests for laurels with the savage, time and applications must not be gingerly bestowed."[*]

---

[*] Keep in mind that only sixty-nine years later, "savage" Hawaii would become America's fiftieth and thus far final state.

An aquatic mailman of Peru, drawn based on a description by Alexander von Humboldt after his South American travels at the dawn of the nineteenth century. According to Humboldt, this postman had descended the River Chamaya and then proceeded down the Amazon, with the help of a log. He carried letters in his turban to keep them dry. *(Science Museum Library/Science and Society Picture Library)*

Dalton's "higher intelligence" approach to swimming is pretty much the same old same old: breaststroke, side stroke, and so forth, with a side nod to "Indian swimming," but he is far kinder to the backstroke than many of his predecessors in the swim-manual trade, even going so far as to offer instruction in a hybrid backstroke that mixes the standard alternate-arm stroke used today with an upside-down frog kick.

However, as befits the head of a volunteer lifesaving group, Captain Dalton is unrelenting on the subject of the need for swimming education:

Few persons know how to swim. By this statement I do not mean to imply that there is not a strong minority among the residents of a sea-coast or a river or lake front who can keep their noses above water for a time, and even propel themselves along at a moderate rate of speed. But of the whole population of a country these swimmers make up only a small fraction, and even among them there are very few who are properly expert in the water. . . .

[And] how many women can swim at all? For a lover of swimming there is something pathetic in a visit to a popular seaside resort, where hundreds of women venture waist deep into the sea, and, seizing the ropes, churn up and down, screaming, partly with pleasure, partly with fear, while a dozen damsels, good swimmers, make triumphant progress to the raft a hundred feet beyond the line of breakers? This state of affairs is wrong.

Dalton was right. This state of affairs was wrong, and kudos to the captain for taking on the challenge.

Empire is what finally got Great Britain out of the swimming slow lane. Intrepid Englishmen and -women were traveling, crossing the Seven Seas, encountering first-person the far-flung civilizations that had never forgotten how to swim. Finally, English speakers could discover the crawl for themselves and claim it as their own.

Three decades after Flying Gull and Tobacco stunned London and offended its swimming sensibilities, John Arthur Trudgen spotted that alternate-arm motion being used by South American Indians and paired it with a scissors kick to create the instantly popular "Trudgen crawl." About the turn of the century, Frederick Cavill, an Englishman starting over again in Australia, modified Trudgen's stroke by substituting an up-and-down flutter kick that he had learned from natives of the Solomon Islands. And with that the Australian crawl was born . . . but slowly.

Another quarter century would pass before anyone attempted to cross the English Channel using the crawl, and then it would be an American, not a British swimmer or an Australian one. And not a man but a woman—in a record-setting time that stood for twenty-five years.

7

DIVING IN FOR DOLLARS AND POUNDS

This was the first, and would, I should say, be the last swimming race for back-swimming—it is so much easier, so much more graceful, so much quicker to employ the ordinary methods of propulsion, that it is a waste of time to bestow much attention on the cultivation of this style.

—*London Society* magazine

Competitive swimming and significant financial reward are rarely associated in the modern imagination. The mother of a child tennis star might dream of her someday taking home the $3.85 million check that nineteen-year-old Canadian Bianca Andreescu won in the 2019 US Open. A golfing dad might use the $1.98 million that twenty-seven-year-old Patrick Reed won in the 2018 Masters Tournament to spur his son to practice more. Parents of preteen soccer wizards who can bend it better than Beckham and 6-foot-6 ninth graders who pass behind the back and play above the rim can hardly be blamed for dreaming of their children as virtual freestanding financial institutions à la Lionel Messi (2018 salary and endorsements: $127 million) and LeBron James ($89 million in 2018 between salary and endorsements).

But a swimming sensation? Perhaps there's a college scholarship ahead—not to be sneezed at, but in-kind money—or even an Olympic gold medal.* USA Swimming, the American governing body of the sport, and FINA (the Fédération Internationale de Natation, which oversees swimming internationally) both run monetary-prize events, and especially in the case of cash-rich FINA, the awards are nothing to sniff at: $20,000 for a first-place finish at the group's biennial World Aquatic Championships, $30,000 for breaking a world record.

Back in April 2019, Australian swimmer Cate Campbell pocketed $37,000 in a single weekend at an invitation-only FINA event in China. As the *Daily Mail* noted, that worked out to $851,118 per hour for the 156.5 seconds Campbell spent in the water during her three events—almost twice what Bill Gates earns an hour, although Gates earns that salary every hour of every day, whether he's awake or asleep.

Maybe like Katie Ledecky, top-tier swimmers will exhaust the competition at the amateur level before they use up their college eligibility, turn pro, pick up endorsements and training support, and even help to launch a bold new professional swimming league to challenge FINA's dominance in the sport. Name power counts, and Ledecky has tons of it. Or like Michael Phelps, they might even become flat-out rich. A decade of endorsements and personal-appearance fees have heaped on Phelps a net worth estimated at somewhere north of $55 million.

But there's only one Michael Phelps in a generation of swimmers, and only the absolute cream-of-the-crop swimmers get to compete for FINA's first-place prizes and world record bonuses. Meanwhile, as of 2018, the median annual salary of the 450 National Basketball Association players was about $2.5 million, and the average salary of the 28 first-team players

---

* Olympic gold medals haven't been all gold since 1912. Today's gold medals are 92.5 percent silver but must contain at least 6 grams of gold—worth about $232 at current spot prices.

on the Manchester United football (aka soccer) team was somewhere over $8.5 million.

Bottom line: In the wide world of competitive sports, swimming is a relatively poor cousin in which only the precious few get any crack at a limited pot of gold. What's more, swimming competitions are among the most closely regulated of any sport. But it wasn't always this way. For nearly a century after swimming reemerged in England, purse races—even handicapped purse races—were commonplace, competitions were often wild and wooly, and hustlers were drawn to the sport like bees to pollen. As was the case with other sports in betting-happy London, wagering on swim races was not only welcome but expected.

One of the earliest accounts of a swimming race with serious money on the line, from the London *Times* of 1791, involved a bet of 8 guineas, about $1,225 in today's dollars. The race was particularly notable because the victor promptly drank himself to death with his winnings. More than fifty years later, in September 1844, two swimmers—young Pewters (about seventeen) and aging Hounslow (circa thirty-eight years old)—met at seven in the morning at the Serpentine, the sinuous man-made lake at the heart of Hyde Park, to settle the Championship of England, with 50 guineas at stake, almost $7,000. (Youth was served: Pewters won by a good twenty yards.)

London Society magazine reported on an 1866 race that combined wagering and street betting with what could easily have been a Monty Python skit.

A gentleman from the other side of the water paid the London Swimming Club a visit, and announced to them that he had practiced—he said "invented"—a new style of swimming, and he was particularly anxious to swim any member of the club for something tangible a-side. The condition was to be that the competitors were to swim on their backs half a mile in the Serpentine—no slight task when one considers that the back of the head is of necessity kept immersed in cold water the whole of the time of the race—a period rather under a quarter of an hour.

The club members accepted the bet and its terms, and then picked their own champion, Harry Gurr, to compete against the "Unknown."

"When the morning came betting was even," the magazine reports. "But after the 'Unknown' had taken a dozen strokes of his extraordinary style, which consisted of an alternate movement of arm and leg, no one could be 'on' at any price, and Gurr won as he pleased."

Sounds like the Unknown was doing modern backstroke, doesn't it? One arm, then the other, with legs going up and down? One guesses Gurr was doing something close to elementary backstroke, which people had been noodling with as far back as Everard Digby at least. Neither stroke, though, had any real future, according to the reporter: "This was the first, and would, I should say, be the last swimming race for back-swimming—it is so much easier, so much more graceful, so much quicker to employ the ordinary methods of propulsion, that it is a waste of time to bestow much attention on the cultivation of this style."

All of which goes to show that swimming predictions are no more reliable than any others.

One other report from that same time tells us that in 1873 the Metropolitan Swimming Association sponsored a series of races at the City of London Baths, in Barbican, which included a 108-yard "handicap race." No word as to how the handicapping was done. Probably the bulk of the competitors started out 8 yards in front, to swim a 100-yard race, while the best swimmers had to swim about 17 percent farther, but why bother to handicap if the organizers weren't intent on making the competition inviting to bettors? The best horses often carry extra weight. Why shouldn't the top swimmers swim extra yards?

Whatever the actual reason, the race was so heavily subscribed that it took eighteen heats to cram all the competitors in. The width of the Barbican pool—11 yards—might have allowed for five competitors a heat, which would accommodate ninety entrants or so in all. That, too, sounds like a purse race, but either way, it was one heck of a lot of swimmers, and they had to be *very* patient.

The surging popularity of swimming in and around London didn't happen in a vacuum. It was pushed hard by a swarm of "swimming professors"—self-proclaimed "professional" teachers who generally operated out of specific pools (or baths, as they were commonly known) and often were behind the purse races on the Thames and in the Serpentine as well as at their own clubs. Typically, the purse would be made up of entry fees paid by the participants, with the professor holding the stakes and helping himself to a cut of the winnings as reward for his troubles. With great regularity, the professors also supplemented their income by authoring pamphlets and sometimes whole books on the subject of swimming, some of them little encumbered by practical knowledge of the sport or even evident experience with it.

In his 1875 contribution to the swimming bookshelf, Eton swimming professor John Leahy cautioned readers about his fellow instructors: "Now that swimming is in such demand, any quack who can swim thinks he can teach the art." Leahy doesn't seem to have fallen into that category. He clearly could swim, and one assumes Eton did due diligence before appointing him, but his warning was timely in the extreme. In the large pond of swimming that was mid-nineteenth-century London, the quacks were out in number.

Captain Stevens offers an early example. The cover to the 1845 second edition of *Captain Stevens' System of Swimming* features a piece of art that could be an outtake from Fellini's *Satyricon,* or maybe another moment from Monty Python: the muscular captain in a vest and with rolled sleeves gripping an upright with one hand and holding a rope with the other as he leans far out over the pool. At the other end of the rope, tied around his waist, is a naked young man presumably learning the Stevens system. Meanwhile, six other naked young men (all properly sexless, I should add) disport themselves in the water, practice diving, or like the two in the foreground wait nervously to be roped themselves and sent out to mid-pool.

Roping new swimmers was a common enough practice in the early days of swimming instruction, and the captain's claims to its efficacy are impressive, although maybe too much so. At one point, Stevens writes that he has taught "during the last nine years upwards of 12,000 to swim." At another junction, he claims to have taught 60,000 people to swim over the last sixteen years. (To spare readers the math, that would mean that for the first seven of those sixteen years he taught 48,000 people to swim, or almost 7,000 a year—19-plus a day for all 365 days of a year, leap years excluded.)

As to what Captain Stevens taught them, I yield to Ralph Thomas, the turn-of-the-century swimming bibliographer: "His 'system' is all humbug."

Roping students to teach swimming was common in London by the mid-nineteenth century, but Captain Stevens—the leaning roper here—might have been singular in his claims to success. According to his advertisements, he taught 60,000 people to swim over a sixteen-year span.

Stevens also seems to have been among the first swimming professors to advertise a "benefit" for himself, an 1842 event of uncertain character. Maybe it was a purse race. Maybe an "entertainment," more about which soon. Or maybe just a flat-out appeal for support by a man in what was still mostly a seasonal business. But the benefit must not have been wildly successful. The following year found Captain Stevens, father of five, in debtors' prison.

Frederick Beckwith appears to have struggled almost as hard as Captain Stevens to make a living as a swimming professor, but he brought a more formidable arsenal to the challenge: a bit of P. T. Barnum, a con man's instinct for the hustle, and four swimming children who regularly advertised his teaching talents in the Thames, the Serpentine, at the Lambeth Baths (his home base), and elsewhere.

An article in *London Society* magazine gives a sense of what life as a swimming prof entailed:

> I once accompanied Fred Beckwith to Southampton, where he had arranged to give a grand swimming entertainment, at which we of course hoped the whole town would be present, and we had, with great care, so managed the proceedings that the fair sex might be represented amongst the spectators.
>
> As bad luck would have it, however, a travelling circus came down and opened the same afternoon, and Mademoiselle Alphonsine and Monsieur Loon took all our contemplated concourse of spectators, and left us only with the lads who came to compete for our prizes, and who had to be admitted free.
>
> . . . There was one foreigner present, and to add to our discomfiture, when Mr. Beckwith made his usual short oration, as to his "swimming any man in the world, from a quarter of a mile upwards, for ever so much a-side," the foreigner sprang forward, and totally disregarding the money consideration, which Beckwith had alluded to, he insisted, in his broken English, on swimming Fred to a pole stuck up in the middle

of the bath, and back, a distance of eighty yards. Fred had to undress and compete with this fierce foreigner, and, needless to add, beat him easily; but it was the last straw, and we shut up our bath, and went to dinner, leaving to others the chance of raising an enthusiasm for the art.

As the vignette above suggests, Fred Beckwith did have legitimate credentials as a swimmer, although he might not have been the national champion he advertised. What constitutes a "champion" was sketchy at best before national governing bodies existed. But we know for certain that Beckwith's Lambeth Baths was one of the most important swimming venues in London, that he staged frequent "swimming galas" there to attract crowds and advertise his teaching talents, and that he and his children were often the stars of the show.

As one enraptured spectator put it: "Among other of the feats [Frederick Beckwith] performs is swimming the length of the bath with his hands and feet tied." Could that be anything other than an early demonstration—far pre-butterfly—of the dolphin kick? His children joined in the fun, leading this same commentator to add: "Had Beckwith and his family lived in the bygone ages, we should have had a good explanation of the notion of the mermen and mermaidens." High praise!*

Fred Beckwith's children more than earned their keep. Willy was only five years old when his father began advertising him as "Baby Beckwith the Wonder of the World." Dad liked to arrange purse races between Willy and whoever might have the gumption (and financial resources) to take the boy on. Dad also didn't mind trying to rearrange these bets in his and Willy's favor—and drum up a larger crowd—when he calculated the boy might be in over his head. Witness this notice that appeared in the London press in July 1873:

---

* Beckwith, it should be noted, had his imitators. At an 1880 exhibition in New York City's Central Park Baths, Prof. Marquis Bibbers of the London Polytechnic Institute performed the same hands-and-feet-tied stunt, but on his back. The professor also ate a piece of cake and drank a bottle of milk underwater, then for good measure smoked a cigar as well, or pretended to by sticking the lighted end in his mouth just as he dashed underwater. The tricks, one reporter noted, were "very pretty, but of no practical use."

The 4,000-foot-long Serpentine in Hyde Park: venue for some of London's earliest and most notable purse swim races. *(Courtesy of author)*

THE LATE CHALLENGE FROM THE BOY BECKWITH TO J.B. JOHNSON AND THOSE WHO SWAM IN THE SERPENTINE RACE.

Professor Beckwith acknowledges having, by some means, made a grave mistake. His son possesses no chance with 20 yards start in 1,200 yards, from J.B. Johnson, but he will take 100 yards in that distance for any fair stake. W. Beckwith is under 15 years of age, and his father sends this challenge, not wishing to run down Johnson's swimming powers. The challenge is correct as regards the other men who contended, and Beckwith will swim Parker 400 yards with 30 seconds start. First come, first served.[*]

One wonders if Willy was in on the con, or his dad simply sprung it on him. Either way, the Boy Beckwith probably swam his heart out.

---

[*] This is quite likely the same "Johnson" who is mentioned elsewhere as being among the best swimmers in England and also handicapped à la Lord Byron.

If anything, daughter Agnes—the "Greatest Lady Swimmer in the World"—outshone even her brother. Agnes was only fourteen in September 1875 when she dove off a boat at London Bridge and swam five miles downstream to Greenwich in a tidy sixty-seven minutes (obviously with a strong tide and current in her favor). Back in the river again in 1878, and with an adoring press looking on, Agnes swam twenty miles—from Westminster to Richmond and back to Mortlake—wearing a little straw hat and a daring fitted amber suit. The next year, she and another noted female swimmer, Laura Saigeman, staged exhibition races at three different London baths, before rapt crowds. An estimated twelve hundred people showed up for their final competition—three races, with Saigeman taking the tie-breaker.

From there, it was on to a professional life of her own. Agnes formed a troupe with other women swimmers, toured the Continent and even America with her aquacades, and kept at it until 1910 when she was almost fifty. By then, though, the bloom seems to have long gone off her act. An 1892 playbill from the Paragon Theater on Mile-End Road in London lists Agnes and another of her brothers, Charles ("Champion Trick Swimmer and Diver of the World"), thirteenth among fourteen acts—that is, somewhere just south of Siberia.

Who was a pro? Who was an amateur? Who was a showman, and who actually knew breaststroke from beeswax? It was all a jumble until the Associated Metropolitan Swimming Clubs (AMSC) of London was formed in 1869, in part to sort out the city's aquatics, but in his *Social History of Swimming in England,* Christopher Love provides evidence that this was a mare's nest not easily untangled.

Could a man who made his living teaching swimming still be an amateur swimmer? How about someone who simply taught lifesaving on the side, as a public service, and collected a few quid for his troubles? Or someone who continued competing in purse races, or had ever once done so? And what about the ornamental swimmers, the ones who picked up pocket change by clowning around in the water: the one-legged swimmer who would coil his remaining leg around his neck; the floaters who struck noble poses—the Dying Gladiator, Jacob's Ladder, and the like—for public amusement; or a man known only as "Old Smith," whose act consisted of diving in wearing a full complement of clothing, then undressing when he floated back up to the surface?

As Love chronicles, rules revision followed rules revision followed rules revision as the AMSC yielded authority to the ASA (Amateur Swimming Association) and the nits became ever pickier. At one point, the whole system threatened to come crashing down over the issue of whether "those who were allowed time off from work, without pay, by their employers to teach swimming to schoolchildren or similar groups should be allowed to receive financial compensation for the hours spent away from work."

King Solomon himself might have been challenged to sort that one out, but such deep regulatory quandaries hardly dampened spirits. Swimming lends itself to a carnival atmosphere, especially outdoors—the sun is shining, water is nearby. Carnivals attract grifters of all sorts along with the teeming crowds. And in this instance, the aquatic carnival with all its problematic questions of professionalism, amateurism, and shamateurism—*and* with all its fun—continued on, in England and in America, well into the twentieth century.*

Nineteenth- and early-twentieth-century America was rarely the scene of frenzied sports betting in the way of London. The first Continental Congress, in 1774, was sufficiently wary of embracing England's sinful ways that attendees addressed the subject in one of the Articles of Association: "Every species of extravagance and dissipation, especially all horse racing, and all kinds of gaming, cock fighting," and the like were to be discouraged. After the Revolution, individual states took up the matter as well, according to their origins, climates, even terrains. Bluegrass

---

* There's a wonderful photo of a "street-clothes" race on Coney Island circa 1910—a long lineup of men in shirts and ties (coats removed) diving off a floating bulkhead. Carnival indeed!

Kentucky encouraged horse racing, while most of New England, raised on Puritanical notions and hardscrabble soil, banned it as an activity likely to promote betting and corrupt the morals of minors and adults alike.

But there were countervailing trends, too. As H. Roy Kaplan notes in an article on work, sports, and gambling in America, lotteries were central to the new nation's founding and survival: "Jamestown, the American Revolution, over forty colleges and universities, and the construction of countless road, bridges, canals, hospitals, courthouses, and schools" were all financed by citizens taking a chance, against improbable odds, on countless lotteries.

Human nature entered into the equation. When John Quincy Adams and other Washington legislators ventured out to the newly opened National Course racetrack in 1802, they found "not only grog, but 'sharks' [bookmakers] at the races." Booze and betting together—who would have thought it possible?

Baby betting steps, of course, especially compared to the Mother Country, but as the world would learn soon enough, Americans like to think big—when it comes to sports purses and, perhaps, to sports-related crime. A May 1880 sculling race on the Potomac River, within sight of the White House, offers a case in point. The contest pitted the reigning world star of sculling, the Canadian Ned Hanlan, sponsored by the local Analostan Boat Club, against a New York contender, Charles Courtney, wearing the colors of the Potomac Boat Club. At stake was a purse of $5,000—huge by modern terms: about $123,000.

Public interest was so high that bleachers were set up along the riverbanks, school was dismissed for the day, and engineers gravely inspected the Aqueduct Bridge (the basis of current Key Bridge, connecting Georgetown and Arlington, Virginia) to make certain it wouldn't collapse under the weight of such a vast throng of spectators.

And then? Hanlan started strong, and Courtney . . . tried a few strokes and promptly quit, complaining of heat stroke, while Hanlan (dealing with the same heat) stroked steadily to the finish line. Did Courtney throw the race? That was the assumption, especially since he and his boat disappeared back to New York City as quickly as transportation could be arranged.

But if the Great Potomac Non-Race disgraced aquatic sports generally, it didn't break the link between water sport and Big Money. Forty-seven years later, in 1927, swimmers on America's West Coast dove into the water in pursuit of what was almost certainly the grandest purse in swimming history.

In America, 1927 was the year in which everything happened: first transatlantic flight, first live TV broadcast, first talking movie. Babe Ruth stroked sixty homers, a record that stood for thirty-four years. Gene Tunney and Jack Dempsey duked it out in Chicago, the famous "long-count" boxing match, before an astounding 105,000 live spectators at Soldier Field. Speakeasies were roaring. People were sitting on poles and swallowing goldfish in the hopes of money. Marathon dancing was all the craze. In the Venice neighborhood of Los Angeles, seven hundred people entered a literal marathon dance contest, with $1,000 on the line for the winning couple. Contestants started at two o'clock on the Venice Pier, then took off for the finish line in downtown LA, seventeen miles away, dancing all the way. By the time health authorities halted the marathon almost twenty hours later, fifty contestants had been hospitalized and, according to the *Los Angeles Times,* "shoeless girls [were] in hysterics." Yet on and on it went—a year of relentless vitality and creeping exhaustion, a last burst before the darkness of Depression and war to come.

Almost forgotten among such wonders was an endurance contest of another sort: the Wrigley Ocean Marathon, twenty-two miles across the treacherous San Pedro Channel, from the Southern California mainland to Santa Catalina Island, with a $25,000 winner-take-all purse—equal to about $360,000 in current dollars—put up by the chewing gum heir William Wrigley Jr.[*]

---

[*] Wrigley offered a separate $15,000 prize to the first woman to finish the swim if the larger prize was won by a man. None did, but he awarded $2,500 each to the two women who came closest.

The race wasn't all about sport. Wrigley had owned the island—the *entire* island, all forty-eight thousand acres of it—since 1919 and had invested millions to turn it into a tourist destination, including moving the Chicago Cubs, which he also owned, there for spring training. The Catalina swim, one more way to draw attention to his investment, was initially meant to be a one-woman show.

In August 1926, Wrigley offered $5,000 to Gertrude Ederle—newly world famous as the first woman to swim the English Channel—to help her prepare for a solo swim to his island. The swim, Wrigley told a *New York Times* reporter, perhaps not accurately, had never been made. When Ederle balked, citing a full schedule of vaudeville dates, Wrigley raised his offer to $10,000. Rebuffed again, he opened the offer up to any taker and eventually raised the prize to $25,000. Still a year away from the actual swim, demand was so great that Wrigley opted for an open race, to be held January 15, 1927.

Of the 153 entrants, only 102 showed up at the starting line. Some entrants, it turned out, could barely swim. A few days training in the turbulent currents had convinced them to keep to dry land. Among the early dropouts was a legless newsboy. Frigid water pared the field further. On the morning of the race, a tugboat measured the water temperature at 54 degrees Fahrenheit. With whitecaps forming in the distance and a fog bank rolling in, betting ran 8-to-1 that *no one* would make it across the channel. Given that every swimmer was required to have a support boat and that beyond that six Coast Guard cutters were on hand to serve as hospital ships, there was also barely room for the swimmers once all 102 of them hit the water and got under way at 11:21 a.m.

Prerace betting had favored three men: Henry Sullivan, the third person and first American to swim the English Channel; Norman Ross, a relative giant of a man, nicknamed Big Moose; and a seventeen-year-old Canadian, George Young, who had the best backstory of any of the competitors. To get to Los Angeles from his home in Toronto, Young and a friend had bought a secondhand motorcycle with a sidecar. When that broke down for good in Little Rock, Arkansas—and this alone suggests

William Wrigley Jr., at left, with a facsimile of the check that is almost certainly the largest purse in swimming history. In current dollars, winning Wrigley's 1927 "ocean marathon" from the California mainland to Santa Catalina Island was worth about $360,000. *(The Catalina Island Museum)*

some shaky geographical knowledge on the Canadians' part—they hitched a ride with honeymooning newlyweds to the West Coast, where Young quickly connected with an agent who put him up and financed his training for 40 percent of his earnings should he win.[*]

On the women's side, absent Gertrude Ederle, the best bets looked to be Clarabelle Barrett, one of Ederle's training partners for the English Channel swim and a person large enough to withstand the cold water and buffeting, and Amelia Gade Corson, a Dane who had married a Baltimorean. Corson had prepped for the event by, among other things, swimming the 153 miles from Albany to New York City in 63½ hours.

George Young, the Canadian, took the opening lead, with Norman Ross on his heels, but the San Pedro Channel was the real winner early on. Three and a half hours into the race, almost half the field—forty-seven swimmers—had dropped out. Still in the lead at three p.m., Young hit an oil slick and had to fight his way forward.

---

[*] One *Los Angeles Times* writer quipped that Norman Ross was sure to win because he "is of Scottish descent and a Scotsman would swim across the Pacific and fight a shark every fifty yards for twenty-five thousand bucks."

By five p.m., only thirty swimmers remained; by eight, only twenty. Henry Sullivan, one of the favorites, gave up the fight at 8:19. By 9:45, the field had been thinned out to a dozen swimmers. George Young, still in front and swimming well, hit a thick patch of kelp at eleven p.m. that nearly did him in. His trainer would later say that he was preparing to pull Young out of the competition when a tug pulled alongside with news from Canada.

"We got a telegram from your mother in Toronto," a voice called out of the near darkness. "She's listening over the radio. Her telegram says: 'I know you will win, George.'" Young, so the story goes, shouted back: "Wire her: 'You bet I will—for you.'" Of such stuff are legends made.

Midnight found George Young a mile and a half ahead of Norman Ross and five and half miles out of Point Vincente, the finish line on Santa Catalina. A trudgen crawler named Meyer held third place, while three women were in fourth through sixth place: Clarabelle Barrett (fourth), Margaret Houser (fifth), and Martha Stager (sixth). Barrett gave up at 1:11 a.m.; Ross, at 2:30. By then, Young was sure to finish ahead, and this was, after all, a winner-take-all race.

At 3:05:30 a.m., after 15 hours, 44 minutes, and 30 seconds of swimming and with fifteen thousand raucous spectators looking on, George Young emerged triumphant from the water at Point Vincente, covered in grease and graphite to fight the cold . . . and otherwise stark naked. In the flush of victory, Young had forgotten shedding his bathing suit two and a half miles back. His $25,000 reward was presented a few days later at Grauman's Egyptian Theatre, a lavish movie palace on Hollywood Boulevard, which had opened five years earlier. In comparative dollars, Young's purse was the largest single payday ever for a swimmer.

In the best spirit of the entertainment industry, his agent took $10,400 of the prize.

8

CLIMB EVERY MOUNTAIN, SWIM EVERY SEA . . .

> At this moment, Captain Webb is probably the best-
> known and most popular man in the world.
> —The *Daily Telegraph*

In the late summer of 55 BCE, Julius Caesar stood on the Gallic coast, at what is now Calais, staring out at an angry sea. Gaul—modern-day France—had been subdued. The empire's bureaucrats were poised to take over. Now Caesar was preparing for his next conquest: Britannia, across the English Channel. On the evening of August 25, he loaded two legions, the 7th and 10th, onto a flotilla of oar-powered transport carriers, and at midnight, the crews began rowing out into the channel, aiming for the White Cliffs of Dover, 20.7 miles away. The invasion was a near disaster.

Caesar's approach had not gone unnoticed. Enemy forces—"barbarians," as Caesar described them in his commentaries—were massed along the cliffs as Rome's flotilla approached. Landing soldiers on the narrow beach would have subjected them to a murderous rain of arrows and spears. Instead, Caesar sent his little navy eastward, in search of a broader and less well-defended beach. The broad strand they found was what historians believe is the modern town of Walmer, but the opposition forces had migrated eastward with the Romans and met them with cavalry and charioteers.

To make matters worse, the legionnaires couldn't make a dry landing. Their transports were designed for deep water. Hulls ground into the sand well short of the beach. Caesar's description of the chaos that followed calls to mind accounts of another channel landing on the French side, the Allied assault on the Normandy beaches on D-Day, June 6, 1944, as German firepower poured down on them:

> Our soldiers in places unknown to them, with their hands embarrassed, oppressed with a large and heavy weight of armor, had at the same time to leap from the ships, stand amid the waves, and encounter the enemy; whereas they, either on dry ground, or advancing a little way into the water, free in all their limbs in places thoroughly familiar to them, could confidently throw their weapons and spur on their horses, which were accustomed to this kind of service.

The channel itself proved a formidable foe. What makes the Calais–Dover crossing so tempting—it's the narrowest point of a channel that broadens to hundreds of miles at the western end—also can make it the most tormenting. The constriction concentrates winds, tides, and currents. Blustery weather is common; rough seas, expected. Several of Caesar's transports hurtled past the landing beach. Others never got there.

Rome's legions did eventually win this battle, although conquest would not follow on this expedition or the one the next summer. Another ninety years would pass before the empire finally secured Britannia, but the Romans who were there for that first landing never forgot the channel they had crossed. It was the *horribilem salum*—the "terrible swell."

On August 24, 1875—almost exactly 1,930 years after the Roman legions first crossed the English Channel—a twenty-seven-year-old British Navy captain stood on the Admiralty Pier in Dover, staring into that "terrible swell" just as Caesar had once done from the opposite shore. Then, at one p.m., he dove in. Twenty-one hours and forty minutes of steady breaststroking later, Matthew Webb stumbled ashore at Calais and became the most famous man in the world.

Every endeavor has its acme accomplishment, and for swimming in the later decades of the nineteenth century, the pinnacle was the English Channel. Crossing it without artificial aids was swimming's Mount Everest, what the Atlantic Ocean would become to solo aviation a half century later and the four-minute mile to runners. In a 2014 article for the *British Medical Journal,* Frances Klemperer and Emily Simon Thomas—both veteran open-water swimmers—enumerate why that should have been so, and why the English Channel remains a worthy opponent today for those who attempt to cross it.

Tides are the first challenge. A superbly conditioned swimmer can ride a slack tide and essentially sprint the twenty-one miles to France in a beeline. The very fastest crossing ever recorded—6 hours and 55 minutes, by Australian Trent Grimsey in 2012—entailed exactly that. Using the tide to his advantage, Grimsey averaged a dazzling 19.76 minutes per mile. Lesser swimmers—almost all the rest of us—must contend with shifting tides that push them here and there, and currents and winds that can turn on a dime. Webb got within seven miles of Calais, two-thirds of the way across, when the tide turned and he spent the next five hours simply fighting to hold his ground.

Because the tides and currents push swimmers so readily off course, the longer they are in the water, the more distance they will have to cover. Webb's first attempt to swim the channel, on August 12, was rebuffed by high winds. By the best estimates, his successful crossing two weeks later covered forty miles in all. The longest recorded crossing, 29 hours, followed a zig-zagging path estimated at sixty-five miles, more than three times the actual distance between Dover and Calais.

The more time spent in the water, the greater the risk of hypothermia, too. The channel is warmest in September when water temperature averages 64.4 degrees Fahrenheit, but by then daylight is limited to only thirteen hours. To avoid too much swimming in the dark, most swimmers, like Webb, shoot for the third or fourth week in August, when the water averages a few degrees colder.

As insulation against the cold, Webb covered himself head to toe in green porpoise grease under a red swimming singlet—imagine a melting Christmas tree—and periodically sipped on hot beef tea, cod liver oil, coffee, pints of ale, and brandy from his support boat. Modern swimmers are more apt to use products like Vaseline and exotic carbohydrates—wetsuits and the like are prohibited for official crossings—but whatever the sustenance and emollients, a healthy body temperature can be sustained only so long in water that cold. As the body temperature skids down from 98.6 degrees Fahrenheit, fine-motor coordination suffers, thinking slows, and eventually gross-motor coordination begins to fail. Below a body temperature of 90 degrees, swimmers are in danger of cardiac arrhythmias. Klemperer and Thomas posit this as the cause of most sudden deaths in channel swimmers, including a friend who collapsed and died during her channel attempt in 2013.

The danger, though, doesn't end when the swimming stops. In the cold water, the body shunts blood from the extremities to the core organs: heart and brain. Out of the water, as the blood rushes back to the extremities, the core temperature is likely to plummet. The same vascular constriction that protects the heart and brain can also lead to pulmonary edema. One would-be channel crosser was forced to quit after he began coughing "pink stuff" out of his lungs.

Lesser dangers include "salt mouth"—after a fourteen-hour crossing, a swimmer identified only as "R" could not fully close his mouth or speak normally for a day afterward—swimmer's ear, and delusions caused by hours upon hours of sensory deprivation. Ten hours into his swim, another channel crosser cited in Klemperer and Thomas's study saw his support boat turn into a huge battleship.

Then there are the jellyfish. Two kinds collect in the separation zone between the north and south shipping lanes: the generally harmless white moon jellyfish* and the very painful lion's mane variety. During practice swims for his channel crossing, Webb ran into a lion's mane jellyfish, quickly exited the water, and soon was vomiting violently. He ran into another lion's mane on his successful crossing and shouted out, "I am stung," according to his support boat crew, but a solid dose of brandy soon eased the pain.

At ten a.m. on August 25, 1875, France hove into view. Soon, a passing mail ship serenaded Webb with "Rule Britannia." A little before eleven, after almost twenty-two hours in the water, he waded ashore at Calais and stumbled into history.

Matthew Webb was already well known to the British public. In 1873, he made headlines by jumping fearlessly from the cruise ship *Russia* into rough waters to save one Michael Hynes, who had fallen overboard. The rescue attempt failed, and Webb lingered in the ocean for more than half an hour until the ship could turn around and find him, but his heroism was well rewarded, first with a £100 gift from the ship's crew and second by a gold medal from the Royal Humane Society.

But conquering the English Channel was heroism of a different order. Webb returned to an England that regarded him with the same awe as the first astronauts to land on the moon garnered almost a century later. At Dover, where his ship docked—this time without the cliffs teeming with barbarians—the mayor gushed, "In the future history of the world, I don't believe that any such feat will be performed by anyone else." The

---

* "Generally harmless" but nonetheless terrifying. Once, backstroking straight out from a beach in North Carolina, I ran into what seemed like an entire great wall of the white moons. "Scared witless" doesn't even begin to describe my reaction.

When Captain Matthew Webb posed for
this photographic portrait, he was the most
famous person in the world. *(CS&PF)*

London Stock Exchange honored Webb with a testimonial fund, and the *Daily Telegraph* assured its readers that "At this moment, the Captain is probably the best-known and most popular man in the world."

"World" it was. London's position as the global journalistic capital ensured that Matthew Webb would become an international icon, the Beatles of Breaststroke. Not only was he lauded everywhere; because the length of his swim was considered well beyond the limits of human endurance, Webb's body was also prodded and poked by eminent physicians, again with good cause: thirty-six years would pass—eighty failed attempts in all—before another swimmer successfully negotiated the channel.

Webb's swim was an astounding achievement, on par with Edmund Hillary's summiting of Everest and Roger Bannister's famous sub-four-minute mile. Yet of all those who have conquered the great physical challenges of humankind, Matthew Webb may have the saddest afterstory to tell. The adoring attention—and celebrity income—waned. Webb was a sailor, not a showman or lecturer. His dogged breaststroke was fine for long distances but gave him no edge in purse speed races. To support his wife and two children, Webb wrote a book—as Vybarr Cregan-Reid acidly notes, "the nineteenth-century's nth book entitled *The Art of Swimming.*" Then, when the income from that petered out, he became a sort of living exhibit, one more novelty in the bizarre world of spectacle, sport, and entertainment of the late 1800s.

In one stunt, Webb floated (for pay) for 60 hours in the whale tank at the Royal Aquarium at Westminster. He more than doubled that time during his first tour of the United States, floating for 128¼ hours, more than five days, and leaving the tank for only 15 minutes every 24 hours to see to the normal necessities of life. Out of the tank, Webb easily swam the ten miles from Sandy Hook, New Jersey, to Coney Island, then was forced to tread water for hours because his contract forbid him from landing until five p.m., when paying crowds would likely be the largest.

Elsewhere in the States, Webb performed in a hotel pool, playing a porpoise and seal as fireworks boomed above him. Back home in England, his appearance at the Scarborough Aquarium was sandwiched between a jump-rope performance and "Little Louie," who had the power of second sight. How awful it must have been for the most famous swimmer in the world.

Finally, desperate for money and deeply dispirited, Webb returned to America and announced that he was traveling to Niagara Falls, where he intended to swim the treacherous rapids of the Niagara River, below the falls.[*]

Webb's business plan, to the extent one existed, was for the railroads that serve the falls to put up a $10,000 reward—chump change given

---

[*] On multiple occasions, the Frenchman Charles Blondin had attracted huge crowds by tightrope-walking over the Niagara Falls. A few months before Webb's attempted swim, Blondin made the crossing with his manager clinging to his back.

all the spectators who would be traveling by rail to watch him. But the railroads balked, generally agreeing with the locals and the national press that any such undertaking amounted to a suicide mission. One newspaper, Chicago-based, opined that "a man might as well jump off the top of the Tribune building." At 4:25 p.m. on July 24, 1883, almost eight years after he had conquered the English Channel, Webb essentially did that, diving into the Niagara River to begin his assault.

A correspondent for the July 25, 1883, edition of the *New York Times* tells the story:

> Capt. Webb started nearly in the middle of the stream, and kept near the middle. He had looked the situation over beforehand, and had evidently regarded that as his only safety. He was carried along apparently with perfect ease, but no one could tell what difficulties he encountered. Occasionally, he would disappear, going under the water, and a few seconds later be seen on the surface again, a long distance below where he went under so swiftly did the current carry him.
>
> When the first rapids were reached he was watched by the spectators with the most intense anxiety. He went under, but seemed to be out of sight but a single instant and reappeared again and passed on as before. . . .
>
> These rapids are at the very neck of the Whirlpool itself, and nearly a mile below the bridge. The river is but 220 feet wide, and rushes violently on. Those waiting near this point saw the swimmer approach, in what condition it was impossible to say. If alive, however, he must have been completely exhausted. On reaching the rapids the water necessarily swept over him as at the rapids above, but he did not appear at the surface again.
>
> The excited spectators watched in breathless suspense. They looked below, to the sides, and all about, but could see no signs of him. They rushed down the river bank as far as they could go, but saw nothing of the strong swimmer. They looked at each other, and said, "The man is lost."

Lost indeed, after only seventeen minutes in the water. Webb's mangled body was recovered four days later and given a pauper's burial at Oakwood Cemetery, near the edge of the famous falls. A quarter century later, a memorial was erected at his birthplace, back in Shropshire, with this simple inscription: "Nothing Great Is Easy." Some things, though, are less-well-thought out than others.*

Except for an impenetrable fog bank, swimming's Next Big Thing might well have been an oversized, toothy thirty-five-year-old would-be opera singer.

The year was 1926. Endurance swimming feats still drew more public attention than standard swim-meet fare. The English Channel remained the gold standard of endurance, and though Matthew Webb had been forty-three years in his pauper's grave, his ghost still hung over the challenge. Four others had crossed it in the years since—two faster and two slower than Webb—but they were all men, and there was the rub.

Clarabelle Barrett was one of a handful of women intent on changing that and breaking the all-male hegemony of channel swims. At 6 feet and 200 pounds, she had the subcutaneous fat to withstand hours in the frigid water. As she would prove the next year in William Wrigley's Santa Catalina purse race, she had the mettle as well, and she had down-to-earth motivation. Barrett was swimming not for fame or fortune, just for enough money to hire a voice coach and fulfill her dream of becoming an opera singer. Of her half dozen competitors for first-woman honors, Barrett was also first in the water. She had everything going for her but good fortune.

---

* Matthew Webb may have suffered a violent death in an impossible pursuit, but his would-be hagiographers would have none of it. In a penny pamphlet titled *The Adventurous Life and Daring Exploits in England and America, of Capt. Matthew Webb, the Swimming Champion of the World,* published shortly after Webb's death, Henry Llewellyn Williams put a far more positive spin on the channel conqueror's last moments: "At first he kept on swimming, but abruptly he threw up his arms and without a murmur, far less a cry, was drawn under to his death."

Clarabelle Barrett entered the channel at Dover at eight in the morning on August 2, 1926. As she swam, a heavy fog settled in. She was two miles from Cap Gris Nez in France when the fog became an all-consuming blanket. At 5:30 a.m. on August 3, exhausted and disoriented, she finally gave up. Barrett had covered forty miles during her 21½ hours in the water, five hours longer than any woman before her, but that was not the distinction she craved. The next day she announced that she would attempt the channel again, soon.

But the window had been left open, and another woman was ready to dive through.

ONLY NINETEEN YEARS OLD, GERTRUDE EDERLE WAS A LITTLE MORE than half Barrett's age, maybe two-thirds her size, and far more versed in competitive swimming. Ederle was still a schoolgirl when she began setting the swimming world on fire—a mere twelve years old when she claimed her first world record, in the 880-yard freestyle; only sixteen when she set seven more world records during the course of a single 500-meter race at Brighton Beach, New York, in 1922.[*]

Ederle won her first Olympic gold medal at Paris in 1924, at age eighteen, on the same US team that included Johnny Weissmuller and a young rower named Benjamin Spock. Those accomplishments earned her plenty of press attention, in a decade increasingly crazy over sports, as did her 1925 attempt to swim the channel. That one ended after 8 hours and 43 minutes when someone on her support boat reached out and touched her, thinking she was drowning. Ederle wasn't, but the rules of channel crossings allow no physical contact whatsoever.

On August 6, 1926, Gertrude Ederle—"the plucky little New York girl," as the *Times* kept calling her—smeared herself with sheep grease,

---

[*] Picking the "greatest swimming performance" in history runs up against a hard wall of variables, but Ederle's Brighton Beach 500 meters has few equals. Maybe the closest was recorded by Laura Val during a US Masters Swimming meet held in San Francisco in January 2011. Over the course of 1,500 meters, Val broke every single freestyle world record in the sixty- to sixty-four-year-old age group. She started the race 0.12 seconds faster than anyone in her age group had ever swum 50 meters and ended it more than a minute faster than any peer had ever completed the 1,500 meters.

dove into the channel off Cap Gris Nez in France shortly after seven a.m., and set off for England doing something no channel swimmer had attempted before her: using the Australian crawl. Behind her, a red ball on the coast served as a small-craft warning that very choppy waters lay ahead.

The seas were as promised. To keep her spirits up, Ederle's father, who was on the support boat, kept reminding her of the red roadster he had promised to buy her if the swim was successful. Occasionally, her mother would chime in from the family home with radio messages. The crew also kept up a near-constant chorus of familiar songs: "Let Me Call You Sweetheart," "East Side, West Side," "The Star-Spangled Banner." Ederle later said that the only real problem she faced during the crossing was a stiff left leg that hampered her swimming for the last five miles, but nothing hampered it much. Fourteen hours and thirty-one minutes after she began, two-thirds the time Matthew Webb had needed, Gertrude Ederle climbed out of the water at Kingsdown on the coast of Kent. Ederle had not only become the first woman to swim the channel but also bettered the record time for a crossing—16:33, set by Enrique Tirabocchi of Argentina in 1923—by almost two hours.

The next day, dressed again in the two-piece suit she had worn for the swim, Ederle sat down in her Dover hotel room with a *New York Times* correspondent. She was, he reported, "looking fit and happy. Her body was brown as a berry but without a bruise or a scar and her skin was as clean as a baby's."

"I will swim another fourteen hours anywhere or anytime you like," Ederle said in that interview, "but never again in the English Channel."

Meanwhile, as that interview was taking place, the *Times* was in a hell-bent race with three other New York dailies—including the pictorial *Daily News*, which had sponsored Ederle—to get the first photos back home of the new most famous swimmer in the world.

Paul Gallico, the sports editor of the *Daily News*, described the race later in his book *The Golden People*. All four papers, it turned out, had placed sets of photographs on four different express liners departing Southampton the same day, all headed for North America. The *News*, though, had chosen a Canadian Pacific liner headed not for New York but for Montreal:

> Traveling the great circle route, [it] reached the rim of the North American continent a day before the others. Employing two aircraft, one a sea and the other a land plane, a racing car with a famous driver, a railroad locomotive and an ambulance for the last leg, the photographs in waterproof wrapping were snatched from the ocean by the seaplane, where they were thrown overboard at the mouth of the St. Lawrence River, and then speeded on their relay through fog and dirty weather, to land in the News office twelve hours in advance of the other.

What Gallico called "the swiftest and most expensive relay in the history of journalism up to that time" won the *News* its scoop and primed the pump for what was to be the most tumultuous welcome home in American history, also up to that time. Steamships, tugs, and barges tied down their whistle cords from the moment Ederle's liner entered New York Harbor, while planes flew overhead, pelting the deck with flowers. Once on the ground, Ederle was greeted with a ticker-tape parade that brought an estimated two million spectators out into the streets of the financial district—the first woman and still the youngest to be so honored individually. (The crowds chanted "Trudy! Trudy!" even though her family had always called her Gertie.)

At one point, the press of the crowd was so great, she had to be rushed into Mayor Jimmy Walker's office in City Hall. Later, there was a visit to the White House with Calvin Coolidge, who marveled "that a woman of your small stature should be able to swim the English Channel." Marriage proposals flooded in by mail. As Webb before her had done, Ederle tried to take advantage of the vaudeville circuit and made a ten-minute movie about herself, but unlike Webb, she seems to have made real money, at least for a while—as much as $3,000 a week.*

---

* Three weeks after Gertrude Ederle's crossing, Amelia Gade Corson became the second woman and first mother to swim the channel, in a time an hour slower than Ederle's but still the second-fastest crossing male or female up to that time. Although Corson missed

Gertrude Ederle was the first person of either sex to swim the English Channel using the crawl stroke and the first woman to ever successfully cross it. Her 1926 channel swim shaved almost two hours off the previous record. *(Library of Congress)*

Eventually, though, the crush got to her. Childhood measles had compromised her hearing. The two channel swims did so further. By 1929, when Ederle appeared in traffic court on a speeding charge, she was nearly deaf. The judge let her off "because you have done so much for your country," but a court attendant had to shout the decision into Ederle's ear to make sure she understood it. Four years later, Ederle slipped on some broken tiles in the stairwell of her apartment building and injured her back so badly that she would spend the next four years in a body cast. By then, she had also been through what seems to have been a nervous breakdown.

None of it seemed to get her down too much. According to Ederle's obituary, for many years she taught children to swim at the Lexington

out on Ederle's lasting fame, Walter Lissberger, who sponsored her swim, made out like a bandit on it. Lissberger placed a $5,000 bet with Lloyd's of London, at 20-to-1 odds against Corson completing the swim, and won $100,000 (about $1.4 million in current dollars) when she reached shore at Dover.

School for the Deaf, in the Jackson Heights area of New York City, near La Guardia Airport. During World War II, she worked at the airport itself, checking flight instruments. Ederle never married, despite all the proposals that followed her channel crossing, but when she died in 2003, at age ninety-eight, she left behind ten nephews and nieces. By then, the most famous swimmer in the world was about to be a strapping, six-foot-four-inch Baltimore-born speed machine named Michael Phelps.

RECORDS FALL. BARRIERS GET BROKEN. PARADIGMS CHANGE. THE CREST of Mount Everest is littered these days with oxygen bottles. As of mid-2018, the Roger Bannister Memorial Sub-Four-Minute-Mile Club was about fifteen hundred strong. In the 143 years since Matthew Webb first crossed the channel, he has been joined by more than eighteen hundred other swimmers, more than a third of them women.* The annual Hellespont Swim Race from Europe to Asia attracts hundreds of swimmers to the 4.5-kilometer course—which swims more like 3.5 kilometers given the favorable tides at race time. (Byron doesn't mention a trailing tide in his account of the swim.) Since William Wrigley Jr.'s first Santa Catalina marathon, which netted one finisher out of 102 entrants, more than two hundred swimmers have made the crossing.

Bottom line: marathon swimmers today have to dream bigger dreams. But where to go? And what's left to conquer?

Not the Great Lakes. Jim Dreyer has already swum across all of them. In fact, he's swum Lake Michigan twice: east to west, for his initial Great Lakes crossing; then north to south, just because it had never been done. When I interviewed Dreyer near the start of this century, Lake Superior hadn't yet entered his portfolio. As the northernmost of the Great Lakes, it has the coldest water and no real chokepoints to make the crossing easy. He was contemplating a forty-eight-mile swim in water that could drop below 40 degrees, with only a single week in mid-August to make it. That

---

* Matthew Webb seems to have gotten the calendar just about right. The most successful day for crossing has proven to be August 22.

obstacle finally fell in 2001. Then he crossed again in 2002. Then, in 2005, he made crossing number three, this time towing his own supplies behind him in a dinghy.

Here's the really remarkable fact about Jim Dreyer: two and a half years before he made that first crossing of Lake Michigan—almost forty-one hours to complete a 43.2-mile swim from Wisconsin to Michigan that weather conditions turned into a 65-mile ordeal—Dreyer, then in his mid-thirties, had no idea how to swim.

"I had a lifelong fear of the water," he told me in the living room of his home south of Grand Rapids, Michigan. "When I was three, I had a near drowning. The family had a cottage northeast of here. Easter Sunday I'm out on the dock, all dressed up in a snowsuit, fishing, when I fall in. My sister saved my life."

That conversation took place in the spring of 2001. When I checked on Dreyer recently, he had just towed a twenty-seven-ton car ferry across Newport Beach Harbor, in California—towed, that is, by swimming. Talk about overcompensating: The Labors of Hercules have nothing on Jim Dreyer. Or on English marathoner Ross Edgley, either.

In November 2018, Edgley completed a 157-day, 1,780-mile circumnavigation of the British Isles, swimming anywhere from six to twelve hours a day, while resting and eating in between on a companion boat. (The eating got more difficult after his tongue partially disintegrated from so much exposure to salt water.) Like Dreyer, Edgley was compensating, too, in this case for his failure the previous year to complete a twenty-five-mile swim across the Caribbean from Martinique to Saint Lucia . . . while dragging a tree trunk behind him.

And then there's Lynne Cox, for whom the word *superhuman* seems insufficient to the cause. Cox's endurance swims—well chronicled in her books—are the stuff of legends. Name an impossible swim, and odds are, she has already done it.

Still in her early teens, she knocked off the English Channel twice, in 1972 and 1973, breaking the speed record both times, and then she got serious about endurance swimming.* In 1974, Cox crossed the turbulent Cook Straits between the North and South Island of New Zealand (10 miles, a little over 12 hours, in 50 degree Fahrenheit water). The next year, she became the first person known to swim the Straits of Magellan, off Chile (4.5 miles, 42 degrees). That same year, she crossed from Norway to Sweden (15 miles, 44 degrees). The Aleutian Islands (also 44-degree water) caught her attention in 1977. In 1978, she sought warmer waters and, in some ways, greater risk, swimming the Cape of Good Hope off the southern tip of Africa (10 miles, 70 degrees; sharks, jellyfish, and sea snakes). And on it goes: Lake Baikal in the former Soviet Union; Lake Titicaca, the world's highest navigable body of water, in the Andes Mountains of Bolivia. In Alaska's Glacier Bay (38 degrees), Cox swam behind a lead boat breaking a path through a quarter inch of ice.

All this would be hard enough—and still undeniably dangerous—if Lynne Cox wore a wet suit in the near-freezing waters and swam inside a cage when sharks lurked nearby. But perish that thought: for her, it's a swimsuit, cap, goggles, support boat and crew, and nothing more. True, she does have an advantage: Cox's body density (36 percent body fat, compared to the normal range of 18 to 25 percent) gives her neutral weight in the water. Translation: She doesn't have to work to stay afloat. All her energy can be expended on moving forward.

She has another advantage, too: intent. Cox's swims are often purposeful as well as daredevil undertakings. In 1994, she swam fifteen miles across the Gulf of Aqaba in the Red Sea between Egypt, Israel, and Jordan. More sharks on that route—nasty ones!—but Cox swam part of the way in the company of dolphins who seemed to appear out of nowhere

---

* Before her first channel swim in 1972, Cox wrote Florence Chadwick—the Gertrude Ederle of the 1950s—asking for advice. Chadwick called Cox not long afterward, inquired about her experience to date and preparations, and followed that with a question Cox never forgot: "She asked if I was swimming for myself or if I was doing it for my parents, and even though I was only 14, I thought, what an insightful question. I said, 'It's my goal, and my parents are supporting me.'"

to help keep the sharks away. If only the dolphins could also help broker peace in the Middle East, but at least Cox tried.

Her most famous swim, in 1987, was one of her shorter ones in terms of distance but long on substance: In almost gelid Bering Strait waters (38–42 degrees), Cox swam for more than two hours to cover the 2.7 miles that separate America's Little Diomede and Russia's Big Diomede islands—a feat that seems to defy physiology but one that also makes an important metaphorical point about the Cold War and arbitrary boundaries.[*]

Cox herself reinforces an important real point about swimming and gender: the longer the race, generally, the narrower the difference in best times. As of late November 2018, the FINA-recognized world record for the women's long-course[**] 50-meter freestyle was 11.7 percent slower than the men's record for the same event. By 100 meters, the record differential had shrunk to 9.3 percent, to 6.7 percent at 400 meters, and to 5.4 percent at 1,500 meters. Stretch that out, and at some theoretical distance, subcutaneous fat becomes more important than sheer muscle mass, both in terms of endurance and speed. Lynne Cox has clearly crossed that point into a realm of achievement that men are unlikely ever to enter.

I asked Cox if there's a Zen-like tranquility to these swims, if her mind was able to float free from her body. Her answer: not exactly.

> I've spent a lot of time before I take a swim thinking about how to organize it, how I'm going to go about it, who's going to be on my crew, and how I'm going to train for it. When I actually do the swim, I'm really

---

[*] These epic endurance swims seem to almost demand some kind of outside motivation. Jim Dreyer's heroic struggles with the American Great Lakes helped benefit Boys and Girls Clubs. When Benoît Lecomte "swam" the Atlantic Ocean in 1998—seventy-two days, swimming six to eight hours a day, protected by a magnetic force field, and riding on an accompanying sailboat when he wasn't in the water—he was raising money for cancer research. His curtailed 2018 similar swim across the Pacific was meant, in part, to spotlight global ocean pollution.

[**] "Long-course" means swum in a 50-meter pool. "Short-course" races are held in 25-meter venues.

focused on making it across. Where am I in relationship to the boat? How fast am I going? Am I holding my pace, holding the straightest line, hitting the current or not? And I'm constantly adjusting my stroke to what the water is doing.

I'm always monitoring. Sometimes I'm really sore or tired, and I have to focus on talking to myself just to keep going. Or I'll stop to have some warm apple juice to keep my blood sugar up. And each swim is different. Going into Antarctica, there was constant concern about how cold the water was and going into hypothermia and dying.

One hates to be trapped in time like the mayor of Dover, in England, who proclaimed that Matthew Webb's 1875 swim across the English Channel would "in the future history of the world . . . [never] be performed by anyone else." Humans may re-evolve, or devolve, toward fish, or evolution and random selection might simply throw off someone (most likely female) better equipped than Lynne Cox to perform such wonders. She seems to think of herself more as a pathfinder than the Evel Knievel of open-water swimming.

"I was able to do swims that no one had ever done before, but now people are thinking, wow, Lynne did that. Maybe I can do this and this too. I have acquaintances from Australia who are now swimming around Shelter Island, off of Juneau, in Alaska. No one would have thought of doing that years ago. There are so many swimmers now around the world who are escaping from the pool, realizing that while it might be a good place to train, there are places they can swim that they had never even imagined."

Still, in the history of distance swimming, Lynne Cox stands alone.*

---

* Diana Nyad and Sarah Thomas deserve nods here as well. In 2013, at age sixty-four, Nyad became the first person to swim the 110 miles from Havana to Key West without the benefit of a shark cage. In September 2019, Thomas completed four continuous crossing of the English Channel—54 hours, 133 miles—two years after being diagnosed with breast cancer.

9

THE GREAT SWIMMING COVER-UP

To be really medieval one should have no body. . . .
To be really Greek one should have no clothes.
—Oscar Wilde

During the Golden Age of Swimming, in the waters around Greece and, later, the baths and pools of Rome and its far-flung empire, women as well as men entered the water naked. Reason dictates that swimming should be done that way. Clothes are an impediment—or were before the invention of skintight, water-shedding synthetics. The Greeks particularly believed that the human form was not meant to be hidden.

The Dark and Middle Ages put an end to that. As Oscar Wilde suggests above, to be medieval requires almost a conscious abnegation of our bodies—of the humanness of being human. Once the Middle Ages yielded to the Renaissance, the clothes began to come off, at least in art. In the English-speaking world, though, the various Puritan movements ensured they would come off only so far, even as the Neo-Golden Age of Swimming was getting under way. Yes, women did return to the water toward the end of the eighteenth century in sufficient numbers to spark a movement, but they returned in costumes—and via elaborate conveyances—that all but guaranteed they never actually learned to swim. Men, too, were expected, and in some instances required, to appear in public decently clad, although what was considered suitable for males was far more variable and lenient.

It's hard to put a start date on this enforced modesty. Prudery has many causes and expresses itself in hydra-like ways. The Puritan movement in Great Britain and the early succession of Great Awakenings in America left little room for frivolity in dress or public behavior. But it wasn't all pilgrims and puritans. Queen Victoria's coronation in 1837 ushered in an era notable for its emphasis on propriety, rigid manners, and at least at the top of the pecking order elaborate dress. For swimmers and swimming, though, 1737—exactly one century earlier—might make the better marker. That's the year that the revived baths of Bath, in England, declared war on nudity. The official notice, from the Bath Corporation, read as follows:

> It is Ordered Established and Decreed by this Corporation that no Male person above the age of ten shall at any time hereafter go into any Bath or Baths within this City by day or by night without a Pair of Drawers and Waistcoat on their bodies. And that no Female person shall at any time hereafter go into a Bath or Baths within this City by day or by night without a decent Shift on their bodies.

Granted, the baths of the eighteenth century were not always the public-spirited playgrounds of ancient Rome, even when they opened among the ruins of such places, as was the case in Bath. As noted earlier, the revived public baths of the late Middle Ages and early Renaissance had a long and justified history as dens of prostitution and forbidden sex. Albrecht Durer's 1496 woodcut "The Bath House" leaves little doubt about the amorous intentions of the men portrayed.

But eleven-year-old boys? Especially at a time when average puberty began years later than today? And "Female persons" of *any* age? Oh, well. If Adam and Eve had to don fig leaves to cover their shame, the least swimmers and bathers could do, presumably, was wear shifts and drawers to cover theirs. As reading primers of the day were quick to remind students: "In Adam's fall sinned we all."

Jump ahead almost four decades, and for women, the suppression of the flesh is in full bloom. By 1776, just as the American Revolution was fomenting, Margate on the coast of Kent was well on its way to being a fashionable resort. Dr. Russell's saltwater cure was all the rage. Margate teemed with imitators. Women and men flocked to its beaches, but the women were rarely seen once they entered the water. This description from the 1776 edition of *The Kentish Traveller's Companion* shows how the system worked in Margate and elsewhere:

> Though Margate, in summer, is a pleasant and agreeable situation, yet what has given it so great éclat in the haut monde, is its conveniency for bathing; the shore being level and covered with fine sand, is extremely well adapted for that purpose. On the wharf are seven bathing-rooms, which are large and convenient. Here the company resort to drink the water, and from whence, in turn, they enter the machines, which are driven out into the sea, often to the distance of two or three hundred yards, under the conduct of careful guides.
>
> There is a door in the back of the machine, by which the ladies descend into the water, by means of a ladder, and the umbrella of canvas is let down, which conceals them from public view. There are often near thirty of these machines employed till near the time of high water.
>
> Mr. Benjamin Beale, a Quaker, was the inventor of them. Their structure is simple but quite convenient; and by means of the umbrella,

In this 1829 illustration titled *Mermaids of Brighton*, formidable older women known as dippers introduce female bathers to the wonders of the sea. The bathing machines were horse-drawn. *(William Heath, altered to black & white)*

the pleasures of bathing may be enjoyed in so private a manner, as to be consistent with the British delicacy.

The "British delicacy" also did not allow for free swims once women were in the water. Commonly, the guides—sturdy local women known as "dippers"—would tilt their charges into oncoming waves or, on still days, push their heads underwater so that they might enjoy the full benefit of a seaside excursion. Three dips was the general rule—Father, Son, and Holy Ghost, perhaps, in keeping with the Christian baptism experience. And then it would be back in the horse-drawn bathing machine, now with the horse on the other end, and back to shore. Not much chance for a swim there. Not much opportunity to swim, either, even if the "dippers" had allowed it.[*]

For starters, female bathers were clothed to a fare-thee-well. Some accounts describe flannel gowns, useful because they weren't see-through when wet. Martha Washington, we know, went down to the Potomac

---

[*] And maybe not very inviting water, either. Thirty horses can make for a lot of floating manure.

River from her home at Mount Vernon in a blue-and-white-checked linen gown similar to a chemise. Photographs of the Victorian era show far more ornate combinations of jackets and petticoats, face-hiding bonnets, even gloves to shield the hands from prying male eyes. Whatever the style, lead weights sewed into the hem kept the assemblage from floating up to the surface. Decorum required it, but like the clothes themselves, the lead weights ensured that women "swimmers" couldn't swim more than a few strokes if their lives depended on it.

And so it went for more than a century. Bathing machines were in active use at Brighton until the 1890s, but it wasn't only at the beach where would-be women swimmers were treated like hothouse flowers while being reported on by the media as if they were chattering magpies.

Witness the *New York Times* July 1870 account of a special "Ladies Day" that attracted between two hundred and three hundred women—"the wives and daughters of working men"—to the newly constructed bathing house at the foot of East Fifth Street:

> Such screaming and splashing about has not been heard in that vicinity for years. Persons standing on the outside of the bath while these timid (?) nymphs were sporting in the water would naturally imagine that some person was undergoing strangulation, or that a menagerie had broken loose from the strange shrieks they make. . . . The Commissioners wish it distinctly understood that in no instance will there be permitted to enter the baths any lewd characters; and, to preserve order and insure perfect decorum, they have secured a detail of four policemen at each bathing-house, part of whose business it will be to prevent disorderly and suspicious characters from intruding.

Then there's John Leahy's 1875 manual, *The Art of Swimming in the Eton Style*. Leahy concludes with a two-page ad for a Ladies Swimming and Bathing Saloon he has opened to meet "the great want of suitable accommodation in Windsor and Eton for the bathing of ladies, and of facilities for learning to swim." His "Saloon," a dolled-up barge, sat moored on the Thames at a spot in the river where the water was only "waist high, with a smooth gravelly bottom, and"—critically—"five hundred yards distant from the nearest male bathing place."

Leahy promises that attentive pupils will attain "the first degree" of swimming in no more than six lessons, although ornamental swimming will take a bit longer. He also warns them (conscious of the continuing "British delicacy") that he "will occasionally put on his bathing dress, to inspire his pupils with confidence, and show them with what ease a practical swimmer can move through the water." Or maybe that's meant to be as much come-on as warning since, as he continues, "All who have seen Mr. Leahy, when swimming and floating, can testify to the surprise and pleasure it gave them." Hmmm . . . *Baywatch*?

Leahy is also careful to observe the social proprieties of the times: lessons and swimming times are offered to "Ladies of the first class" between eleven in the morning and one thirty in the afternoon and, for half a shilling less, to "Ladies of the second class (which comprises tradespeople only) between 2 and 5:30 pm."

As to the bathing dresses the ladies are expected to wear, Leahy provides some guidance in a sketch elsewhere in the book: a blouse cinched tight at the waist with short-sleeve arms, and full trousers with only the ankles exposed. By High Victorian standards, it's almost racy—even though the nearest male gawkers were five football fields away—but imagine trying to swim in even that pared-down outfit. As Vybarr Cregan-Reid notes in his essay on swimming in the nineteenth century, it's a costume that far better serves the needs of a rising consumerist culture than swimming itself.

Men got off easier. For them, the new prudery was at least initially mostly an inconvenience. The Frenchman Melchisédech Thévenot laid down the marker for male swimming in his 1696 manual when all forty of his how-to illustrations used nude males, clearly endowed with the normal male furniture. At least on the Continent, things hadn't changed much a century and a half later. In his 1844 book, *Paris dans l'eau,* Eugene Briffault notes that in the swimming baths introduced to Paris four decades earlier, swimming drawers were available to those who could afford them, but added that the majority made do without this "vain ornament."

Englishmen seem to have been equally reluctant to embrace the new prudery. In spite of caning threats, maybe even because of them, inebriated Oxbridgeans continued to swim naked, and too often drown naked, in the Cam and Thames rivers—or the Isis River, as the Thames is known in Oxford. Men and boys of all ages and of all stations rarely bothered with clothing at lakes, ponds, and other inland and rural water holes.*

Seaside swimming was a more complicated matter for men, especially at the swankier ocean resorts, but the outcome was much the same. In his 1771 novel *The Expedition of Humphry Clinker,* Tobias Smollet describes how a gentleman might enter the sea at Scarborough, Weymouth, Brighton, and the like:

> Imagine to yourself a small, snug wooden chamber, fixed upon a wheel-carriage, having a door at each end, and on each side a little window above, a bench below—The bather, ascending into this apartment by wooden steps, shuts himself in, and begins to undress, while the attendant yokes a horse to the end next the sea, and draws the carriage forwards, till the surface of the water is on a level with the floor of dressing room, then he moves and fixes the horse to the other end—The person within being stripped, opens the door to the sea-ward, where he finds the guide ready, and plunges headlong into the water.

---

* The Jane Austen Society of Australia would like it known that the producers of the 1995 BBC mini-series based on Jane Austen's *Pride & Prejudice* got this fact wrong in the scene in which Colin Firth (as the brooding Mr. Darcy) plunges fully clothed into a lake, then with his shirt still dripping wet, unexpectedly encounters Jennifer Ehle (Miss Bennett). "In the interests of historical accuracy, we should have seen much more of Colin Firth—his wet-shirt scene should have been a nude scene. Drawers . . . did not become widely used until the 1860s." Jane Austen's novel was published in 1813. When I checked the wet-shirt scene out on YouTube, I was viewer number 6,574,058.

And then the gentleman, having swum buck-naked, would dress again as he was being pulled back to shore and step out of his snug wooden chamber fully and properly clothed.

Not all bathing machines, of course, were created equal. Those used by King George III and his court at Weymouth had "God Save the King" inscribed over all the windows. In a 1789 letter, the satirical novelist Frances Burney recorded that the motto was to be found elsewhere as well.

> Those bathers that belong to the royal dippers wear it in bandeaus on their bonnets, to go into the sea; and have it again, in large letters, round their waists, to encounter the waves. Flannel dressed, tucked up, and no shoes or stockings, with bandeaus and girdles, have a most singular appearance; and when first I surveyed these loyal nymphs it was with some difficulty I kept my features in order.
>
> Nor is this all. Think but of the surprise of His Majesty when, the first time of his father, he had no sooner popped his royal head under water than a band of music, concealed in a neighbouring machine, struck up "God Save Great George our King."

Burney, then serving as Keeper of the Robes to Queen Charlotte, makes no mention of whether the king that God was to look after was clothed or not when the band started to play, but odds are he was royally in the buff.

American men were no more likely than their English cousins to dress for swimming. Recall Benjamin Franklin's stripping on the spot and diving into the Thames when he was working in London in the 1720s. During the Revolution, George Washington objected to the troops under his command swimming naked in ponds and rivers—and presumably never did so himself—but more for decorum's sake and skewed health reasoning.

Too often, Bonnie Ledbetter writes in her essay "Sports and Games of the American Revolution," Washington's soldiers celebrated after their swims by running naked up to nearby houses "with a design to insult and wound the Modesty of Female Decency." Just as important, Washington was convinced that swimming in the heat of the day inflamed the blood and contributed to the fever outbreaks that plagued his camps. Finally, he formalized his various concerns into an official order:

> There is to be no bathing between the hours of 8 and 5, and the custom of remaining long in the water is to be discontinued, as it is too relaxing and injurious to the health. It is also expected that the soldiers in this kind of recreation will observe more decency than they usually practice.

The order, however, must not have been overly obeyed. The Commander in Chief of the Continental Army and future first president and Father of his Country had to reissue his swimming ban in various forms summer after summer while the war ground on.

One of Washington's successors as president and himself the son of a president, John Quincy Adams (1825–1829), apparently suffered no such qualms about the ill effects of swimming on a hot day. Adams used to beat the capital's stifling summer heat and humidity by walking down to the Potomac, stripping to his birthday suit, and diving in.* According perhaps to legend, the intrepid journalist Anne Newport Royall found Adams there one day and sat on his clothes until he agreed to an interview.

That's a scene to cheer any naturist, but the anti-barbarians were waiting at America's gate, armed with all the righteousness of the Victorian Age. In their 1846 manual *Orr's Book of Swimming as practiced and taught in civilized nations . . .* (the subtitle is telling), J. W. Orr and N. Orr agree that male "bathing is best done when quite naked." However, since "decency forbids entire nudity, a kind of short drawers is worn . . . and where ladies and gentlemen bathe in company, as is the fashion all along the Atlantic coast . . . shirts and trowsers are worn."

---

* The Potomac River was closer to the White House then than now. Much of the National Mall is in-fill from later in the nineteenth century.

Over the decades ahead, the minimal "short drawers" would expand to singlets—think of the "onesies" or unitards high school and college wrestlers still wear in competition—that covered not only the upper thighs but also most of the torso. As late as 1917 the American Association of Park Superintendents was promulgating regulations for all swimming under its aegis, forbidding men from exposing any flesh beneath a line connecting their armpits.

The all-male, mostly all–East Coast and WASP, and definitely uptight power structure of the Amateur Athletic Union of the United States—the dominant force in American swimming in the first half of the twentieth century—didn't make life any easier for would-be women swimmers either. Not long before his death in 1914, AAU kingpin James Edward Sullivan threatened to expel the Rye Beach, New York, Swimming Club from the organization if it allowed even one female to swim in its pool. Sullivan also excoriated E. C. Brennan of the American Life Saving Society for holding "school boy races with open races for women in the same tank on the same day—absolutely something that should not have been done." A year after Sullivan's death, another AAU big shot crusaded for ending women's competitive swimming altogether after witnessing a "wholly immodest bathing suit on a girl."

In some ways, things were even odder Down Under. By 1912, when women's swimming (freestyle only) was added to the Olympic Games to be held in Stockholm, Australia had become a female swimming stronghold, as might be expected of an island nation, but would-be Aussie female Olympians faced a daunting catch-22: The New South Wales Ladies Swimming Association, home to some of the country's best female swimmers, forbid its members from appearing in competitions where men were present, but to be chosen for the team, women had to compete before all-male Olympic selectors. In Stockholm, too, they would have to compete in front of a mixed audience if chosen.

That rule was eventually rescinded, but not before the president of the Australian ladies association, Miss Rose Scott, resigned in protest

Tipping point: Great Britain's gold medalists in the inaugural women's 4 × 100-meter freestyle relay at the 1912 Stockholm Olympics are all dressed for the twentieth century, while the stern matron behind them reminds that the past lingers on. *(Library of Congress)*

and went public with her complaints: "I think it is disgusting that men should be allowed to attend. . . . I think it is horrible. We cannot have too much modesty, refinement, or delicacy in the relation between men and women. There is too much boldness and rudeness now, and I am afraid that new decision will have a very vulgar effect on the girls, and the community generally."

Perhaps as a sop to such sensibilities, an Australian female competitor was expected to always wear a cloak from the dressing room to the starting blocks and keep it on until just before the starter raised his gun, at which point she would pass it to the cloak-maid stationed behind her.

The prudes and censors didn't have it all their way, though, or maybe they just couldn't be everywhere at once.

During the two years (1845–1847) that Henry David Thoreau famously spent on Walden Pond, swimming became part of the ritual of his life. Most mornings he would rise early, walk the four hundred feet from his front door to the gravelly beach at what became known as "Thoreau's Point," and dive into the deep water there. It was, he wrote, "a religious exercise, and one of the best things I did." And he did it naked as the day he was born.

Walt Whitman was another great admirer of nude swimming, and unclothed swimmers, for that matter. In his poem "I Sing the Body Electric"—included in the 1855 edition of *Leaves of Grass*—Whitman waxes lyrical about "The swimmer naked in the swimming-bath, seen as he swims through the transparent green-shine, / or lies with his face up and rolls silently to and fro in the heave of the water."

The Frenchman Paul Valéry, who was only twenty when Walt Whitman died in 1892, was even more specific about the sheer sensual (and sexual) joy of swimming in the buff: "To plunge into water; to move one's whole body, from head to toe, in its wild and graceful beauty; to twist about in its pure depths, this is to me a delight only comparable to love." Nor did the high moral standards of the era deter Thomas Eakins from his masterful 1874–1875 painting *The Swimming Hole*, with five nude young men lounging on and diving off a rock promontory in an isolated river setting. Indeed, it might have encouraged him.

In a 1995 article for the *Oxford Art Journal*, Randall Griffin writes that Eakins's painting can be seen as the artist's modern take on "an ancient Greek sculptural frieze"; as an echo of Whitman, whom Eakins greatly admired; as a kind of sacred ritual, given the solemnity of the swimmers and divers; or as a homoerotic fantasy. (Eakins himself is the sixth figure in the painting, watching perhaps too closely from the water, in the bottom right.) But at a far more basic level, *The Swimming Hole* also depicts in beautiful fashion how young men away from populated venues swam in those days.

Ironically, though, it might have been those overclothed, undertaught, hothouse-flower Victorian female bathers who did the most to democratize swimming. In early 1901, *Womanhood,* a high-end British magazine, read by royals and swells, asked its readers to weigh in on the subject of mixed sea bathing, not *mixed* in the sense of male and female bathing machines going into the water side by side but *mixed* in the sense of actually swimming side by side, within sight and even touching distance of one another. The responses were telling.

One woman wrote: "I can see no objection to ladies and gentlemen bathing together. . . . It is natural that they do so; also it is safer. I cannot imagine when or why there came to be a necessity for separate bathing places." Other correspondents noted that "the Continental fashion" of side-by-side bathing was already an accepted feature at numerous English seaside resorts.

Even when responders favored separate bathing, they hinted at a robust swimming-meet culture already in place for women. The Portsmouth Ladies Swimming Club counted upward of five hundred members, many actively engaged in a competition circuit that included clubs in Bournemouth, Exeter, Salisbury, Southsea, Brighton, Worthing, and London. The Duke and Duchess of Connaught had begun providing an annual silver trophy for the Portsmouth club's ladies open-sea championship. That same year, 1901, the sport's national governing body, the Amateur Swimming Association, began awarding prizes in various parts of the country to the winners of all-female races at 100 yards.

In part, this was the popular doctrine of muscular Christianity conferred on both British and American womanhood—God wants us all, both sexes, to be strong and active in body, mind, and faith—but on both sides of the Atlantic, people were voting on women's competitive swimming with their time and attention, as well. A 1919 barnstorming tour of America by two of Australia's most prominent swimmers, Fanny Durack and Mina Wylie, was a complete logistical mess, but when the two squared off against some US swimming stars in a pontoon-enclosed "pool" in the Atlantic Ocean, just off Manhattan Beach in New York City, "10,000 aquatic enthusiasts circled the course and rooted themselves hoarse," according to the *Brooklyn Daily Eagle*.

Ten thousand! Surely, this was a milestone moment for women and for swimming generally, but full liberation was still pending on either side of the Atlantic.

On May 30, 1919, 182 years after the Bath Corporation banned nudity in virtually any form, and three months before that cheering horde of swimming fans showed up at Manhattan Beach, the *New York Times* noted that Sheriff Samuel Mitchell of Queens had appointed "a score of women Special Deputy Sheriffs" with orders to patrol the Rockaways for fellow women "wearing bathing suits of diminutive proportions." A month further on, now into the summer of 1919, the *Times* reported that Coney Island police had arrested one Anna Goldman for daring to wear a bathing suit *under* a sweater and skirt. The costume ran afoul of an ordinance forbidding anyone to walk along Ocean Parkway in other than complete street attire. Anna, her husband, and a friend, Nicholas Christy, all objected to the arrest and got themselves hauled in for disorderly conduct as well. But this was far from a clean win for the censors. A few days later, in the Coney Island court, Magistrate Geismar upbraided the arresting officers for raising Anna Goldman's dress to see if she was in violation of the clothing code.

"You had no business to see if she had on a bathing suit," the magistrate said, "If she did have a bathing suit under her sweater and skirt, she had a right to go anywhere she pleased. If she wants to go shopping in such attire, she was at liberty to do so. It is a man's privilege, if he wishes, to go to business wearing a bathing suit under a sweater and trousers."

In short order, charges of violating the clothing ordinance were dismissed and sentences suspended for the disorderly conduct.

Jump ahead another eight years, and the battle over swimming and the censors continued, in a more public fashion. The original regulations for William Wrigley Jr.'s high-stakes Santa Catalina swim held that contestants could wear "any non-floating form of suit they desire, or if they prefer, no suit at all." One would guess that regulation was meant for male contestants only—recall that George Young actually finished the race in the raw—but it was actually written at the request of one of the female contestants, Charlotte Moore Schoemmell, a New Yorker, who contended that a suit would hinder her swimming and chafe her body. Within weeks, the Women's Christian Temperance Union was all over the matter, citing no less an authority than Gertrude Ederle in a resolution printed in the *Los Angeles Times*:

Believing that the request made by certain entrants in the Catalina swimming contest to be granted nudity for that occasion should be positively denied, in that Miss Gertrude Ederle the world champion swimmer, is competent authority for saying that lack of swimming raiment is not needed and absolutely not to be countenanced, and being confident that such brazen vulgarity is not considered necessary on part of said entrants, but is desired for the publicity such a shameful act would bring. Therefore, be it resolved: that we of the Los Angeles W.C.T.U. County Executive, a body of Christian women toiling in every way possible to uplift humanity, protest against nudity in any contest particularly in the Catalina race now being arranged for January 15, 1927.

Ederle herself chimed in on the subject during a visit with Wrigley on his island, referencing her own recent conquest of the channel: "Personally, I believe there is room for modesty in swimming as in everything else, and I would not think of swimming unclad. I wore men's athletic trunks and a brassiere. I think this is the ideal costume."

As for Charlotte Schoemmell, she abandoned her campaign to swim naked and instead covered herself with not only a bathing suit but ten pounds of black axle grease—to keep warm, she told reporters, and because she believed sharks did not go after dark bodies in the water. (They do. Just ask seals.) And it wasn't only women who suffered. Not until 1937 did Atlantic City, New Jersey, allow men to go shirtless on its beaches. Up until then, the "no-nipple" rule was strictly enforced up and down the Eastern Seaboard.

The photographic record confirms what news accounts tell us—that the prudes, the censors, the guardians of public morality were everywhere to be found in and around American swimming venues deep into the Roaring Twenties and beyond: a stern-faced female measuring the depth of bathing-suit armholes to ensure that no hint of flesh showed through them, a policeman kneeling on the sand in Palm Beach tape-measuring how far above the knee a woman's swimsuit began, two bathing-suited women in Chicago being perp-walked off a Lake Michigan beach for showing too much in suits that would be laughably oversufficient today, another would-be female swimmer in the Windy City being hoisted in the air by a beefy cop, on her way to a nearby paddy wagon.

But it was all a futile, rearguard action—nostalgia for a swimwear Maginot Line that had already been breached in a way that could never be closed again. What's more, the damage had been done by the most perfectly formed woman in the world.

10

AN AUSSIE WRECKING BALL GOES ROGUE

I can't swim wearing more stuff than you hang on a clothesline.
—Annette Kellerman

The history of swimming is rich with mostly forgotten heroines. Some we have already met: Cloelia, who rescued her fellow Roman hostages from the Etruscans; Agnes Beckwith, with her little straw hat; Gertrude Ederle, who not only became the first woman to cross the English Channel but also destroyed Matthew Webb's record time by the simple expedient of using the crawl instead of the breaststroke; Lynne Cox, who has fashioned a spectacular career out of long distances, cruel conditions, and seemingly impossible accomplishments.

Other heroines have thus far swum below the radar in this telling or been submerged in a footnote: diminutive Aileen Riggin, who stood 4 foot 8 inches and weighed all of 65 pounds when she won the Olympic 3-meter diving gold medal in 1920 at age fourteen, and four years later added a silver in the same event and a bronze medal in the 100-meter backstroke; another American, Florence Chadwick, the Gertrude Ederle of the 1950s, who swam across the mouth of San Diego Bay as a ten-year-old—yes, ten!—and later became the first woman to swim the English Channel from both directions (and set a new record each time); Janet Evans, the wind-milling American freestyler, whose Olympic records in the 400-meter and 1,500-meter freestyle events, set in 1988, stood for eighteen years and nineteen years, respectively.

The list goes on. They are all deserving of a better place in modern memory. But none changed the social history of swimming more than Annette Kellerman.

Kellerman emerged at just the right moment—as the rising popularity of women's swimming competitions was colliding with the ridiculous encumbrances of Victorian morality—and she had the moxie and entrepreneurial savvy to smash two centuries of prudery to pieces and come out rich and happy on the other end.

Born in Sydney, Australia, in 1886, to musician parents—her father was a violinist, her mother a piano teacher—Kellerman was hit early by what might have been polio or perhaps rickets. Either way, she suffered as a young child from weak and deformed legs. At age two, she was fitted with clunky leg braces and would wear them for the next five years. When they finally came off, her doctor recommended swimming to strengthen her legs, but little Annette wanted nothing to do with it. Terrified of the water, she begged her mother and father not to take her into the ocean. Her parents, though, persevered with the therapy, and soon they could hardly keep her dry. Fortunately, too, turn-of-the-century Sydney had plenty of opportunities for swimming lessons. Kellerman became a regular at Cavill's Floating Baths, founded by the British émigré Frederick Cavill, who had twice nearly swum the English Channel prior to Matthew Webb's successful crossing.

Practicing in an enclosure surrounded by shark-proof netting, Kellerman got to know Cavill's dynastic swimming family: Ernest, who became the New South Wales 1,000-yard champion at age fifteen; Charles, the first person known to swim the Golden Gate in San Francisco; Percy, Kellerman's main teacher and the first Australian to win races abroad; Arthur, known as Tums, another New South Wales champion and one of the first swimmers to use the Australian crawl; and Sydney, who played a key role in developing the butterfly. Another Cavill's Baths regular, Freddie Lane, won two gold medals at the 1900 Summer Olympics in Paris.[*]

Kellerman got to emulate the best, and she was a quick study. In 1902, age sixteen, she set new world records for the 100 yards and mile swims at the New South Wales championships.[**] Three years later, now living in Melbourne with her parents, she swam record times for five, ten, and fifteen miles on the Yarra River. By then, she had also launched herself into the aquatic entertainment business, giving diving and swimming exhibitions around Melbourne, miming a mermaid at one entertainment center, and swimming with the fishies at the Exhibition Aquarium.

Part of that was for sheer fun—Kellerman was a born entertainer—but part was also from economic necessity. Her parents' small musical academy in Sydney had been hard hit by the economic turndown of the 1890s, and the move to Melbourne hadn't gotten them out of debt. To get right with the family's creditors, Kellerman and her father used scarce remaining funds to sail for England in April 1905 in hopes of launching her career as a professional swimmer. To that end, Kellerman announced herself loudly to Londoners by swimming for three and a half hours down the Thames, from Putney Bridge to Blackwell. The

---

[*] As dynastic as they were, the Cavills were also a star-crossed family. In addition to his two failed attempts to swim the English Channel, patriarch Frederick spent the last thirty years of his life crippled by rheumatism; Charles drowned at Stockton Baths in California one year after crossing the Golden Gate; Percy coached for fifteen years in America before disappearing and later reemerging as a beachcomber in the Bahamas; and Tums froze to death trying to swim across Seattle Harbor in 1914.

[**] Or what were thought to be new world records of 1:22 and 33 minutes, respectively. No official sanctioning body for swimming records existed for many decades to follow.

swim was anything but pleasant: the water, Kellerman would later say, was polluted and she had to dodge tugboats and barges. But the crowds who watched from the shore along the way were sufficiently large and enthusiastic to catch the attention of the editor of the *Daily Mirror*, who offered to back Kellerman if she wanted to become the second woman ever to try swimming the English Channel.

Kellerman took the offer seriously, training for a month and a half, sometimes up to a hundred miles a week, before joining three men on the beach at Dover on August 25, 1905—the thirtieth anniversary of Matthew Webb's triumph. None of the four made it, but in Kellerman's case, it wasn't for want of trying. The *Daily Mirror* was paying her by the mile, and she logged as many as she possibly could before giving up. (According to one account, the cocoa provided by one of her other sponsors made her sick.)

Kellerman would try the English Channel twice more, without success. "I had the endurance," she would later say, "but not the brute strength." Even her failures, though, won her front-page coverage. As she would for the rest of her career, Annette Kellerman relentlessly built her brand, and finally it paid off.

"[My father and I] had fame," she told a *Boston Globe* reporter in 1953, "but we were still just about starving after the Channel attempt when I was asked to give a performance for the King and Queen of England at the Bath Club. At a preview, it was decided I must cover up my 'limbs' for their majesties. We had no money for a proper costume, so we hit on the idea of sewing silk stockings to the racing suit I always wore, and that's really how the one-piece bathing [suit] was launched."[*]

But it wasn't only the one-piece suit that had wings—Annette Kellerman was launched, too.

---

[*] Kellerman was in her mid-sixties when she gave this account to the *Boston Globe*. Other versions of the story have the invitation coming from the Duke and Duchess of Connaught, who as we saw in the last chapter were great supporters of women's swimming. Either way, the outcome is the same.

IN PARIS THE FOLLOWING YEAR, *L'AUTO* NEWSPAPER BACKED HER IN A seven-mile race down the Seine River. Kellerman, the only female in an otherwise all-male field, finished third, with hundreds of thousands cheering along the way. From there, it was on to Austria, where she locked horns with Walpurga von Isacescu, sixteen years her senior, who had been the first woman to attempt the English Channel. Their twenty-eight-mile river race down the Danube from Tulu to Vienna was a rout. Kellerman won by a good forty-five minutes, but the conditions—icy water, swirling whirlpools, sharp rocks—made for a painful victory. Briefly back in New South Wales, she competed behind locked doors before thousands of cheering women at the Ladies' Amateur Swimming Association championships. (Locked to prevent men from attending.)

THE NEW SOUTH WALES MEET CAME NEAR THE END OF HER LIFE AS A competitive swimmer—even though she was only twenty years old by then—but it was just the beginning of an entertainment industry career that in some ways was unmatched across the first half of the twentieth century. The woman was a human whirlwind, and a fearless one at that.

In London, Kellerman elevated the "ornamental swimming" of the previous century to its own art form, performing underwater ballet in a glass tank at the London Hippodrome. (Think of the synchronized swimming of Olympics fame.) Out of the water, she dove from 60, even 90, feet into pools small enough to draw terrified gasps from the audience. (For comparison's sake, the highest Olympic platform diving takes place from ten meters, about 33 feet, or only slightly a third the height of Kellerman's most dramatic dives.)

In 1907, in search of richer pastures, the Kellermans, father and daughter, carried her vaudeville act to America. At the White City Park in Chicago, she found herself on a playbill between the "Educated Flea Circus" and "Mundy's Trained Wild Animal Arena"—shades of Matthew Webb's depressing vaudeville introduction to the United States. Kellerman, though, always provided value for the entertainment dollar. Soon, she had set up shop at the New York Hippodrome—more water

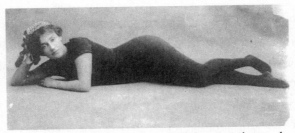

No one did more than Annette Kellerman to change the social history of swimming. In 1910, the head of Harvard's Hemenway Gymnasium declared Kellerman the "most beautifully formed woman of modern times." *(Library of Congress)*

ballet, more swimming with fish, more death-defying dives, this time from a tight rope at the very top of the theater.

Audiences oohed and aahed at the daring feats—and maybe oogled more at her curvaceous body. Forty years later, Paul Gallico remembered as a boy seeing Kellerman at the Colonial Theatre on Broadway and 62nd Street: "The sellout attendance had come ostensibly to see her doing the crawl, the backstroke, the jackknife, and the swan dives, but nobody at the box office was being kidded. The original Annette Kellerman bathing suit was still a slightly bulky affair of jersey wool, even though skirtless and sleeveless. Nevertheless, it made the question of how ladies were put together no longer a matter of vague speculation."

But away from the world of theater and its libertine ways, Kellerman couldn't ignore the reality that women who sought to do any sort of swimming or public bathing were required to dress from neck to feet, as if they were heading into an ozone hole in the dead of winter. Or maybe she simply couldn't ignore the publicity potential inherent in that state of affairs.

Either way, Kellerman had had enough. In July 1907, she walked out onto Revere Beach, in Boston, wearing what newspapers described as a "maillot pantaloon"—basically, a self-designed, one-piece bathing suit that revealed her bare legs and well-endowed body—and the battle was joined. Whether police might have been already alerted, and by whom, is open to question, but it didn't take them long to arrive at the beach and promptly arrest Kellerman on charges of indecent exposure.

Years later, Kellerman would describe the incident as a "big mistake." She was simply headed to the water to train for a long-distance swim, she said, and never intended to shock or offend a soul. More likely, she had a larger purpose in mind. "I can't swim wearing more stuff than you hang on a clothesline," she reportedly said, just before her arrest. Either way, as John Lucas writes in a lengthy essay on Kellerman, the indecent exposure "may have been her most publicized performance." And the wide press coverage cost her not a single thing, not even a small fine.

At her trial, Kellerman admitted to the charge, but didn't stop there. "What difference is there from these legal [bathing] costumes than wearing lead chains around our legs?" she asked the judge, and how many more women were bound to die either because they didn't know how to swim or couldn't swim in all the clothes they were legally bound to wear?

Both arguments seemed to carry the day. The judge vacated the charges against her on the single stipulation that, next time, she wear a cape to the water's edge. More happily for Kellerman's bank account, a new swimsuit line soon followed, marketed as "the Annette Kellerman,"

Women's swimming-lib, 1916-style: The suits were inspired by Annette Kellerman, and there's not a matron in sight at the start of this open-water race in Sheepshead Bay, off the south end of Brooklyn, New York. *(Library of Congress)*

and became an instant sensation. In 1912, when women's swimming—the only sport other than tennis open to women—made its Olympic debut in Stockholm, Kellerman was no longer racing, but all the women Olympians wore some version of the liberated swimwear that she had debuted in Boston five years earlier.

Annette Kellerman was already a vaudeville hit before Boston. Her arrest made her a headliner, and her indefatigability began to make her rich. For two solid years, the Australian Mermaid or Diving Venus, as she was known, did two shows a day, fourteen a week, in New York, all around America, as well as Europe, New Zealand, and her native Australia.

In New York she won a popularity contest by a fifty-thousand-vote margin, picked up a peach-colored Buick for her reward, and rode through Times Square on an open float, dressed as a mermaid with a long "seaweed" wig and an estimated two hundred thousand adoring fans cheering on all sides. (It was "beastly cold," she remembered. "I shivered, but the johnnies didn't know that.") On another occasion, she paraded around New York on a white horse, following a band led by John Philip Sousa. ("His feet hurt from the pavement, and he envied me on the horse. Poor Mr. Sousa. His feet always hurt.")

And then, as if that attention wasn't enough, Dudley A. Sargent—director of the Hemenway Gymnasium at Harvard College—declared Annette Kellerman almost perfect.

In a lengthy, heavily illustrated December 4, 1910, article in the *New York Times*, Sargent laid out for the press the results of his decade-long quest to find the "most beautifully formed woman of modern times." His purpose, Sargent assured readers, was of the noblest sort. He wanted to rescue women from the tyranny of corsets and girdles and reacquaint them with the superior beauty of the ancients.

"At the time of the worship of the beautiful by the Greeks, women quickly discovered the harmonious curves and symmetrical lines that received the approval of the men of that age, and fashioned themselves accordingly," Sargent told the press. "Then, as the moral fibre of the Greeks grew lax, the courtesans set the fashion." Waists were cinched. Corsets became ever tighter, so much so that Hippocrates "vigorously reproached the ladies of Cos for too tightly compressing their ribs and interfering with their breathing powers." And so things were to remain for thousands of years.

To prove the ill effects of corseting, Sargent had women from nearby colleges run for two minutes and thirty seconds, wearing regular gym clothes and then, after a good rest, their corsets. The results? The corsets reduced lung capacity by about one-fifth. Or as Sargent put it: "The tightly corseted woman throws away 20 percent of the air she breathes."

As for what the perfectly proportioned woman should look like, Sargent posited the Aphrodite of Milos, better known as the Venus de Milo, including her missing arms. Next, he built a database of index cards recording the exhaustive measurements of over ten thousand coeds—from Wellesley, Radcliffe, Smith, Vassar, and other collegiate points far and wide: twenty-five data points in all, everything from girth of head to circumference of the left and right calves. And then, late in the game, along came Annette Kellerman, and Dudley Sargent knew he had found his winner. Kellerman's major measurements—weight 137 pounds, height 64.5 inches, chest 35.2, waist 26.2, hips 37.8—weren't entirely perfect. Only the Venus de Milo can be the Venus de Milo. But the measurements were close enough, and to Sargent they were also evidence of the superiority of swimming for physical conditioning and the ultimate superiority of women to men as swimmers, at long distances, largely for the reasons cited in the previous chapter: that annoying and wonderful subcutaneous fat.

Kellerman herself couldn't have agreed more. "The fact of the matter is that women are naturally better for swimming than men," she wrote in a 1915 article for the *Ladies' Home Journal*. "In almost every other line of athletic endeavor, women are outclassed by men. But it is not true of swimming. On account of their small bones and frames, which are more fully padded with soft, buoyant flesh, they do not sink so readily as most men, and so little of their strength needs to be spent on merely keeping up their bodies."

NOT SURPRISINGLY, KELLERMAN'S VAUDEVILLE CAREER SOARED EVEN higher after being declared so beautifully formed. At its peak, she was making $1,500 a week from her appearances—$78,000 a year, over $2 million in current dollars. But trouble was brewing. Kellerman got caught up in a power struggle among theater magnates B. F. Keith, William Morris, and Edward Albee.* Once the dust settled, Albee threatened to cut her weekly salary in half. But as always seemed to be the case, Kellerman was ready to move on, and by then, her brand was almost impregnable and deeply engrained in the male libido.

Back home in Peru, Indiana, in the summer of 1912, a budding Yale songwriter penned lyrics for a proposed musical to be produced that fall by the Delta Kappa Epsilon fraternity. The show never made it to the stage, but the subject, naturally, was women, sex, love, high society, and college high jinks. Cole Porter called his song "She Was a Fair Young Mermaid":

> **Verse:** *When a fellow immature*
> *I had one affaire d'amour*
> *About as queer as e'er befell a man.*
> *I was strolling by the tide*
> *When I suddenly espied*
> *A pretty dear—an Annette Kellerman.*
> *She was sitting nonchalantly,*
> *Quite undraped and all alone.*
> *And I thought some debutante, she*
> *Has escaped her chaperone.*
> *But while I gazed at her pulchritude celestial,*
> *I perceived she was a girl—but not terrestrial.*

---

* The recently deceased playwright Edward Albee was the theater magnate's grandson—adopted by Reed Albee as an infant.

Chorus: *She was a fair young mermaid,*
A debonair young mermaid. . . .
Yes, a veritable Venus,
Was my mermaid love.

Kellerman seems to have suffered for about six seconds from the screws being turned on her vaudeville career. She had been experimenting since the end of the first decade of the new century with short movies filmed in California and back home in Australia. In 1914, she decided to dive deeper into those waters. With Leslie Peacock, she coscripted an underwater fantasy film titled *Neptune's Daughter* and naturally featuring herself. Made on a relatively low budget of $35,000, the film grossed over $1 million in ticket sales. Kellerman helped keep costs down by doing all her own stunts, including leaping from a cliff while fighting off the film's villain—a bit of bravado that left her unconscious at the water's edge. Along the way, she was also badly cut when the underwater tank in which she was acting burst from the pressure.

Her next movie was another matter altogether—the 1916 extravaganza *A Daughter of the Gods* with twenty thousand extras, sets said to stretch half a mile long, and a budget of over $1 million. This time studio executives nixed a proposed death-defying waterfall dive, but Kellerman still did her own stunts—including diving into a pool of live crocodiles—and this time moviegoers got to see even more of Kellerman's beautiful form, thanks to several in-the-buff scenes (with her long hair artfully spread) that sparked a formal ban on nudity across the movie industry.* Unchastened, probably even emboldened, Kellerman laughed all the way to the bank.

For the next decade, over the course of four more movies, frequent live performances, a best-selling book on beauty tips, and public lectures

---

* In his book *Players: 250 Men, Women, and Animals Who Created Modern Sport*, Tim Harris tells the story of an Ohio man who was so taken with Kellerman that he sat through three successive showings of the movie, only to be confronted and murdered with a potato masher by his enraged wife when he returned home.

on the importance for women of exercise and physical education, Kellerman reportedly earned as much as $5,000 a week, maybe the highest-paid working woman in the world and definitely one of the most savvy, too.

Airport courtesy lounges these days crawl with branding consultants. Whole libraries could be filled with books on the subject. But Kellerman needed none of that: she was a wholly intuitive branding genius. Even when she was long gone from performing, Kellerman made sure that her brand was treated right. When MGM was filming *Million Dollar Mermaid*, a biopic of her life that landed in theaters in 1952, Kellerman was on hand to counsel the great film choreographer Busby Berkeley on the water scenes, and she made certain the role of herself was played by the leading swimmer-turned-actress of a new generation: Esther Williams, who might well have claimed an Olympic gold medal of her own if the 1940 Olympics hadn't fallen to World War II.[*]

Annette Kellerman was of Hollywood, but not Hollywood. That's a cliché, but an accurate one. Her biographers Barbara Firth and Emily Gibson compare Kellerman favorably to Mary Pickford, Charlie Chaplin, and Douglas Fairbanks in terms of the control she exercised over the films she starred in. She could fight it out with the best of them, and she never backed down from a stunt. But she also lived in two worlds. In 1912, she married her manager, James Sullivan, and the two lived happily together for sixty years, until his death in 1972. By then, she was living back in Australia, in an oceanside home on the Gold Coast, still advocating for swimming and for women and for physical education.

"When I die," she told one reporter, "I hope to leave a cup for girls' long-distance swimming. I feel distance swimming is very important, not only as exercise but as a character builder. Once you've accomplished swimming a great distance, anything else in the world seems easy by comparison."

---

[*] In addition to Esther Williams, *Million Dollar Mermaid* got the full-star treatment, with Walter Pidgeon playing Kellerman's father, Frederick, and Victor Mature as her husband, James Sullivan. Total cast credits run to 141 names.

When it came to exercise and keeping fit, Kellerman also followed her own advice: she swam daily in the ocean, and in her high-sixties, she could still get a straight leg up in the air, well over her head.

In her later years, Annette Kellerman offered various "greatest moments" to those who came to see her. "My chief pride and pleasure," she told one audience, "has been the knowledge that my work has stimulated an interest in swimming as a woman's sport." On another occasion, visiting New York in 1953, she told columnist Meyer Berger her greatest hour was a 1917 soldier benefit staged at the Metropolitan Opera House. Three stars of the day did scenes from *Madame Butterfly,* followed by Fritz Kreisler playing Toscanini, backed by a ninety-piece orchestra. Then it was Kellerman's turn, not to do ornamental swimming this time but for a bit of land ballet made famous by one of her own great heroes, Anna Pavlova—the death scene from Tchaikovsky's *Swan Lake:* "I did Pavlova's Swan," she told Berger. "I'd always wanted to. Got a great hand with it."

For an epitaph, though, I'll take what a *Boston Post* reporter wrote about Kellerman decades earlier, reviewing one of her public appearances: "After seeing her, one may feel like defying any ten-foot man in the audience to declare that the sex of which she is an ideal example hasn't the courage to fight or the ability to vote or do anything else they choose to do." Like, for example, swimming in a "bathing costume" not designed to drag you down to the bottom of a pool or the depths of an angry ocean.

Of course, by the time of Kellerman's death in 1975, "bathing costumes" had been reduced to their bare essentials.

11

NYLON, WWII, JAMES BOND, AND THE G-STRING

> It was an itsy bitsy teenie weenie yellow polka-dot bikini /
> That she wore for the first time today.
> —Vocal by Brian Hyland, lyrics by
> Lee Pockriss and Paul Vance

Two photographs: One is of my mother, her older brother, and their father—my grandfather and namesake, John Howard Bursk. The date must be somewhere around 1913–1914. My mother, holding her father's left hand, would have been five or perhaps six years old. Her brother, my Uncle Ed, holding his father's right hand, might be all of eight. Both children are barefoot in the sand, wearing some sort of variation of a sailor suit. Between them stands my grandfather, posed for the camera—ramrod straight, broad-shouldered, still muscular in his thirties. (He had played football in college.) Behind them is a long stretch of white sand and, off to one side, a pier stretching out into the Atlantic

Ocean. In the very background, waves are beginning to crest, decent rollers by the looks of them. I can only guess, but from family history, this should be the southern New Jersey coast, two train rides away (via Philadelphia) from the family home in Lancaster, Pennsylvania.

I never knew my grandfather—he was dead long before I was born—but I can see my face and my brother's in his, especially the long upper lip. But it is his outfit I'm concentrating on: a singlet such as a wrestler might wear, but more full. The pant legs stretch down to the knees. His chest is completely covered, too, up to a slight scoop neck. His arms are

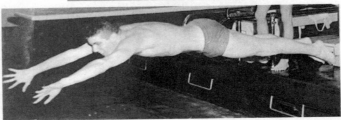

Two family photos: The author's uncle, grandfather, and mother on the New Jersey coast circa 1914. Men were not allowed to show any flesh beneath a line connecting the armpits. Below, the author, far more lightly clad, leaving a high school starting block in 1961. *(Courtesy of author)*

exposed from the shoulders down, but the top is cut so that his axilla, or armpits, are not visible.

The singlet is made of wool, of that I feel certain, and probably high grade. A few years earlier, my grandfather had launched his own whole-sale sugar company: imported sugar from Cuba, sales to confectioners nearby in south-central Pennsylvania, including Milton Hershey. Business was good. The family had money then. He and my grandmother would not have gone cheap on beachwear. Who knows what the American oligarchs were wearing that same summer, but this was state of the art for the kind of people I come from.

The second photo is of me. I'm stretched out almost perfectly flat above the water, only a second or two after the gun has fired. The starting block is right behind my feet. My arms are reaching as far as they can get in front of me. This is 1961, a photo for the J. P. McCaskey High School newspaper, *The Vidette*. The photo is marked on the back to run at 27 picas—4.5 inches wide, a big deal. Except for the relatively narrow band of nylon around my hips, covering my front and buttocks—and it is nylon, made by Jantzen, as all racing suits seemed to be before Speedo got in the game—I am, of course, completely naked, exposed in a way that I'm sure my grandfather never could have contemplated.*

What happened in the roughly four and a half decades between those two photos? Well, World War I, the Roaring Twenties and Olympic Games, Tarzan, the Great Depression, E. I. du Pont de Nemours and Company, World War II, Nagasaki, Hiroshima, postwar atomic bomb testing in the Pacific, liberated France, *From Here to Eternity,* rock 'n' roll, teenagers, *Beach Blanket Bingo,* James Bond/Sean Connery/Ursula Andress, and of course (by now, deep in the background) Annette Kellerman.

All of those elements and much more played a role—swimming is a magnet that draws much to it—but at the center, connecting them all,

---

* The dive alone would date the photo even if the baggy nylon racing suit didn't. I'm trying to land as flat on the water as possible and as far out from the starting block as I can get. Competitors today take advantage of the reduced resistance underwater by diving beneath the surface and undulating dolphin-like for the allowed 15 meters.

was swimwear. And swimwear, in part, was driven as all fashion is by the larger confluence of history, materials, technology, and shifting public morality.

In antiquity, among the Greeks and Romans, swimwear had basically a negative market. A nearly two-thousand-year-old mosaic in the Villa Romana del Casale, in Sicily, does show ten long-limbed women in skimpy, two-piece outfits, caught in the middle of some kind of game. Today's beach volleyball players come readily to mind. But this is a rare exception to the norm: ancient swimmers preferred no swimwear at all.

In the Middle Ages, as we've seen, swimwear had no market either, at least among Europeans. The record suggests that only royalty took the occasional dip, and royals can wear anything they want to, or nothing for that matter. It's up to The Majesty to decide.

The revival of swimming that began with the Renaissance did create a clothing market—waistcoats and drawers, for those little boys at Bath; shifts for the girls; and upward from there—but the market had very little to do with swimming, per se. Among men, skinny-dipping was still expected, away from crowds and especially on brilliant, sunlit days. Among women, for propriety's sake, limbs were to be covered, and the covering grew ever more elaborate as the Victorian era moved along. But fashions fade. Eras scud past. Queen Victoria died on January 22, 1901—after almost sixty-four years on the throne, then the longest reign of any British monarch, since surpassed by Elizabeth II—and a couple of German Americans way the heck and gone in Portland, Oregon, were well positioned to take advantage of the pending paradigm shift in fashion.

Carl Jantzen and John Zehntbauer would go on to dominate swimwear for over half a century—first as the Portland Knitting Company, which they founded in 1910, and later as Jantzen Inc., but they got their start with rowing outfits, not bathing ones. In 1913, a fellow member of the Portland Rowing Club stopped by their small factory to request a specialty item: rowing trunks that would stay up without a drawstring and that would retain body heat on the chilly Willamette River. The solution—trunks made with a stitch like that of a sweater cuff—was so successful that soon the entire Rowing Club was wearing the Portland Knitting trunks. That's when the same customer returned and asked for bathing trunks in the same material.

John Zehntbauer picks the story up from there, in a 1928 article for the company paper, the *Jantzen Yarns*:

> When he came back, he came into the store and told us that [the suit] was heavy and one could not swim well in it, but that he was well satisfied because it was so much warmer than any suit that he had ever had before that it made ocean bathing a pleasure. . . . This experience gave us the idea that a bathing suit made of this stitch only lighter in weight would be an excellent garment. We discussed this between ourselves and decided that we would order a needle bed for our sweater machine that would be fine enough to knit a rib-stitch bathing suit in a weight that would be comfortable. [Carl] and I were constantly in the water in those days, either in the YMCA pool or in the river, and we began to experiment for our own use on swimming suits made of this fine elastic fabric. We soon developed a suit that we found was the most excellent garment for swimming that we had ever seen.

The suit Portland Knitting came up with was not significantly different from the one my grandfather is wearing in the photo I mentioned earlier: a one-piece, all-wool suit that was far more form-fitting than previous iterations of the unitard, thanks to the rib stitching. In fact, if I'm off by a year or two in dating that photo, my grandfather's suit might actually be a Jantzen. It hugs him tightly, and the company's new swimsuits went into production in 1915. As spiffy as they looked, though, the new suits had the drawback of absorbing large quantities of water once they got wet—eight pounds in all, a significant handicap. Like generations of bathing suits that had preceded it, the new Jantzen was better made for land than for water. But the company was now in the swimwear business and ready to make the most of it.

In the general American euphoria following the end of World War I, Jantzen began advertising its suits nationally, in *Vogue, Life* magazine, and elsewhere. Invariably, the ads were accompanied by what would in just a few years become the company logo, a diving girl in a red swimsuit. In the original illustration, her bust was slim, her hips somewhat wide, and for modesty's sake, she wore a bathing cap and red-tinted stockings, but none of that prevented the logo from becoming a national sensation: taped to windshields, plastered on train windows.

More important in the long run: the diving girl is stretched out over imaginary water—a swimmer, not a bather. Jantzen's earliest ads for its outfits had followed the conventions of the day: The models in those ads stood demurely at the water's edge. One woman is holding a parasol. A male model leans on an oar, homage to the swimsuit's roots. But Jantzen's new diving girl in the red swimsuit means to do more than just get wet. She's going to hit the water any second and take off across the pool or lake with a stroke that would do Annette Kellerman proud. Within a year, the company had followed up on the logic of that with a new advertising tagline: "The Suit That Changed Bathing to Swimming." And that, really, was a seismic shift in the history of the sport.[*]

Again, John Zehntbauer:

> It was not until 1921 that Mr. Dodson [the manager of one of the company's retail stores] first conceived the idea of using the name "Swimming Suit" instead of bathing suit. Up to this time we had never heard the name "swimming suit" used, and we had been selling bathing suits for years and had come in contact with all kinds of advertising of these garments. . . . I remember distinctly the twinkle in [Mr. Dodson's] eye as he suggested the use of the name in our advertising.

---

[*] In her very earliest rendering, the Jantzen diving girl is accessorized with a little knit swimming cap complete with pom-poms and calf-high swimming socks, but those disappeared as the Roaring Twenties caught fire.

Why the big deal? Because having established via its advertising that swimming was an active sport, not an exercise in hygiene or simply cooling off, Jantzen would then populate its further advertising with sports heroes of the day, such as Duke Kahanamoku, the Hawaiian swimming champion and godfather of surfing, and the undisputed world's fastest man of his era, Johnny Weissmuller, later to star in a dozen *Tarzan* movies without the bathing-suit top that convention still required. (In his very first movie, 1929's *Glorifying the American Girl*, Weissmuller, as Adonis, wore only a fig leaf. Imagine Tarzan swinging from vine to vine in *that*!)

America's success in the 1924 Olympics in Paris helped accent the ad campaign: nine of eleven golds, with Weissmuller taking first in half the events swum, and Duke Kahanamoku, then an ancient age of thirty-four, finishing second to Weissmuller in the 100-meter freestyle. So did the 1928 Olympics in Amsterdam, when the USA team (now including women) captured a third of all the medals awarded, including six of the eleven golds.[*]

Swimming was hot—as sport, recreation, and mass entertainment—and it stayed hot even through the Great Depression. In the 1930s, Jantzen's ad campaigns pivoted toward the movie stars who helped ease the pain of deprivation: Loretta Young, Joan Blondell, Ginger Rogers, Dick Powell, and others. On the live stage, *Billy Rose's Aquacade*, an extravaganza that combined music, dance, and swimming and that starred Weissmuller and another Olympic gold medalist, Eleanor Holm, was a huge hit at the 1937 Great Lakes Exposition, held on the shores of Lake Erie at Cleveland.[**]

---

[*] In the looser spirit of those earlier Olympic Games, Johnny Weissmuller helped entertain the large crowds in Paris by taking part in diving exhibitions—off the 3-meter springboard and the 10-meter platform—between his swimming events.

[**] Eleanor Holm is worth a book, or maybe just a tabloid, of her own. Favored to repeat as Olympic champion in the 100-meter backstroke at the 1936 Games in Berlin, she was kicked off the US team after getting severely intoxicated on the cruise across the Atlantic. Not long afterward, she married her lover, the Aquacade impresario Billy Rose. At their divorce in 1954, Holm was awarded alimony of $30,000 a month—$280,000 a month in current dollars.

Two years later, Rose brought the show to New York, for the 1939 World's Fair, and by now he was thinking *really* big. Five thousand applicants showed up for tryouts for the five hundred positions as swimmers, dancers, and actors. Holm, now Mrs. Billy Rose, remained with the show, as did Weissmuller though he would soon be replaced by yet another piece of Olympic beefcake, Buster Crabbe. The real headliner for New Yorkers, though, was their own local hero, Gertrude Ederle, by then almost deaf as a post from her English Channel swim but apparently still able to hit her marks on stage. And what a stage it was: 300 by 200 feet, a huge pool, two illuminated curtains of water 40 feet high, all fronted by an Art Deco amphitheater that held eleven thousand people and was often filled for its thirty-nine shows a week. Beyond doubt, the Aquacade was the hit of the fair.

By then, too, college swimming had a Billy Rose of its very own. Bob Kiphuth is remembered today mostly for his innovations as a swimming coach—land exercises, weight training—and for his unparalleled success. In his forty-two years as Yale's head coach, his teams compiled a win–loss record of 528–12. Kiphuth coached the US Olympic team in 1928, 1932, and 1936, and again in 1948 when the Games resumed after World War II. But the annual Water Carnivals he staged at Yale gave proof that he also had a showman's flair for the sport that fit perfectly with the times.

Rediscovered footage of the 1935 Yale Water Carnival tells the story. The venue is the Bob Kiphuth Exhibition Pool at the university's vast Payne Whitney Gymnasium: six lanes wide, flat starting blocks, twenty yards long, with stadium seating for twenty-two hundred. The show begins with young swimmers diving in, spelling out YALE, and then splashing in the water to the tunes being played by the poolside Yale jazz band.

One race pits college swimmers breaststroking with kids on their back; another has kids holding a tow rope as they surfboard behind the tethered swimmers. Larry Griswold, "the world's greatest comedy diver," performs, along with real divers and Ivy League relay teams. In one of the concluding events, Kiphuth's team members change into nightgowns, dive off the three-meter board, race to the shallow end, blow up balloons until they burst, and race back to the deep end, where they are handed lit candles and sent back up the pool one more time. Some serious racing gets done. An assault or two is made on national records. But what looks to be the closing act is Smith College swimmers doing kaleidoscope-like formations that call to mind the old June Taylor dancers. It's entertainment through and through—and every one of the twenty-two hundred seats is full . . . and raucous.

Meanwhile, and interrelated, swimwear was becoming ever more clingy. Prior to World War I, America had virtually no synthetic fiber industry of its own. Clothes were made of all-natural materials: wool, silk, cotton, or linen. Rayon—"artificial silk," as it was known—had been around for many decades, but it had to be imported from abroad, mostly Germany. The British blockade of German ports during the war put an end to that and spurred the creation of a domestic rayon industry, which did little good for swimming in and of itself. Straight rayon made for a nice, tight fit, but the material proved too fragile for swimwear, especially when it got wet. But rayon combined with cotton or silk had more wear and tear in it, and from rayon, manufacturers could venture out to other stronger and more elastic synthetic fibers.

Lastex, basically extruded rubber surrounded by fiber, helped mold swimming suits to the body wearing them, but its elasticity was transient. Then in 1935, DuPont came up with a new nylon it called 6,6 polymer, a mildew-resistant, durable, high-strength, and highly flexible plastic useful for everything from toothbrush bristles to sheer women's stockings to swimsuits. Dacron, Orlon, Lycra, and Spandex would all follow, but the 6,6 polymer was grandmother to them all.

Jantzen's red diving girl logo from the very early 1940s looks to be clad completely in it: more shapely at the bust (probably helped by wire and padding) and across the hips, slightly more arched as if the nylon were actually bending her backward, and no longer with shoulder straps, thanks to the reliability of 6,6 polymer nylon and an ingenious hidden drawstring above the bustline that the company called the "Shouldaire."

The war soon to come, of course, changed everything. Jantzen continued to make swimsuits, but they were short-legged trunks for the US Marine Corps. The company's nylon stock was used for parachutes; its knitting machines were retooled for sleeping bags, mufflers, gas-mask carriers, army-green sweaters, and the like. Then came peace and a return to normalcy, and swimwear designers looked over the vast array of new, war-inspired materials at their beck and call, contemplated the pent-up demand for such goods, and decided to start making suits that used almost no material at all.

Two-piece women's swimsuits were not invented post-WWII. They had become a fairly common fashion statement in the late 1930s and got a big boost when the US War Production Board imposed a 10 percent cutback in the fabric used for women's swimwear. Lana Turner, Rita Hayworth, Ava Gardner, and other celluloid beauties of the day were all photographed wearing them, and where Hollywood went, fashion followed. But compared to what was coming, these were modest outfits in the extreme: some flesh exposed below the halter tops, but not much more than the lower rib cage. The bottoms started at the very top of the waist and extended below the hips, sometimes as shorts or with a little skirt attached—Dorothy Lamour subbed a sarong for the two-piece bottom in 1937's *Hurricane*. Most important was the navel: the Hays Code, which then governed on-screen morality in Hollywood, forbid its display, and fashion followed there, too.

And then, in the summer of 1946 on the Riviera at Cannes in newly liberated France, the flesh started flying. Whether fashion designer Jacques Heim or mechanical engineer Louis Réard invented the bikini is an open question. Heim was first, in May 1946, to release a design for a two-piece swimming suit that he named the *atome*, maybe because it was so small or pretty women were known as "bombshells," or perhaps—with the A-bombs that fell on Hiroshima and Nagasaki in mind—he wanted to capture the explosive effect the new design would have on male libidos. But, in fact, Heim's design wasn't all that daring: Breasts were more isolated but still protected. Haunches didn't hang out the sides. Looked at one way, Heim's suit was simply a rational response to the postwar material shortage that would persist in France and elsewhere for many, many months to come.

Louis Réard pushed the envelope much harder when he unveiled his new suit two months later. The navel was exposed as were large swaths of the buttocks, and a generous helping of the breasts, too. Even the name was daring (if somewhat derivative of Heim's *atome*): *bikini*, taken from Bikini Atoll, part of the Marshall Islands chain in the central Pacific Ocean. Only four days earlier the atoll had been the site of the first of what ultimately would be twenty-three nuclear weapons tests conducted over a dozen years. Now it would become an integral part of fashion history, even as the atoll after which it was named became uninhabitable and remains that way to the present day.[*]

So controversial was Réard's design that he couldn't find a runway model willing to wear it when the new bikini was unveiled at the Piscine Molitor in Paris on July 5, 1946. Instead, he hired a nude dancer from the Casino de Paris, Micheline Bernardini, to debut his creation. In a news photo that quickly circled the globe, Bernardini is holding in one hand a tiny box that the suit—thirty inches of fabric in all—is said to fit inside.[**] Later, Réard claimed that a real bikini had to be small enough to pull "through a wedding ring." There was little mention in the press coverage of actually swimming in the suit, but swimming probably wasn't the point anyway, then or now. One survey found that 85 percent of bikinis never go in the water.

---

[*] When bikinis first surfaced, news outlets generally capitalized the "B" after the proper name of the island, but the "bi-" soon came to be understood as "two"—i.e., the top and the bottom. Thus, when Rudi Gernreich introduced his topless women's one-piece suit in 1964, he cleverly called it a "monokini." Two decades later, Gernreich dubbed his new extreme-thong-style one-piece outfit the "pubikini," for obvious reasons, and the atoll connection was lost for good.

[**] Micheline Bernardini would soon fade back into obscurity, but not before receiving some 50,000 fan letters from men and women all around the world.

Shock value aside, reception of Réard's creation was neither im-mediate nor universal. For Roman Catholics, Pope Pius XI's January 1930 decree on modesty still obtained. Parents were to be wary of letting their children even attend athletic events and gymnastic competitions, much less participate in them. Dresses, bathing attire included, were to conform to the "Marylike standards" established by the pope's Cardi-nal Vicar: not cut deeper than "two finger breadths under the pit of the throat." Even had the Vatican suddenly decided to go rogue, the ravaged economies of Europe were in no position to launch a fad, even one sup-posedly built around postwar shortages.

Yesteryear's beauty icons didn't all fall in line either. Annette Keller-man, the world's most perfectly portioned female as of 1910, the woman who first liberated swimwear from the tyranny of Victorian morality, had a low opinion of Louis Réard's invention. "The Bikini bathing suit is a mistake," she told the *Boston Globe* in 1953. "Only two women in a million can wear it. And it's a very big mistake to try. The Bikini shows too much. It shows a line that makes the leg look ugly, even with the best of figures. A body is at its most beautiful when there is one beautiful, unbroken line."

Liberation, though, was in the air, in fashion as in lifting the yoke of war. Even as Annette Kellerman was bad-mouthing bikinis, they had begun to storm the beaches of the French Mediterranean, led boldly by attention-grabbing film stars like Brigitte Bardot. The Iberian autocrats—Francisco Franco in Spain and Portugal's António de Oliveira Salazar—cast a cold eye on bikinis. Other seaside destinations either followed or were unwelcoming to them, but German-speaking Europeans didn't need material shortages to justify scant outfits—for men or women—or no outfits at all, and they seem to have been irresistibly drawn to the sun after often bitter war winters.

In October 1952, *La France* reported that an estimated thirty thou-sand nudists, many from the north, had made summer visits to the Île du Levant, off the western edge of the Riviera. By comparison, a bikini was almost dressing up. Brazilians would soon go all in for the diminutive swimwear as well—and even more so for the bikini's still-briefer spawn, the G-string.

The British and US markets, by contrast, largely resisted, at least in the short term. Anglicans and their American cousins, Episcopalians—the "Frozen Chosen," as they are sometimes known—are congenitally slow to yield on matters of propriety. Both cultures, too, continued to be shaped by the residue of Puritanism and low-church movements for whom the thought of even swimming on a Sunday, much less doing so in almost nothing, was anathema. But in the English-speaking world, and particularly in America, sex, swimming, and popular culture were converging in ways not to be denied.

In the 1953 film *From Here to Eternity*, based on James Jones's novel of the same name, Burt Lancaster (in what was then a brief, tight swimsuit) and Deborah Kerr (in a one-piece cut deeply in the front) don't actually have sex near the end as they lie in the Hawaiian waves embracing, but as Samuel Wigley noted in a sixtieth-anniversary look back at Fred Zinnemann's famous film, they might as well have. "The orgiastic music, the thunder of the waves, trembling bodies, the looks of intent in their eyes—this was strong stuff for films of the time." Even as a nine-year-old, I had some sense where that scene was headed.

Ex–Disney Mouseketeer Annette Funicello lacked Deborah Kerr's raw allure, and she seemed to always be dressed in pink bikinis that might have been approved by a particularly conservative religious sect, but her seemingly endless run of beach-party movies in which she costarred with rock idol Frankie Avalon ("Venus, goddess of love that you are . . . " / no Burt Lancaster either) cemented the equation of teenage expectation: skimpy swimwear + sand + enough water for splashing = happiness. Brian Hyland's 1960 hit single "Itsy Bitsy Teenie Weenie Yellow Polkadot Bikini" even put some suspense into the equation: Was she afraid to come out of the water because (a) modesty was reasserting itself or (b) because that itsy-bitsy teenie-weenie top was hard to keep in place and, after all, she was wearing it "for the first time today"?

Actress Ursula Andress, as Honey Ryder, in the very first James Bond movie, *Dr. No*, from 1960. Andress emerged from the Caribbean in a slim white bikini and walked into the dreams of a generation of schoolboys. *(Everett Collection, altered to black & white)*

And then, that same year if you were the right age (I was by then, at fifteen), Ursula Andress (as Honey Ryder but ever thereafter for much of my generation Ursula Undress) walked out of the water in the very first James Bond movie, *Dr. No*, wearing nothing but a thin white bikini accented by a knife sheath, and, well, it was hard to get over. Suddenly, swimming had a purpose far greater than ribbons, medals, and the occasional trophy.[*]

When, six years later, Raquel Welch donned a tattered fur bikini for the anthropological epic *One Million Years B.C.*, it seemed somehow anticlimactic. Ditto for *Sports Illustrated*'s first swimsuit cover, which

---

[*] Ursula Andress's *Dr. No* bikini eventually sold at auction for $35,000. The top was one of the actress's own bras, fronted with ivory cotton.

launched in 1964 with "A Skin Diver's Guide to the Caribbean." Cover model Babette March is cute as a button and like Ursula Andress in *Dr. No,* she is wearing a white two-piece, but she is to Ursula as hand-holding is to heavy necking—that is, no contest.*

---

* Simultaneously, and especially in Europe, men's swimwear has been shrinking to the point where beaches are now crowded with bathers who look as though they have dressed for a Mr. Universe contest, frequently without the bodies normally associated with such an activity. Here, too, the English-speaking world has largely trailed behind, for many of the same reasons that slowed the advance of bikinis among British and American women: vestigial prudery, self-consciousness, low-church influences, etc.

I was once on a beach on the North Sea where the men were oddly divided between those wearing almost nothing and others, like me, in loose-legged boxer trunks.

"Want to play Spot-the-English-Speaker?" a friend asked.

"How do you do that?" I replied.

"I'll give you a hint," he said. "We're not talking about the guys wearing banana hammocks."

An evocative phrase!

12

SWIMMING TOGETHER, SWIMMING ALONE

> He seemed to see, with a cartographer's eye, that string of swimming pools, that quasi subterranean stream that curved across the county.
> —John Cheever, "The Swimmer"

Swimming pools predate the Greeks and Romans by thousands of years. The Great Bath at Mohenjo-daro, in the Indus Valley of what is now Pakistan, was built in the third millennium BCE, and it was great in every way for its day: size (12 meters × 7 meters × 2.5 meters deep), construction (the bottom and sides are made of bricks and mud, overlaid with plaster and a waterproof tar), design (bathers entered via wide staircases at either end, and the pool was surrounded on at least three sides by brick colonnades), even mystery (no one knows for sure what the bath was intended for, but most likely it was purification rituals, not morning laps).

Two thousand years later, the Greeks raised swimming to a civic virtue. The capacity to move gracefully through water foreshadowed moving gracefully (and usefully) through life. The Romans added plumbing and engineering finesse to the equation—heated water, for example—and made their pools communal so long as you weren't a slave from some newly conquered land.

While Europe was cloaked in the Dark and Middle Ages, China got into the pool business with the Taiye Pond in the Imperial City, begun during the Jin Dynasty (1115–1234 CE). Or at least the semi-pool business. The Chinese characters for *Taiye* translate as "Great Liquid Pool," but the pool was closer to an artificial lake. Nonetheless, the Taiye was so admired for its beauty that Kublai Khan sited his palace to take advantage of the view, after his Mongol hordes had overrun the country.

The English, as we've seen, took advantage of the Thames and other rivers to create floating pools, or they diverted the river to ditches to form pools sided with mud and clay, with a nice gravel bottom if you were lucky. By the start of the nineteenth century, the budding natators of Harrow School, Lord Byron among them, could take advantage of an oblong muddy-water ditch known as the "duck-puddle" to perfect their breaststrokes, although apparently they had to share the "pool" with eels and water rats in addition to the ever-instructive frogs.

The practical Swedes along with the well-organized English and others introduced infrastructure to pool life in the nineteenth century, creating swimming associations and indoor pools specifically for competition. Meanwhile, the French, being French, added panache to pool architecture. The 1929 Piscine Molitor, where Louis Réard first introduced his new bikini, was designed by architect Lucien Pollet to echo an ocean liner and fitted with Art Deco stained glass by Louis Barillet, a noted French artist of the day. Another indoor pool from the same era, in the small town of Roubaix, far in the north of France, was such a stunning and lush example of Art Deco that, rather than tear the pool down when it fell into disuse, the locals converted it to a museum that draws over two hundred thousand visitors a year.

Less densely settled than Europe, more rural generally, and blessed with an endless array of natural swimming holes—more holes than able swimmers, as witness the high drowning rate of the nineteenth century—America was a Johnny-come-lately to the pool business. Such indoor pools as there were at the beginning of the twentieth century were largely the work of the Young Men's Christian Association. Begun in London in 1844, the YMCA arrived in North America seven years later, first in Montreal and then, a month later, in Boston.

The Civil War decimated the organization and its "young men" membership, but by the early 1880s the YMCA was fully established in the United States and on a building boom. Large urban Ys went up in city after city—multipurpose buildings with indoor pools, rooms for rent, often cafeterias and duck-pin bowling alleys, even auditoriums. If my own family history is correct, it was just about this time that my great-grandfather, Daniel S. Bursk, is said to have walked the thirty-eight miles from Lancaster, Pennsylvania, to Harrisburg to ask the Philadelphia department store magnate John Wanamaker for help funding a local Y.

Why he might have walked, I have no idea. Maybe it was a publicity stunt—a way to get the attention of Wanamaker, who was then serving as president of the American branch of the YMCA. Maybe walking thirty-eight miles didn't seem that big a deal back then—my great-grandfather had walked considerable distances daily as the commissary sergeant for his Pennsylvania regiment during the Civil War. But whatever the intent, it seems to have worked. The Y got built, a great hulking structure one block off the central Lancaster Square, and seventy-plus years later I spent endless late afternoons practicing in its 20-yard-long, four-lane, heavily chlorinated tank of a pool. Today, all that remains of the building is a rescued stained glass window donated in honor of my great-grandfather.

Following the British model of providing sanitary bathing for the poor, the New York state legislature—in the flush years for the North after the Civil War—passed a bill mandating free bathhouses in cities with populations in excess of fifty thousand. Stanley Fox's drawing of the interior of one such swimming bath—from the *Harper's Weekly* of August 20, 1870—shows at least half the boys swimming, jumping, and roughhousing naked. Again, following the British model, New York City also began introducing floating baths along both the Hudson and East Rivers. As in England, too, the baths went out of use as river pollution mounted.

A 1900 survey found a total of sixty-seven public pools in the United States, indoor and outdoor, or one public pool for every 1.14 million Americans, hardly oversaturation. But change was on the way. The first indoor collegiate pool opened just before the turn of the century, in 1896, at the University of Pennsylvania. Brown University followed with a second pool a decade later.

Almost simultaneously with the Brown University swimming facility, Teachers College in New York City got its own indoor pool, part of a newly constructed gymnasium that was then the largest such facility for women in the nation. Six years later, the famed architect Cass Gilbert proposed a Pompeii-like bath/pool, richly decorated with mosaics, for the basement of the new Woolworth Building at 233 Broadway. As befit the most successful retailer in America, Woolworth did the building as a whole on the grand scale, but it went cheap on the flourishes for Gilbert's pool. Still the pool thrived for most of the twentieth century, falling into permanent decay long after the five-and-dime stores that built it disappeared from the urban landscape.

As the early part of the twentieth century moved along, swimming pools began to outstrip technology. The more they were used, the more bacteria and other ills accumulated in the water. A 1915 report cited nineteen separate medical authorities and laid out a dire catalog of swimming-pool-related ills: venereal, ocular, aural, and intestinal diseases. As we will see later, the fear of contagion has never really disappeared, but over the next eight years, three groups with exhaustive and fearsome names—the American Association for Hygiene and Baths, the Committee on Pool Standards of the American Public Health Association, and the Conference of State Sanitary Engineers—all produced reports on physical, chemical, and bacteriological standards for pools.

By 1929, this triad seems to have actually combined forces and made headway on effectively treating pool water. The Ambassador Hotel, which opened that year on K Street in downtown Washington, DC, boasted that the water in its new indoor pool was chemical-free, treated by ultraviolet radiation just like home well water today. Water quality, though, would soon be the least of America's problems. The Roaring Twenties were about to crash, and once again, swimming is a useful index of conflicting forces.

The plus side of the Roaring Twenties is demonstrable. The American excesses of the decade created huge swimming superstars like Gertrude Ederle and Johnny Weissmuller, and swimming pools that were equally huge in every way—size, attendance, you name it.

The numbers defy easy imagination. The Raven Hall Baths in Coney Island, New York—60 yards by almost 30 yards—drew 16,000 paying customers on July 15, 1928, the year the baths opened. (If the pool remained open from, say, ten in the morning until eight at night, that averaged out to 1,600 customers an hour, or 27 customers a minute pouring through the front gate.) Fleishhacker Pool, in San Francisco, established in 1925, billed itself as the largest heated saltwater pool in the world: 1,000 feet long, 300 feet wide, 6.5 million gallons of filtered seawater pumped in from the Pacific Ocean. A dozen lifeguards were on duty at all times, while lifesaving rowboats prowled the waters. Fleishhacker bragged that it could accommodate up to 10,000 bathers at any one time.[*] The twenty-five-cent admission (fifteen cents for children under twelve) came with a large dressing room with showers plus the loan of a bathing suit and a large towel guaranteed to be sterilized between uses.

Out in St. Louis, the auditorium where Woodrow Wilson was renominated for the presidency in 1916 got converted to a massive pool within a pool, 100 feet by 200 feet in all. The larger outer pool was from two to five feet deep, ideal for beginners and toddlers. The inner pool, for real swimmers, was a uniform nine feet deep, with one- and three-meter

---

[*] In theory, if the pool was completely filled, each of the 10,000 swimmers would still have 30 square feet and 650 gallons of water to her- or himself.

diving boards and two diving platforms, 15 and 25 feet high. (Generally speaking, it takes a fool, a daredevil, or an Annette Kellerman to dive from 25 feet in the air into a 9-foot-deep pool. Kids, Do Not Try This at Home.) The pool even brought a touch of faux ocean to the landlocked Midwest: its six hundred thousand gallons of water were turned into a buoyant saline solution with rock salt from Avery Island, Louisiana, better known today as the birthplace of Tabasco brand pepper sauce.

And so it went. The 100-yard-long Lakeside Pool in Salem, Virginia, used river water, pumped in at the rate of twenty thousand gallons an hour. Price Run Pool in Wilmington, Delaware, oddly built in the shape of a human foot, was 160 yards from end to end. As a municipal pool, it was also open to the public free for two hours every morning, plus from two to five p.m. on Saturdays.

Down in Fort Lauderdale, Boy and Girl Scouts could swim free every Saturday morning at the new ten-lane Casino Pool next to the Las Olas Casino.* Further south in Florida, in 1924, real estate developer George Merrick turned an abandoned quarry in Coral Gables into the elegant and vast Venetian Pool—four acres big, 820,000 gallons. In the old days Venetian-style gondolas traveled the waters. Occasionally, the pool would be drained so the Miami Symphony could take advantage of the quarry's acoustics. The pool was added to the US National Register of Historic Places in 1981 and remains the sole swimming facility on that roster.

Developers and pools were pairing up on the West Coast as well. Out in Riverside, California, would-be real-estate moguls made the Lake Norconian Club swimming and diving pools the centerpiece of a proposed million-dollar resort. The thirteen-year-old girl in a publicity photo doing a swan dive off the thirty-two-foot tower (into, thankfully, 16 feet of water, not 9) clearly went to school on Jantzen's diving girl in red. All around the country, realtors were doing the same thing: starting with a pool, *then* developing a community around it.

---

* Decades later, sale of the Casino Pool site would help fund the creation of the International Swimming Hall of Fame in Fort Lauderdale.

If you build it, they will come—so went the reasoning, and with good cause. Just as this privately funded pool-building boom was reaching its peak, the Committee on Curriculum Research of the Society of Directors of Physical Education announced that, compared to all other forms of recreation, swimming and diving scored highest "on the basis of their contribution to physical and organic growth, traits and qualities of good citizenship, social and moral ideals, psychological development, [and] skill for self-protection and aid to others."

Quite an honor—almost the Nobel Prize of Sports, a boom activity if ever there was one! A 1927 survey counted 3,212 public, for-profit, and private pools in US cities of over five thousand in population—one pool for every thirty-seven thousand Americans, a huge leap forward from the 1900 survey.

Then along came Black Monday and Black Tuesday—October 28 and 29, 1929, when the Dow Jones Industrial Average plunged by almost 25 percent—and all the easy money that had funded the rapid private-market expansion of swimming pools and so much else during the Roaring Twenties was suddenly gone. And strangely enough, the growth of swimming and swimming facilities barely missed a beat.

Of course, almost everyone and everything suffered in the Great Depression, but swimming suffered less than most, especially once Franklin Roosevelt became president, three and a half years into the debacle. His predecessor, Herbert Hoover, believed America could save its way out of financial calamity; FDR believed in spending the country's way back to the high ground.

More to the point maybe for these purposes, Hoover was a baseball fan—he had played shortstop at Stanford University before dislocating his finger, after which he became the team's business manager. As president, he threw out the opening pitch for the Washington Senators all four years in office. Roosevelt played no ball sports. Polio had left him with very limited use of his legs. Instead, for recreation and for therapy, he swam. FDR had been in office only a few months before the first

White House indoor pool opened, between the White House itself and the West Wing, funded not by government but via a campaign launched by the *New York Daily News*.

Two years later, on May 6, 1935, Roosevelt founded the Works Progress Administration as a centerpiece of his New Deal. Over the next four years, the WPA put millions of Americans back to work, building roads, schools, and other public projects; and pools for the masses were near the top of the WPA's must-do chart.

The list goes on and on: the Anacostia Swimming Pool and Bathhouse and the Banneker Recreation Center and Pool, both in Washington, DC; a bathhouse and pool for Electra, Texas, and for Carver Park and Kosciuszko Park in Milwaukee. Highland Park in Guthrie, Oklahoma, got the same treatment. So did the Schiller Park in Buffalo, New York, and the Washington Memorial Park in Buffalo, Wyoming. Hellenback Pool in Wilkes-Barre, Pennsylvania; City Pool in Winter Garden, Florida; Island Park Pool in Fargo, North Dakota; Long Meadow Pool in Durham, North Carolina; Chaffee Public Pool in Chaffee, Missouri; the appropriately named Roosevelt Pool in Susanville, California—they all were courtesy of the New Deal.

In New York City alone, in the single summer of 1936, the WPA got eleven new pools up and running. Combined admissions at all eleven totaled just shy of 1.8 million people; six hundred thousand kids under fourteen got to swim—and *learn* to swim—at no charge weekday mornings.

And even that only scratches the surface. WPA pools—sometimes built in cooperation with the Civilian Conservation Corps—blanketed the country, but it wasn't just summer entertainment that the agency was providing. The WPA added pools to the University of Mississippi campus, the University of New Hampshire, and the State Training School for Girls in Chalkville, Alabama. It also built high school after high school, and in many of those spanking new schools, it included an indoor pool, often state of the art for the late 1930s. As a teenager, I graduated from practicing in a cramped, seventy-five-year-old, 20-yard pool at the bottom of the local YMCA to practicing and competing in a more spacious

WPA-provided 25-yard swimming pool tucked off at the end of a high school the WPA finished in 1938. Like the façade and entrance of the school and its massive auditorium, the pool had Art Deco touches. The Works Progress Administration did things right.

America wasn't alone in its pool building. The 160-foot-long Brockwell Lido swimming pool, in the Herne Hill area of London, opened in 1937. That same year a 60-meter by 30-meter pool came on line at the Earls Court Exhibition Center, near central London. When not in use, the pool could be covered with a 750-ton retractable floor. The Derby Baths pool measured 50 meters long by eight lanes wide, with a diving well and seating for 1,800 spectators—Olympic caliber, in short. It opened in Blackpool two years later, in 1939, just in time for war.

The Germans also have a long history of municipal and public pools. Berlin's indoor Stadtbad Neukölln, opened in 1914, might be the most beautiful pool still in use in Europe: marbled pillars, an arched ceiling, intricate tile work, and at the center of it all a four-lane 25-meter pool that must be bliss to swim in. While Franklin Roosevelt was ramping up his Works Progress Administration, Adolf Hitler's engineers and architects were ramping up for the 1936 Olympic Games with a spectacular 50-meter pool at the center of a stadium that also featured a diving tower for the men's and women's 3-meter springboard and 10-meter platform events. (Americans swept all but two bronze medals.)

Unlike England, Germany, and the rest of Europe, however, the United States did not have a war fought on its own land to savage its cities, cripple its economy, and set public amenities like swimming pools back at least half a generation. Swimming in America also developed uniquely within the flow of the nation's social history, for good and for ill.

IN THE ROARING TWENTIES AND EVEN THROUGH THE GREAT DEPRESSION, the driving idea behind these massive pools—public and for-profit—was American togetherness, the fabled Melting Pot, community, fun writ big. They were not just places to cool off for an hour or two. They were celebrations of urban life. Some were surrounded by sand or large swaths of lawn. Others had fountains to lure the timid into the water. For more bold swimmers, there were also likely to be terrifyingly long sliding boards at one end of the pool and 1- and 3-meter diving boards at the other, deep end, maybe several of each.

One such pool where I worked as a lifeguard in the early 1960s had a water-cooled metal slide that must have been forty feet high, reached by a long set of open stairs and exited at the bottom at top speeds into three feet of water. What were the odds of injury there? High! Another pool where my summer AAU swim team practiced, also built pre–Great Depression, complemented its low and high boards with a 5-meter platform, halfway to the 10-meter towers used in Olympic competition. Another warning: Kids, Do Not Belly-Flop from Here!

Such amenities have, of course, disappeared, victims of crippling liability riders. The last time I dove off a 3-meter springboard, it was bolted to a privately owned floating dock in Narragansett Bay. Tides had the board situated on a north–south axis. Waves had the dock tilting back and forth east and west. The combination made for an interesting walk to the end of the board, especially after the side railings terminated. I might have chickened out if my daughter hadn't raced out and done a perfect dive just in front of me.

But the massive pools themselves have almost disappeared as well, done in by suburbanization, health scares, the decay of so many of America's inner cities, boutique community pools, shifting understandings of "community" itself, and—to get to a more basic level—gunite and its later iteration, shotcrete.

Let's start with the country club movement. Urban men's clubs and rural fox-hunting packs were commonplaces of American life, at least for the upper classes, in the decades just after the Civil War. The former was likely to be only a short walk from the office, perfect for a midday meal; the other commonly required a weekend stay in the country. Golfing, though, was different—less expensive than keeping a horse and/or a second home, more active than lunching and dozing off in a leather chair—and golf grew explosively at the end of the nineteenth century, from a single course in 1885 to over a thousand courses by 1900.

Many of these early courses were haphazard affairs—sand greens and the like—but as the first decades of the twentieth century wore on, clubs began to accrue around these courses, and the clubs themselves often aspired to be mini-resorts with not only golf but also eating facilities, maybe tennis courts, and of course a pool. What's more, as the clubs spread and grew in number, they reached ever deeper into the rising middle class for members. At the start of the century, one survey found at least one country club in all forty-eight states. By 1915, that number had swelled to about a thousand such clubs, and by 1927, it reached fifty-five hundred with 2.7 million members.

The Depression devastated those numbers. By 1939, forty-seven hundred clubs had managed to keep their doors open in one form or another, but total membership had plummeted by almost 80 percent, to a little under six hundred thousand. Still, Americans had gotten a taste of the club mentality. The huge urban pools of the twenties and thirties had been all for one, one for all, just be careful where you dive. The country clubs, by contrast, were rife with covenants and codicils: no blacks; no Jews (except in the all-Jewish country clubs that sprang up in response); dress whites for the tennis courts, and so on. Turns out, a lot of people liked it that way.

The various polio scares during the first half of the twentieth century and just beyond—sixty thousand cases were reported in 1952 alone—didn't help either. Polio was a summer disease. It tended to peak in July and August, then back way off in the winter months. Naturally, swimming pools were suspected as fomites—and the bigger they were and the more they catered to a lower-middle-class clientele, the more suspect they were. In the summer of 1954, as the polio season heated up for one last time (Jonas Salk's vaccine was waiting in the wings), the two sprawling public pools in my hometown closed their doors, while my local country club pool stayed open, a refuge not only from the masses but from their diseases.

That thinking was, in fact, wrong on multiple levels. Polio did spread through contaminated water, but chlorine, by then used in just about all swimming pools, is polio's mortal enemy: it inactivates the poliomyelitis virus practically on contact. Also, country clubs were no refuge. The people I know who came down with polio that summer—my older sister (a mild case, fortunately) and a sweet girl my age (much more severe)—both swam no place other than our country club.[*]

The country club movement was one death knell for swimming together in America. It robbed the big for-profit pools of customers and robbed the municipal pools of an influential political constituency. Ironically, the GI Bill, meant to democratize educational and housing opportunity, was another, much louder knell.

Officially known as the Servicemen's Readjustment Act of 1944, the GI Bill provided a variety of benefits to the nation's fifteen million World War II veterans, men and women, as they returned home from combat: tuition-free college or vocational education plus a cost-of-living stipend (almost half of all students entering college in 1947 were veterans), unemployment compensation for up to a year as the veterans looked for work ($4 billion paid out from 1944 to 1949), and government-guaranteed loans to purchase homes, farms, or businesses. The first of those provisions, the education benefits, probably did more than any other factor to create the prosperous middle class of the postwar years. The low-cost housing loans, though, created the suburbs, and the suburbs atomized swimming even more.

As I've already indicated, I claimed multiple summer pool venues while I was growing up: a country club my parents had belonged to since

---

* There's always something to worry about. An article in the January 2012 issue of *Environmental Health Perspectives* reported that boys ages fourteen to eighteen who had been swimming regularly in chlorinated indoor pools since younger than age ten had testosterone levels 20 percent lower than similar boys who swam in pools disinfected with copper-silver ionization and were three times more likely to have abnormally low levels of the hormone.

the late 1930s, a huge twin pool once I was old enough to lifeguard, and another huge relic of the 1920s where my AAU team practiced. The country club remains. The others are long gone.

My own children grew up mostly in Bethesda, Maryland, in a suburban world that was almost a perfect expression of what swimming pools had become. The houses in our neighborhood were nearly all just-post-WWII—smallish ranches and split levels, priced for returning GIs with their low-cost loans and entry-level workers for a rapidly expanding federal government. At the end of our street, three blocks downhill, was a community swimming pool with a very active swim team that competed against teams from other, almost identical communities: a multiblock cluster of houses, a pool within walking distance—or easy biking distance—of everyone meeting the residential requirement for membership.

The six-lane pool at our community club and the L-shaped diving well (low board only, now no more) were typical, as well, of the pools at all the surrounding clubs. Any one of them would have fit inside a teeny corner of those great sprawling urban pools of the 1920s.

And then there's gunite. Essentially concrete blown out from a pneumatic gun, gunite dates back to 1910, the invention of a Pennsylvania taxidermist. Prior to World War II, it was used primarily for repairing and shoring up sewer tunnels, reservoirs, dams, and the like, as well as lining furnaces. During the war, it proved invaluable for quickly restoring damaged runways. Postwar, the same properties that made gunite so useful in other endeavors—easy application, fast drying—combined with the housing boom (first fueled by the GI Bill), the rapid expansion of commuter highways, and an increasingly supercharged economy to create a sub-boom in home pools. Who needed 30 square feet of a 300,000-square-foot pool filled with a motley array of wet strangers when you could have 300 square feet of pool in your own backyard, filled with family and friends, with a grill waiting on the deck at one end and, to get a little wild, a tiki bar at the other?

A near century of swimming pools: the massive Fleishhacker Pool in San Francisco, opened in 1925, with a ten-thousand-swimmer capacity [top left]; Berlin's 1930 glass-enclosed Stadtbad Mitte [middle left]; the 160-foot-long Brockwell Lido in London from the mid-1930s [bottom left]; the gunite-enabled amoeba-shaped pool that brought swimming to the American backyard [top right]; and a contemporary indoor resistance pool—with room for only one [bottom right]. *(Backyard swimming pool photograph: James Lee, on Unsplash, altered to black & white; resistance pool photograph: Laura Dabinett)*

As communities grew ever more atomized—gated entrances, for example—pools atomized along with them and became an anecdotal barometer of economic health. Before the financial collapse of 2008–2009, all those glistening backyard dots of blue you saw as you descended into McCarran International Airport testified to the boom economy of places like Las Vegas. After the bust hit and the housing market collapsed, just the opposite was true. Pools sat empty or stagnant and untended for blocks and blocks. In Fresno, California, enterprising skateboarders turned the pools of foreclosed McMansions into makeshift ramps and parks.[*]

The economy recovered. Abandoned pools were filled and blue again, but as that happened, a new best seller, resistance pools, reduced swimming to its smallest and most private molecular structure yet: lone swimmers doing battle against a predetermined current, often in the indoor privacy of their own dwelling. Talk about swimming alone! But swimming alone had already found its bard: John Cheever.

Cheever's masterful short story, "The Swimmer," which first appeared in the July 1964 *New Yorker*, begins innocently enough, even boldly. Neddy Merrill, sitting by the edge of a friend's pool one late morning with a gin in his hand, conceives of swimming the eight miles to his house in Bullet Park via a succession of private pools—fourteen in all, most belonging to people long known to him—and one unavoidable public pool. "He seemed to see, with a cartographer's eye, that string of swimming pools, that quasi subterranean stream that curved across the county," Cheever writes.[**] And with that, Neddy plunges into the pool, swims to the far end, pulls himself out, cheerfully informs those present that he is swimming home to his wife and two daughters, and the adventure begins.

---

[*] Two decades earlier, the elegant Piscine Molitor in Paris had also been taken over by skateboarders and graffiti artists after closing its door in 1989. The pool reopened again in 2014—at the equivalent of $245 for a one-day swim pass.

[**] I learned after I chose Cheever's quote for the opening of this chapter that it had also been the inspiration for *Waterlog*, Roger Deakin's wonderful 1999 account of swimming through Great Britain.

The early pools are pleasant; his friends, surprised but glad to see him. Some are pouring midday cocktails. Drinks are offered. Neddy takes one and moves on. But the story quickly darkens. A storm passes through, cooling the air. Shivering, Neddy discovers that the Welchers' pool is dry.

Worse is coming. Crossing Route 424 is a disaster. Traffic is heavy. Neddy, barefoot, wearing only his swim trunks, is jeered as he waits first on the shoulder, then on the median, to cross. With no entry money, he has to sneak into the public pool but is soon found out. At his next stop, Mrs. Hollaran tells Neddy she was terribly sorry to hear about his "misfortunes." What misfortunes, he wonders?

(By now, in the 1968 film version of *The Swimmer*, Burt Lancaster—as Neddy—has switched from a jaunty crawl to a doleful, barely moving breaststroke.)

Two pools later, Grace Biswanger is openly rude to Neddy and calls him a gate crasher. The final pool before his own house is that of his old mistress.

"What do you want?" she asks.

"I'm swimming across the county."

"Good Christ. Will you ever grow up?"

And then he's at his own house, or what once was. A rain gutter is loose, hanging down in front. The door is locked. He pounds on it, tries to force it open, then, "looking in at the windows, saw that the place was empty."

The National Swimming Pool Foundation tells us there are now more than 360,000 public pools in the United States that are open year-round and a staggering 10 million swimming pools in all, one for every thirty-three citizens. Here's hoping the swimming is happier in all 10 million of them.

One more word on swimming alone: many of us who are ardent lap swimmers essentially do it all the time even when we are in a crowd, or maybe especially when our lanes are crowded. Across several articles for learned journals, Susie Scott, a professor of sociology at the University of Sussex in England, has explored the idea of the swimming pool as a kind of communal exercise in self-governance, a place where order is constantly being adjusted among people who are often intentional strangers.

"Even more intriguing," Scott writes, "is the fact that each of these actors is nearly naked, but that nobody refers to this: It is a polite fiction that must be maintained for the show to go on. The swimming pool operates as a local social world, with its own set of norms, routines, and tacit stocks of background knowledge shared between participants. It functions as a negotiated order that is precariously upheld by its participants and subject to continual revision."*

Lap swimmers forced to share a lane with more than one other swimmer must keep carefully to their side of the pool. Swimmers pass carefully in the middle. They constantly adjust their speed to the others around them, all the while avoiding physical contact at the turns, intrusive eye contact, and with no time, space, or maybe incentive to stop and have a quick chat at the end of the workout if the lane is still in use or others are waiting to get in.

Add in the inevitable sensory limitations of the sport and the reality that lap swimming locks you in your own small, repetitive world—counting laps, singing songs to ourselves to set the rhythm of our stroke, or just tuning out as we plow along—and hundreds of thousands of us around the world are essentially swimming alone even as we swim together.**

At least, though, we have a chance to get in the water.

---

* For ease of reading, I have omitted Scott's many citations in the quoted passage.

** Susie Scott's articles draw heavily on "field notes" from her own lap swimming. Among my favorites: The man who accidently kicked her on his turn, then "looked really embarrassed and apologized profusely as if I might think he was trying to touch me." The fellow regular at her pool who "complimented me on stamina and asked how many lengths I do, to which I replied, 'I don't know. I don't count.' This surprised him, as it does every male swimmer I've spoken to—why do they always want to compare lengths?" And: "Home safely. Pervert parade tonight—they all crawled out of the woodwork. The 'reclining' one swam only three lengths. I counted."

13

THE LAST TABOO

Sometimes, I feel like I'm alone on an island. Reporters ask
me questions that other swimmers, white swimmers, are
never asked. . . . I'm not the voice of Black America.
—Simone Manuel

The massive American swimming emporia built in the first three decades of the twentieth century that I wrote about in the last chapter
were pleasure palaces, caste and class levelers, expressions of the American Experiment, of the boundless optimism of an emerging nation. They
were also, whether they were municipal pools or private enterprises, almost entirely for the use of white patrons only.

African Americans piled into the rapidly expanding cities of the
North, the mid-Atlantic, the Midwest, and the Great Lakes states during
the same time period these pools were built. They lived under the same
hot summer sun as other residents of New York, Pittsburgh, Cleveland,
Chicago, Detroit, Milwaukee, Kansas City, St. Louis, and on and on.

If anything, their ghetto homes were likely to be even more sweltering, given a general absence of circulating air.

In a number of these cities—Wilmington, Delaware, for example—blacks even had a small public pool set aside for their use. But *small* and *few* were the operative words, and in many ways the whole point. In St. Louis, a city blessed by the mid-1930s with not one but two aquatic pleasure palaces, blacks made up 15 percent of the total population but took only 1.5 percent of total swims—in a single cramped indoor pool available for their use. By 1940, almost 30 percent of Washington, DC, residents were African American, yet blacks had access to only three small indoor pools and two outdoor ones, while whites had their choice of some fifty pools indoor and out, public and private. For blacks, there was an urban water world of sorts, but it was a world far removed from the water resorts on the other side of town.

It hadn't always been that way. In his 2007 book, *Contested Waters*, Jeff Wiltse tells the story of an 1898 visit to Philadelphia made by Daniel Kearns, secretary of the Boston bath commission, to study the nine public baths there. All but three, Kearns reported back, were sited in residential

Municipal pool, Washington, DC, 1942. Nearly one in three Washingtonians was African American at the start of World War II. All these municipal swimmers are white. *(Library of Congress)*

slums and used by only "the lower classes or street gamins," who made no effort to rinse off before plunging in. "I must say that some of the street gamins, both white and colored, that I saw, were quite as dirty as it is possible for one to conceive."

Daniel Kearns, of course, was focusing on the sanitation issues involved—microbes, urine, feces, and the like. But Wiltse notes that Kearns mentions the baths' racial diversity without a note of surprise and only in passing, which is how the poor people of Philadelphia generally seemed to have taken the matter. Men and women swam on separate days, as they did in England, Australia, and elsewhere into the twentieth century, but within the same sex, blacks and whites swam together. Far from controversial, the baths were a smash-bang hit: on average 144,000 swimmers per summer, 1,500 a day, and apparently uncontroversially mixed race.

Jump ahead forty years, and the story gets told differently. A poster put up by the New York City Department of Parks in the late 1930s boldly announces a "Learn to Swim Campaign" to be held June 3 to June 22 with "Classes for All Ages Forming in All Pools." The dominant image at the center is of a white male with brown hints (or a brown male with white hints) bent over, as if learning to dive, seemingly an artistic nod to racial diversity. Behind him, though, on the left side of an arcing diving board, are five white children; and on the right, six black children. It's a beautifully designed piece of poster art. The cause is a good one: teaching children water safety is desperately needed to this day. But the poster artist seems to have gone out of his or her way to say that though both races need swimming education, they wouldn't be getting it together.[*]

Leap forward another decade, and in many northern and midwestern cities, pools were already segueing into racial battlegrounds. In the summer of 1949, after St. Louis officials decreed that the city's pools could no longer be segregated, fifty black swimmers showed up at the luxurious

---

[*] Jeff Wiltse, it should be noted, used this poster as cover art for *Contested Waters*.

Fairgrounds Park pool, where they were attacked by almost two hundred white teenagers carrying baseball bats and sticks. The next day St. Louis mayor Joseph Darst rescinded the desegregation order. And so history goes.

A 1960s "wade-in" at Biloxi Beach, on the Gulf Coast of Mississippi, led to some of the worst racial violence in the state's long and bloody history of opposing integration. An Associated Press photo from 1964 shows a white police officer jumping angrily into a kidney-shaped pool in St. Augustine, Florida, to arrest a mixed group of black and white men who had staged a "dive-in" at a local motor lodge. In 1966, after race riots had ripped apart Chicago, Mayor Richard Daley sought to cool tempers by appropriating $10,000 to purchase ten plastic pools to be distributed throughout the city's sprawling ghettos. Ten? Plastic? Could Mayor Daley have meant that as anything other than an insult?

Move ahead to our own time, and it's still going on. There are no more Woolworth lunch counters to compare those 1960s sit-ins with today, but look around inside any McDonald's, even in the Deep South, and you are likely to see tables of blacks and whites side by side. Big Macs, bags of fries, mega-doses of Coke—these are the great social levelers of our time. Not so swimming. Witness in the summer of 2018 alone (and you could witness on cell-phone video in both cases) the fifteen-year-old black boy who was verbally berated and struck by a white woman at a South Carolina community pool and the white man in North Carolina who demanded a black woman produce her ID before she could use a pool. In both instances, the African Americans under assault were doing nothing wrong. The fifteen-year-old was a guest of a pool member; the black woman lived at the apartment complex and had entered the pool with an electronic key given to residents only—but never mind. Swimming is the last taboo.[*]

---

[*] Give Fred Rogers credit for trying to ease the taboo. In a 1969 episode, Mr. Rogers invited an African American recurring character, Officer Clemmons, to join him in soaking their feet together in a wading pool on national TV.

What went wrong? Endemic racism in American society aside—and it's a big aside—what has arguably made swimming such a difficult racial issue is the very success of the liberalization of the activity, on multiple fronts. Mixed bathing, unthinkable through much of the nineteenth century, brought the sexes together. Annette Kellerman and others helped liberate the female form from the complicated layers and entanglements of Victorian bathing costumes. Near the end of the 1920s, men finally got to show their naked upper bodies—not always a blessing, one might add. And as the pool resort boom of the 1920s and the WPA-fueled pool saturation of the 1930s rolled on, all these forces began to flow together.

One 1935 survey found that swimming and moviegoing were equally popular, at the top of the nation's recreation activities chart and for much the same reason probably: They were a diversion from hard times. Both were a communal activity in those days when going to a movie entailed massive, often beautifully appointed theaters, and they were both, for lack of a better word, sexy. There was, though, one big difference: In a movie theater, however scantily clad the actors and actresses on-screen might be, the people watching were generally fully clothed. In a pool, as the century rolled on, people were ever closer to being totally naked.

As Caleb Smith writes in a 2012 article for *Southern Geographer*, a pool incorporates many elements: the politics of wherever it is located, the societal pressures of coming together in a confined space, the physicality of recreation, and "a heavy dose of sexual overtones" combined with the theory especially prevalent in but certainly not confined to the Deep South "that the Negro man was a sexually latent savage."

Black men, white women—this was really the problem with pool integration. And the racial tension that spawned became a powerful force multiplier for all the other factors that atomized swimming and swimming pools as the twentieth century moved forward: country clubs and their covenants, suburbanization and community pools, the plowing under of municipal pools in the South in the face of court orders to open their doors to everyone, the failure of the remaining urban municipal pools for lack of civic and governmental support, gunite-construction, private pools, and so forth.

Caleb Smith's article is accompanied by two maps that compare public swimming pools in Mississippi in 1965, just before court-ordered integration, and public pools as of 2010. For the earlier date, the map shows at least one public pool in more than half of the state's eighty-two counties; by 2010, only about one-third of Mississippi counties offered a public pool.

Blacks can't swim, we're told. But where would they learn?

IT'S NOT ACCURATE TO SAY THAT SWIMMING IS THE WHITEST OF THE MA-jor sports. Japan has been prominent among Olympic medalists since the late 1920s. China was slower off the mark. Prior to the Revolution, the Republic of China sent three delegations to the Summer Olympics without winning a medal. Post-Revolution, the People's Republic of China sent one delegation to the summer Olympics, in 1952, then boycotted the next seven Games because the International Olympic Committee continued—along with most Western political powers—to recognize the defeated government-in-exile in Taiwan as China's official representative. Finally, reality trumped hope. The PRC became a regular Olympic participant in 1984 and has been a formidable force in international swimming and diving ever since.*

For its part, the racially scarred United States can point with justifiable pride to Simone Manuel, who became the first African American woman ever to win an Olympic gold medal in swimming, when she tied for the top spot with Canadian Penny Oleksiak in the 100-meter freestyle at the 2016 Games in Rio. Or to Maritza Correia who, at the 2002 NCAA Championships, became the first black women to break

---

* Credit for China's emergence as a swimming power often goes to Chairman Mao, who was ardent about the water but questionable when it came to self-locomotion. During Mao's famous seven-mile "swim" down the Pearl River, he floated all the way, "his big belly sticking up like a balloon, legs relaxed, as though he were resting on a sofa," according to his doctor.

US swimmer Simone Manuel and Canada's Penny Oleksiak embrace after tying for the gold medal in the 100-meter freestyle in 2016 at the Rio Olympics. *(UPI/Alamy Stock Photo, altered to black & white)*

an American record—two, in fact, in the 50- and 100-meter freestyle events. But we can also sympathize with Manuel when she laments, as she did in an online "letter to her younger self," that reporters are more inclined to ask her about social justice issues than about her own remarkable swimming accomplishments.

"Sometimes," she wrote, "I feel like I'm alone on an island. Reporters ask me questions that other swimmers, white swimmers, are never asked. They want me to talk about social justice issues. . . . I want to contribute to the conversation and lead, but I'm not the voice of Black America." Nor should she have to be.

Look at tennis (Althea Gibson long before the Williams sisters). Look at track (Wilma Rudolph three decades before Florence Griffith Joyner, aka Flo-Jo). Look at basketball. African American women have dominated in all three.

Or for that matter, compare British swimmers to England's World Cup footballers, or soccer players, as Americans think of them. The swimmers, men and women, are captured in a photo on the British Swimming website: twenty-three of them, eleven women and fourteen men.

Among them are Siobhan-Marie O'Connor, who barely missed a gold in the 200-meter individual medley at the 2016 Rio Olympics, and backstroker Georgia Davies, winner of five firsts in international competition. The men's side includes James Guy, who took two relay silvers in Rio, and Adam Peaty, the world's fastest-ever sprint breaststroker. They are a handsome crew and a talented one, and they are all to a person decidedly white. Meanwhile, the forty-six footballers on England's most recent World Cup entries, men and women, sprawl across the race-and-ethnicity spectrum (more so by far on the men's side, admittedly) in a way that captures the full range of the British population, not just its white majority.

Why such a discrepancy between activities that both demand strength, stamina, and endless dedication? Swimming is no harder, nor easier, than football/soccer to star in. It isn't a specialty sport like, say, curling. As with any common activity taken to an elite level, competitive swimming can get expensive. Speedo's drag-reducing (and, critically, legal) LZR Pure Valor technical racing suits can cost upward of $350 for boys and over $450 for girls and women. Its Fastskin Pure Focus goggles retail for $85. But Nike's LeBron Soldier XI basketball shoes can cost nearly $400, and Under Armour's Curry 3 shoes, as much as $425.

Tennis rackets break, and tennis often requires a club membership. Golf for those who want to be the next Tiger Woods takes a whole bag of clubs and sleeves upon sleeves of golf balls just to get started. Swimming, by contrast, has almost no start-up costs at the entry level—a basic racing suit, some ten-buck goggles. You can worry about the LZR suits (and the fact that they wear out their form-clinging elasticity in a hurry) later. What's more, swimming is an activity nearly as old as human history—a sport with a ten-thousand-year story to tell—and black athletes are just now beginning to make an appearance in it.

When I was a kid swimming in meets on the summer AAU circuit around the mid-Atlantic states, adults used to explain the near-total absence of African American competitors by such factors as bone size and density: blacks' bones were too thick; those extra-heavy femurs and tibias and fibulas sank them too deep in the water. Blacks were made for running and jumping, not pools. Swimming is a "white thing." The underlying assumptions are often ugly, but science might actually lend some weight to the premise itself.

In an article for the *International Journal of Design & Nature and Ecodynamics,* Adrian Bejan, Edward Jones, and Jordan Charles write that performance in both sports is determined by the center of mass. The fact that the center of mass in blacks is, on average, 3 percent higher above the ground than that of whites gives African Americans an edge in running because track is a lean-in sport and bodies in which the center of mass falls forward from a greater height get propelled faster than bodies less advantaged. The lower average center of body mass in whites, on the other hand, allows the upper torso to rise higher above the water than that of black swimmers, and thus to meet less resistance. The exact edge according to Bejan et al. is a 1.5 percent speed advantage in either direction.

Even if we accept the science, though, such an edge is hardly an insurmountable disincentive to competition. As I write, the world record for the 200-meter freestyle is 1:42.96, held by Michael Phelps. A 1.5 percent handicap for an African American swimmer would add only 1.5 seconds to his time. Swimmers of that caliber can make up half of that difference with a great start and a couple top-notch turns.[*]

Besides, history argues in the opposite direction. Earlier, I cited Kevin Dawson's account of how astounded European colonizers often were by the swimming skills of native Africans. That talent—and amazement—didn't disappear once those Africans became an enslaved population in the New World. Dawson's article is full of examples. Here is Dr. George Pinckard's 1804 description of a Barbadian slave amusing himself in the water:

"He was quite at play in the water, and diverting himself in all kinds of antic tricks, and gambols. He dived to the bottom—swam in a variety

---

[*] Looked at from the other direction, 1.5 percent of Usain Bolt's world record for the 100-meter dash, 9.58 seconds, equals 0.14 seconds—a teeny bit longer than a single blink!

of ways—walked or paddled along like a dog—concealed himself for a long time under water—laid himself at rest upon the surface, and appeared as much at his ease, in the ocean, as if he had never breathed a lighter, nor trodded a firmer element." Sounds like Benjamin Franklin's diverting antics during his 1726 three-mile swim in the Thames, from Chelsea to Blackfriars, doesn't it?

Elsewhere in that same journal entry, Pinckard writes that such swimming expertise "renders the negroes peculiarly useful in moments of distress, such as in cases of accident at sea or in the harbor."

An account from the mid-eighteenth century, set in Beaufort, South Carolina, tells of a slave named May who leapt onto the back of a manta ray, speared it with a harpoon, then swam back to the boat he had jumped from. "Had he belonged to the Saxon or Norman race," one witness wrote, "he had probably been knighted, and allowed to quarter on his shield the horns of the devil-fish, in token of his exploit."

In 1790, Dawson notes, a traveler to the West Indies was so awestruck by slaves who waded into the Caribbean to do battle with sharks that he feared for slavery itself: "If they can go into an unnatural element, in quest of hideous monsters, for the sport of engaging with them, it will leave us to wonder at their submission to the yoke of slavery, to wonder that ever a rebellion can be suppressed." (The adjective *unnatural* nicely captures the European fear of water.)

Clearly, even if blacks do have a higher center of mass than whites, that didn't prevent them from becoming proficient swimmers in their native Africa or remaining so for multiple generations in the New World. If they are collectively worse swimmers than whites today—and they are demonstrably so, much worse by many measures—the reason must be that over a century of being denied access to decent swimming pools and decent instruction, African Americans collectively have *unlearned* how to swim, with consequences severe in the extreme.

Overall, the drowning rate for African Americans is 40 percent higher than that for whites and Hispanics. The only ethnic groups more likely to drown than blacks are Alaska Natives and American Indians, another population that has unlearned swimming over the course of the last century and a half and for similar reasons—lack of access to swimming pools and to swimming education, plus all the socioeconomic disparities with whites that implies. But wander into the weeds a bit deeper, and there's much to learn.

According to the Centers for Disease Control and Prevention, accidental drowning deaths in the United States number about thirty-five hundred a year—almost ten a day—the second highest cause of accidental deaths generally among all Americans age nineteen and younger. Proportionally, though, the threat is far greater to black children than to white ones. Black children ages five to fourteen drown in swimming pools at a rate more than three times that of white children. Stretch that to black children and teens ages five to nineteen, and they drown at a rate five times that of their white counterparts, not because they roughhouse more in the water or run heedlessly on the deck or don't listen to lifeguards as well as white children but simply because far too many black children simply cannot swim.[*]

In one study, almost 70 percent of black kids said they were unable to swim or felt uncomfortable in the deep end of a pool, compared to 31 percent of white children. Other studies put the swimming illiteracy rate at 64 percent for African American children, 45 percent for Hispanic/Latinx, and 40 percent for Caucasian youth. Some of that is a matter of definition. Maybe the key and most telling statistic is that four in five children from households with annual income below $50,000 have little to no swimming ability. That's scary in its own right, but the problem is also generational and thus structural. A USA Swimming Foundation study found that only about one in eight children of parents who don't know how to swim will ever learn to do so themselves.

---

[*] Teenage boys white, black, Hispanic, Native American, and so on are far more apt to drown than teenage girls, largely because teenage boys whatever their race or ethnicity are often terrible decision makers.

Simone Manuel and a few others notwithstanding, blacks are enormously underrepresented in the top tiers of American swimmers, despite all the black success in other sports. African Americans make up a tiny fraction of the membership of USA Swimming—the Big Kahuna of the sport for precollege athletes and the gateway to Olympic competition. Blacks are the needle in that haystack, and the severe underrepresentation filters down through swimming generally and becomes a kind of self-fulfilling prophecy, or maybe just a closed loop.

Lifeguards are generally drawn from the ranks of able swimmers, and they are local heroes (or at least I felt like one when I was occupying a lifeguard chair many, many decades ago). Lifeguards spur emulation. Emulation, in this instance, spurs younger kids to take swimming seriously. As far as anti-drowning goes, this is a virtuous circle. But African Americans, for the same reasons they are underrepresented in USA Swimming, are underrepresented here as well. And the absence of significant numbers of those role models echoes far and wide because swimming is important not just in saving lives or preventing drowning but also in good health generally: cardiovascular benefits, reduced obesity and more easily controlled diabetes (both health issues more likely to affect African Americans than whites), and well beyond.

In 2003, an article in the *British Medical Journal* reported on an effort in three very remote Aboriginal communities in Australia to use new swimming pools as a kind of sociological intervention. The pools were 25 meters long, partially shaded; and the study was as much interested in medical matters common to the Aboriginal population—skin and middle-ear infections, particularly—as about the sociological effects of the new pools. But the sociological effects garnered the most notice. School attendance went up after the local authorities instituted a "No Pool/No School" policy. Children looked and acted happier and healthier in addition to learning how to swim. One parent said the pool had kept children out of mischief. Police also said they had logged a noted decline in petty crime.

In the United States, public schools have been going in precisely the opposite direction. I'll never forget the day nearly six decades ago when my tenth-grade gym class of maybe forty-five boys was marched down to the basement and ordered to strip naked and report to the pool deck. Collectively, we must have been a horrifying sight, especially for the kids who were overweight, the ones with sunken chests, the underendowed and not yet fully pubescent—all the things that haunt fifteen-year-olds. But at least the school was trying.

Boys who couldn't swim the length of the 25-yard pool or refused to attempt it got six weeks of swimming instruction while the rest of us played volleyball or wrestled or whatever the phys ed department concocted to exhaust our testosterone. And I'm willing to bet that at least one of those boys who remained behind—and the odds are disproportionate that he was an African American—lived to adulthood because of the effort the school made.

In fact, one of them might well have been Stanley Brown. Four years earlier, he had been my bunkmate for two weeks at a YMCA summer camp and was adept at most things campers do but terrified by the daily "free-swim" half hour. At the swim test when we were tenth graders, he wouldn't even consider going near the edge of the pool. Either he learned to swim in the lessons that followed or he stayed away from water for the rest of a longish life because, last I knew, a decade or longer ago, he was still with us.

Girls, by the way, took the same test, but not in the buff. Instead, they were issued knitted wool bathing suits color-coded by size. The suits, one of my classmates assures me, were "horrible."

Drowning, after all, is preventable, and it doesn't take an Einstein or a Stephen Hawking (who couldn't swim for lack of muscular control) or an Aristotle (who definitely did know how to swim) to teach it. Relax, get over your fear, put your face in the water, know you can float so long as your lungs are inflated, roll on your back so you can more easily do just that—the protocol is basic, the results clearly successful. The YMCA still understands this. Youth groups in various locations have embraced the value of swimming. The USA Swimming Foundation, through its Make a Splash program, has even brought Olympic glamour to swimming education, mounting annual tours that have included, among others, the African American 2008 gold medalist Cullen Jones, who nearly drowned as a child. All power to every one of them, but at the local public school level, swimming is still too often a losing fight.

The practical effects of this lethal stew of lack of swimming education, lack of public pool facilities, racism, and the fear that always grows in a climate of neglect and ignorance were on hideous display in Shreveport, Louisiana, in August 2010 when six black teenagers from two families who had been wading on a sandbar in the Red River drowned while trying to save one of their own who had slid into deeper waters.

DeKendrix Warner was the first to get into trouble. Takeitha Warner, age 13; JaMarcus Warner, age 14, and JaTavious Warner, 17, followed, unable to save their sibling or themselves. Three brothers and cousins—Literelle Stewart (18), LaDairus Stewart (17), and Latevin Stewart (15)—failed, too, and in the same way for the same reason: none of the victims knew how to swim.

Nor did any of the family picnickers, watching horrified from the shore of the Red River. Marilyn Robinson was among them: "None of us could swim. They were yelling 'Help me! Help me! Somebody please help me!' It was nothing I could do but watch them drown one by one."

DeKendrix Warner, who began the whole chain of drownings, was the only survivor, pulled out of the water by a brave passing stranger. But by then, passing strangers were the only hope of rescuing the others. When no one present and engaged can swim, when so many witnesses are afraid to even wade into water for a rescue chain, when fear trumps the primal need to help, something is deeply wrong in the Wonderful World of Swimming—or the still deeply Medieval World, at some level.

Are we getting better at teaching people to swim? Yes, undoubtedly, at the competitive level. Proof of that is to follow. But when I plugged "swimming education" into Amazon recently, one featured book and seven additional "Customers Who Bought This Also Bought" titles popped up. In all cases, the books were sensibly geared to kids and their parents—Ground Zero in the fight against drowning. On two of the eight, the cover image was a cartoon—a frog in one case, a duck in the other. On the other six, the image was either a photo or an illustration. Either way, all of the children portrayed were white.

We can do better. In fact, we must, and maybe we finally are.

In 1603, the Japanese emperor Go-Yōzei ordered that all school-children must learn to swim and take part in inner-school competitions. Absolute rulers get to decree such things, absolutely. Messy democracies have to work harder to achieve such goals. They have to work harder still when the groups most in need of learning to swim—African Americans, American Indians, poor people generally—are also the most underserved by the public education system and have the least access to swimming pools. But some countries seem determined to turn the tide.

In England, swimming instruction has been part of the National Curriculum since 2012—the only sport included in the physical education wing of the curriculum. Specifically, every eleven-year-old is expected to leave primary school able to perform self-rescue in various water situations, swim a competent 25 meters without stopping, and use more than one swimming stroke effectively. According to Swim England, the national governing body for the sport, more than half of all students don't actually get there. Costs interfere as do other curricular demands and lack of facil-ities, but credit England for trying at the national level. Even flawed as it is, the effort probably helps explain why the United Kingdom has one of the lowest drowning rates in the world, a third that of the United States.

My WPA high school, the one where I milled buck-naked with forty or more of my tenth-grade peers waiting to try a length of the pool, gave up on that humiliating but important swimming test long ago. In New York City, as Jim Dwyer pointed out a few years back in a *New York Times* column, "a few high schools [still] require students to pass a swimming test or take lessons, but, unlike proper use of condoms, it is not part of the curriculum required of the city."[*]

Save a life, prevent a pregnancy—that sounds like it should be a tie.

But places like my old high school might also be leading the way back, on a crucial battleground. People tend of think of Lancaster County, where I grew up, as Pennsylvania Dutch through and through: buggies, farmers' markets, *Witness,* the Ultimate Amish Experience. But the city that gives the county its name is nothing like the Lancaster I knew, or thought I knew.

Some 80 percent of students in Lancaster's city schools are black or Hispanic; 92 percent qualify for free-breakfast and free-lunch programs. Demographically, this is *the* prime drowning cohort, and one that has been largely abandoned nationwide—via both tax distribution and civic interest—by those who can most afford their own swimming instruction: white suburbanites, private-school parents, and the like.

What to do? In my hometown, the turnaround is taking place on two interrelated fronts. The school district has formed a coalition with the local YMCA, a recreation league, and the Boys and Girls Club to provide mandatory swimming instruction for second graders at all thirteen of the district's elementary schools, with total implementation set for 2022. Meanwhile, a dynamic physical education teacher, Suzie Holubek, has revived the fortunes of the McCaskey High School boys and girls swimming team, growing its total membership from twenty-two kids in her first year to thirty-four in year two and coaching the team to its first winning season in practically anyone's memory.

Holubek is also working to bring the two initiatives together. Her swimmers put together a one-week clinic for community eight- to twelve-year-olds. For an hour every evening, team members taught eighteen

---

[*] To give New York City proper credit, the parks department runs a summer swimming education department that serves with varying degrees of success some 30,000 people, mostly children, but in mid-summer of 2019, the waiting list for the program ran to almost 2,500 others. Meanwhile, total public school enrollment in the city is about 1.1 million.

younger children water safety, how to float on their stomachs and roll over on their backs, how to go under water, kicks and strokes. In 2020, they are planning to offer the same program for four weeks, twice a week, to kids from six months to thirteen years old. It's all basic stuff, but who knows how many of those six teenagers in Shreveport, Louisiana, might have been spared if a similar effort were made in their hometown.

Holubek's team hasn't done much statistically to mend the school's racial divide when it comes to swimming. Her swimmers are whiter than the student body as a whole and in 2018–2019 included eight team members from two other schools—one a Christian academy, the other a private day school—that don't offer swimming themselves. But by interacting freely with younger kids who have almost no access to the sport, they are providing the sort of local role models that can help break the cycle of swimming illiteracy across multiple generations. And that's important for both public health reasons—fewer drowning tragedies—and simple character development.

Competitive swimming can be a crushing sport. So often, you are racing against your own expectations. Not to meet them stings. But swimming also teaches self-reliance, maybe more so than any other sport. As they churn out lengths, swimmers are alone with their thoughts, unable to hear anything other than the splash of their arms and legs, with nothing consistent to look at except the black line on the bottom of the pool or, for backstrokers, the ceiling tiles or passing clouds and the flags that warn "Turn Ahead!" If you can't rely on yourself in an environment like that, there's very little else to rely on at all.

"A lot of my swimmers are honor students," Holubek told me. "It takes a special person to be able to swim-flip, swim-flip, swim-flip. You're doing it on your own"—a useful skill to hone.

Sportswriter, author, and US Masters swimmer John Feinstein said much the same thing:

> To be a successful swimmer, you have to be disciplined. You have to be willing to deal with PTA—pain, torture, and agony. Most parents

also have to be willing to make major sacrifices. The meets can be tor-
turous, but getting their kids to practice at 5 in the morning day after
day is far worse. It's a chicken-and-egg thing. Does swimming give you
the discipline that helps you succeed in life, or do you have to already
have that discipline to succeed in swimming and then in life? I don't
know the answer, but I have known very few successful swimmers who
weren't also successful as people.

14

GROWING PAINS

Had the first modern Games been held in Tokyo instead of
Athens, Olympic swimmers today might be diving into the pool
wearing armor, with swords sheathed on their backs.

The earliest swimming education for the masses had little to do with
strokes and almost nothing to do with endurance or speed. The goal
was far simpler: survival. People went to sea. They took excursion rides on
lakes or along the coast. Decks were swamped by ferocious storms. Boats
broke up on hidden shoals. Steam boilers exploded while paddle wheelers
made their way downriver or up. When such misfortunes happened a
century and a half ago, disaster was almost assured. Vast swaths of the
population had no more chance of surviving in the water than those six
unfortunate teenagers in Shreveport, Louisiana, did just a decade back.

People who earned their living on and from the water were often no
better than the landlubbers they left behind. In 1838, *Sailor's Magazine,*

published by the New York City–based American Seaman's Friends Society, exhorted its seafaring readers to learn to swim: "For want of knowledge of this noble art thousands are annually sacrificed, and every fresh victim calls more strongly upon the best of feelings of those who have the power to draw the attention of such persons as maybe likely to require this art, to the simple fact, that there is no difficulty in floating or swimming."

A half century later, Lieutenant Commander Theodorus Bailey Myers Mason, the founder and first head of the United States Office of Naval Intelligence, was still lamenting the state of swimming education in America: "The great majority of people cannot swim, and strange as it may seem to you, there are many who follow the sea as a profession who cannot swim a stroke." For starters, Mason suggested teaching swimming to all plebes at his alma mater, the US Naval Academy.

About the same time, a magazine put out by England's national lifeboat association editorialized in favor of swimming instruction for lifeboat men, very few of whom could swim, a shortcoming that must have seriously compromised their missions.

In case anyone missed the point, newspapers in Europe and America offered up constant reinforcement of the need—grisly accounts of death on and in and under the water.

On September 3, 1878, the *Princess Alice*, a pleasure steamer, pulled out of dock on the river Thames for a day trip down to the sea. The outing was cheap, about two shillings; the day, bright and sunny. No passenger log was kept, but the estimates are that some 750 people were on board as the *Princess Alice* returned to London that evening. At 7:40 p.m., Alfred Thomas Merryman was idling on deck when he saw a large coal carrier, the *Bywell Castle*—more than three times the size of the pleasure cruiser—bearing down on the *Princess Alice*. Minutes later, the coal boat slammed into the *Princess Alice*'s starboard side and sliced the smaller craft neatly in two.

"The panic on board was terrible, the women and children screaming and rushing to the bridge for safety," Merryman would later recount. "I at once rushed to the captain and asked what was to be done and he exclaimed: 'We are sinking fast. Do your best.'"

Sink it did, and fast indeed. Those who could jumped ship, but few knew how to swim, and even those who could were weighted down by clothing and shoes and further challenged by the tons of raw sewage that poured into the Thames near the scene of the collision. In the end, an estimated 650 people, including 400 women, died—the worst inland maritime disaster in British history. Some perished from the collision, most from drowning, although the riverbanks were for even a barely competent swimmer near at hand. Others died more slowly and painfully from having ingested the putrid water.*

Many of the same factors were in play a quarter century later, on June 15, 1904, when the *General Slocum*, a side-wheel steamer, left its dock on New York's East River at nine a.m., headed for an excursion along the North Shore of Long Island. Like the *Princess Alice*, this outing was dirt cheap—the local Saint Mark's Evangelical Lutheran Church had chartered the boat for $350, roughly 25 cents for each of the 1,358 passengers aboard. The air was festive; women and children made up most of the passenger list. But this time disaster didn't tarry until day's end.

Within half an hour of pulling into the river, the *General Slocum* erupted in flames, and passengers leapt overboard to avoid the conflagration. Again, the clothing conventions of the late Victorian period made swimming difficult. Again, too, the banks of the river were tantalizingly close. And again, women and children—almost universally uninstructed in swimming at the start of the twentieth century—died in industrial numbers. In this instance, though, we have an exact figure: 1,021 dead, a gruesome total, but *not* the worst maritime disaster in US history.

That questionable honor belongs to a little-remembered moment of horror on the Mississippi River, and this time, nearly all the fatalities

---

* The sole female to survive, an eighteen-year-old identified only as Miss Thorpe, swam directly to shore as soon as she entered the water. Her brothers, ages nine and seventeen, were able to swim in the river until rescue boats arrived. Despite the disaster, a jury looking into its cause apparently rejected the suggestion that a rider be attached to its verdict stressing the necessity of a more general knowledge of swimming.

were men. The *Sultana*, another side-wheel paddle steamer, left Vicksburg, Mississippi, at ten p.m. on April 24, 1865, carrying as many as 2,500 people, on a ship with a listed capacity of 376 passengers. Perhaps 2,300 of the passengers were soldiers—no exact count was made at boarding—and of those the vast majority had been recently released from the Confederate prisons at Andersonville, Georgia, and Cahaba, near Selma, Alabama.

The Civil War was over. The men on board were destined for Camp Chase, in Ohio, to be demobilized, and then headed home, wherever that might be. Most never got there.

In the very early morning of April 27, as the *Sultana* rounded a bend some nine miles north of Memphis, a boiler that had been hastily patched in Vicksburg gave way. Two other boilers exploded almost simultaneously with it, ripping a huge hole in the vessel, setting fire to its wooden decks, and sending literally thousands of men leaping into an unwelcoming river.

The neglect brought on by the Civil War had left the dikes and levees along the Mississippi unprepared for the spring thaw of 1865. The river stretched some four miles across where the *Sultana* went down, with a water temperature in the range of 60 degrees, and many of these were damaged men to begin with, victims of inhumane prison conditions and the famine that had settled across the entire South in the closing year of the war.

But the Mississippi was soon full of floating debris as the *Sultana* broke up. Even a rudimentary sense of how to swim or float would have given a man a chance at survival. Few seem to have had even that slim hope on their side. Bodies continued to wash up at Memphis and elsewhere for weeks afterward.

Because no exact count was made of the passengers who boarded the *Sultana*, the number of dead in the aftermath can only be estimated. Some say eighteen hundred; others go as high as twenty-two hundred. Whatever figure is used, low or high, the explosion resulted in the greatest loss of life ever in US waters. Only four battles of the Civil War claimed more Union soldiers: the Wilderness, Spotsylvania, Gettysburg, and Antietam.

Unlike the *Princess Alice* or *General Slocum* disasters, though, and dramatically unlike those Civil War battles, this event was quickly forgotten. Six hours after the *Sultana* exploded, Secretary of War Edwin Stanton sent word that John Wilkes Booth had been flushed from a burning barn near Port Royal, Virginia, and shot through the head. With that, the *Sultana* sank like a stone off the front page.

Such colossal and lethal ignorance of swimming sparked the first efforts at organized instruction for the masses. Humans run instinctively from fire, but they don't swim instinctively toward shore or anywhere else when disaster sends them scurrying into the briny deep. As we've just seen, most didn't even float instinctively until help could arrive. Instead, they panicked, replaced the naturally buoyant air in their lungs with water, and sank. Job one was to teach them to keep themselves alive in the ocean, lake, river, or pond into which they had plunged. Strokes (breaststroke, in most cases at first) followed from there, and competition—whether of endurance or speed—from strokes.

Sweden's Uppsala Swimming Society typifies the evolution.[*] Founded in 1796 at Uppsala University, itself established in 1477 and much lauded, the society claims to be the oldest such organization in the world and in its initial years confronted a deeply wary audience. "Swimming was not embraced by the Swedish public," one history reports. Only Russian prisoners swam, and "Swedes looked upon them with astonishment even though most could only swim dog paddle."

The Uppsala swimmers persevered, however, and by the mid-to-late nineteenth century they had spread out across the country, teaching "front swimming, front swimming with clothes, backstroke, floating, treading water, carrying a person, moving a large stone, swimming for distance, diving, [and] jumping from a high board," first in rivers and then, beginning in 1841, at a new pool facility in Svartbäckstullen.

---

[*] Or, more accurately, Upsala Simsällskap. The proper name uses the old spelling of Uppsala, with one *p*.

Gradually, too, some of the Uppsala instructors peeled off from the society and began spreading its mission and methods across Europe and to America. By the 1890s, Eric Helsten, offspring of Uppsala's lead instructor in the 1850s, was advertising his Helsten Method in newspapers all across the United States. The method, he noted tersely, was "Worth knowing. Saves lives. . . . The wonderful discovery of the age. How to make a drowning person buoyant. . . . Full instructions." All for a measly dollar.

Not until the start of the twentieth century did the Uppsala Swimming Society become a training grounds for competitive swimmers. But training for what? For another half century that was a hard question to answer.

What's so startling about swimming is that, for an ancient sport, it's surprisingly new and still evolving. Running—the "track" part of track and field—has barely changed since the original Olympics and almost not at all since the first modern Olympiad. In 1896, men (and only men) competed at five distances—100, 400, 800, and 1,500 meters plus the marathon and a 110-meter hurdles event. Track events had more than doubled by 2016 in Rio to include relays, walking, and a greater variety of distances for both hurdles and pure running, and of course, women had long been included. But basically the races were still a matter of laying down one foot after another, as fast as possible, over the prescribed distances, pretty much what cavemen did fleeing a saber-toothed tiger.

Competitive swimming, by contrast, is just settling down. Not even 150 years have passed since an otherwise forgotten New Yorker named Edward A. Cone began trouncing the competition in sidestroke races by the simple expediency of not holding his head out of the water the entire race. (Cone didn't really have a choice: He had only one arm and had to fashion a stroke to accommodate his disability. Necessity truly is the mother of invention.)

Another enterprising American, Chicago newspaperman Jamison "Jam" Handy, compensated for his physical shortcomings—he was

4 foot 11—by endlessly tinkering with the timing between the breast-stroke kick and stroke and won a bronze medal in the 440-yard event at the 1904 Olympics for his troubles. Handy also had the bright idea of painting lines on the bottom of a pool so swimmers wouldn't have to be constantly looking up to see where they were headed.[*]

Like the proverbial camel, the butterfly stroke appears to have been put together by committee—in this case, an international one. Credit for the double overarm stroke goes to an Australian, Sydney Cavill; or maybe to the American Henry Myers; or to a German, Erich Rademacher. Or maybe the butterfly armstroke was just sitting there in the chlorine cloud that hung over swimming pools in the late 1920s and early 1930s, waiting to be discovered, because all three men seem to have been experimenting with it around that time.

The dolphin kick of butterfly has a more exact father, Volney Wilson, then a young physicist and swimming enthusiast, and later a collabora-tor on the Manhattan Project that produced the first atomic bomb. As Marie Doezema tells the story in the August 11, 2016, issue of the *New Yorker*, Wilson was hanging around the Shedd Aquarium in Chicago in the summer of 1934 when he noticed that fish propelled themselves by swinging their vertical tails laterally, from side to side, but dolphins (and by extension whales and other cetaceans) undulated their way forward by moving their flat, horizontal tales up and down. If aquatic mammals, why not would-be aquatic humans, Wilson wondered, and soon he had mas-tered a similar undulating, up-and-down kick in the pool of the Chicago Athletic Club.

Other sources, I should add, credit the kick to David Armbruster, swimming coach for almost forty years, beginning in 1917, at the Uni-versity of Iowa. Either way, though, there was a problem. Cavill et al. paired their new overarm stroke with a traditional breaststroke kick, with predictable results. Butterflying breaststrokers took an early lead, thanks

---

[*] Twenty years later, the diminutive Handy won a second bronze medal at the Paris Olympics as a member of the USA water polo team. He was a dynamo.

to the more powerful arm stroke, but often failed to hold it in longer races because the stroke and the required kick paired up so poorly and sapped energy in the mismatch.

Footage of the 200-meter breaststroke finals at the 1936 Berlin Olympics tells the story. A "butterflying" American leads the pack for the first 100 meters, then tires and reverts to a standard stroke for the rest of the race, while three start-to-finish traditional breaststrokers from the future Axis powers claim all the medals (first and third for Japan, second for Germany) as a beaming Hitler looks on at the Olympiapark Schwimmstadion.[*]

Volney Wilson, on the other hand, paired his new, fluid dolphin kick with the traditional breaststroke arm movement—a better match but also a bit of a camel since the front and back ends of the stroke didn't complement one another. In any event, Wilson's hybrid was largely useless for competition since the powers that be wouldn't allow it.

Who put the two together and turned this camel into a racehorse? The International Swimming Hall of Fame hands that honor to Japan's Jiro Nagasawa, a traditional breaststroker who switched to the dolphin kick and simultaneous-overarm stroke in the early 1950s to save his arthritic knees, just as butterfly was being liberated from the confining rules of breaststroke and recognized as a stroke in its own right. When butterfly was finally allowed in Olympic competition, at the 1956 Games in Melbourne, it was quick to flaunt its speed advantage. American William

---

[*] The swimming side of 1936 Olympics is almost as notable for a woman who refused to compete as for the swimmers who did: Judith Haspel. Born in August 1918 in Vienna, Haspel began her career at a local Jewish athletic club—other such clubs being forbidden to Jews and sometimes dogs—and by 1935 held every Austrian women's freestyle record from middle distances and up. The following year, she was selected to join the Austrian national team heading to the Olympiad in Berlin. When Haspel refused to perform in front of Hitler, she was banned from competition in Austria and eventually had her records erased and name expunged from the books when she emigrated to Palestine. Her story, along with that of her Austrian Jewish teammates, gets told in the 2004 documentary *Watermarks*.

Yorzyk's winning time in the 200-meter fly was more than fifteen seconds faster than the winning breaststroke time at the same distance.[*]

Rather than standardize swimming—which might have been expected of an august quadrennial international competition—the Olympic Games, at least in their early years, pulled the sport every which way but loose.

The 1896 Games in Athens were a threadbare nod to the rising popularity of swimming in Europe and America: three freestyle events open to everyone and another freestyle race for Greek sailors only, all held in the Bay of Zea. Only nineteen swimmers participated—one each from the United States and Hungary, two from Austria, and fifteen from Greece. All but the US and Hungarian swimmers competed in the raw. The American, in fact, barely competed at all. He jumped off a float to start the race and jumped right back out again. The water, he explained, was Way Too Cold.

The swimming side of the second Olympiad, the 1900 Games in Paris, was more like an aquatic carnival, and not only because events were held in the Seine River. Organizers added backstroke (upside-down crawl then), a 4,000-meter freestyle race (about two and a half miles), and a freestyle relay, but they didn't stop there. Novelty events included a 200-meter obstacle race in which swimmers first had to climb over a pole and a row of boats, then later swim under another row of boats. Frederick Lane of Australia, who had won the 200-meter freestyle in a time of 2:25.2, took the gold in this event as well, in 3:04. There was also an underwater swim, won by Frenchman Charles Devendeville, who managed 60 meters without breathing.

In the same anything-goes spirit, the 1900 Games also included water polo, the first team sport added to the Olympics. A Scottish invention

---

[*] Butterfly for women was also introduced at the 1956 Olympics, but limited to 100 meters. Not until Mexico City in 1968 would women butterflyers compete at 200 meters. The winning time in the 2016 women's 200-meter fly was almost fifteen seconds faster than the winning men's time in 1956.

of the mid-nineteenth century, water polo originally had very little to do with swimming. The game did take place in rivers and lakes, but the rules were far closer to rugby than to anything we would recognize as a swimming-based competition today, or to modern water polo, for that matter. Players could hold their opponents underwater until they coughed up the India rubber ball, like a scrum but including oxygen starvation. As with rugby, too, players scored by placing the ball down in an end zone, in this case a deck at either end of the aquatic field of play. With good cause, as late as the 1870s the activity was regularly referred to as "football in the water."[*]

As the sport spread throughout the British Isles, then to Canada, the United States, and Europe, rules accumulated, and the playing became more refined, but the first Olympic water polo games were still wet brawls played with competing equipment—the Americans favored a semi-inflated rubber ball, the Europeans a leather one—with lots of holding and pummeling. The general improvement of swimming skills in the decades ahead and the introduction of (and agreement upon) a fully inflated rubber ball brought finesse to the game. But it was the invention—in 1928 by the great Hungarian coach Béla Komjádi—of the so-called dry pass that turned water polo into the fast-paced aerial game we know today and made Hungary itself the giant of the sport, including nine Olympic gold medals. (In this case, "giant" can be taken literally as well. Of the thirteen members on the Hungarian national team as of 2018, the shortest five were all six-foot-four.)

Water polo was an Olympic swimming oddity that stuck. The plunge, introduced at the 1904 Olympiad in St. Louis, had no such luck, but it can probably claim to be the weirdest swimming event to ever grace the Games, although technically no swimming at all was allowed.

The plunge required contestants to dive into the "pool"—in the case of the St. Louis Games an artificial lake—from a height of exactly 18 inches and float as far as they could, with absolutely no attempt at

---

[*] The "polo" part of water polo comes from the Tibetan-Kashmir word *pulu*, which simply means "ball." *Water* was added because horse-based polo had already claimed the name.

locomotion, for a full minute, and no more. Winning distance of this once-and-done Olympic plunge: 62.5 feet, recorded by American William Dickey. The current world record, 86.6 feet, was set by the Englishman Francis Parrington in 1933. By then, the event had faded almost completely from competitive sports. The women's record, 71 feet, was set by Hilda Dand even earlier, in 1925. Both records would seem to be begging for a modern assault.[*]

An Olympics-like games, never officially blessed by the Olympiad itself, was staged back in Athens in 1906, but neither the timing nor the venue did swimmers or swimming much good. Events were held in the Neo Pharilon Bay off the coast of Athens, rather than the nearby Bay of Zea, but the elements and curiosity still took most of the medals. Gale-force winds shut the competition down completely for two days. Even on "good" days, choppy seas choked the swimmers, and private boats crowded the swim lanes when the water was tolerably flat.

Back on the quadrennial cycle, the 1908 Games in London, still all-male, looked more like modern Olympic swimming. The aquatic steeplechase and underwater swim had disappeared along with the plunge; 100-meter backstroke and 200-meter breaststroke had been added. Appropriately, given the British Isles' claim to being the birthplace of breaststroke, two Brits, Frederick Holman and William Robinson, finished one-two in the initial breaststroke event, but the English dominance in the "English stroke" quickly faded. Another sixty-four years would pass before Great Britain would claim another breaststroke medal.

For the first Olympic time ever, swimmers also had a pool, 100 meters long, in the center of the track-and-field oval, and the United States finally got a genuine, certified aquatic hero—the newest world's fastest man.

---

[*] By its very nature, the plunge favored the corpulent. After my very obese bachelor cousin Parker died in Philadelphia in the early 1960s, I helped my mother go through his dresser drawers. Buried beneath the socks was a medal won at the University of Pennsylvania circa 1919. "Parker?" my mother said. "A sports medal? He never played anything." We turned it over and on the back was engraved "2nd Place. The Plunge." More than half a century had passed. He must have wanted to keep it.

Three scenes from 1908 Olympics in London. [top left], competitors in the 200-meter breaststroke take off from a bulkhead draped with towels to keep from slipping. [bottom left], water polo had been introduced to the Games in 1900, but it was nothing like the fast aerial game we know today. The ball was only semi-inflated: players could grip it in one hand and carry it underwater. At right, dapper American Charlie Daniels, the 100-meter freestyle champion and newly crowned as the fastest swimmer in the world. *(Daniels photograph: Library of Congress)*

Swimming out of the New York Athletic Club, where he also was a squash and bridge champion, Charlie Daniels had performed more than admirably in the 1904 Olympics, winning the 220- and 440-yard free-styles but losing both the 50- and 100-yard freestyle races to the Hun-garian sprinter Zoltán Halmay. In the 1908 Games, after tutoring from the Australian swimming champion Barney Kiernan (who soon after died of complications of appendicitis surgery), Daniels came entirely into his own, winning the 100-meter free in a stunning world-record-busting time of 1:05.6.[*]

---

[*] For comparison purposes, the best-ever 100-meter free time for eleven- and twelve-year old American swimmers as of early 2019 was more than ten seconds faster—0:55.3,

Swimming retreated to open water at the 1912 Olympics—events were held in Stockholm Harbor, average June water temperature about 56 degrees Fahrenheit—but by then, international competition was becoming standardized, beginning with the need for an exactly measured pool. Still, Olympics swimming has continued to evolve, adjust, and change ever since, including returning to open-water racing at the 2008 Games in Beijing with a 10-kilometer marathon for men and women.

Absent a sanctioned butterfly, the medley relay as we know it (backstroke, butterfly, breaststroke, and freestyle) could not come into Olympic existence until 1960. Nor could the 400-meter individual medley, which reverses the front two strokes—butterfly and backstroke—so competitors can dive in rather than leap backward from the wall. That didn't make the grade until 1964. Its shorter cousin, the 200 IM, made a brief Olympic appearance in 1968 and then disappeared until the Los Angeles Games in 1984.

The 300-meter medley relay and the similar-distance individual medley—medleys without the outlaw butterfly—were once common enough events in national competitions, but world records for both have long since withered on the vine.

Also long gone or in permanent retirement is a whole slew of American records calibrated to the 20-yard pools that were once commonplace and meant to create a near equivalency between American races (measured in yards) and European ones (in meters): the 220-yard freestyle, the 440, and 880. For a time after 20-yard pools disappeared, racers would sometimes cross a hastily put up finish line in the middle of the pool. Meanwhile, other pools were being standardized downward. When I was a preteen, I swam my miles in a 35-yard pool—fifty lengths in all, a hundred yards longer than the 1,500-meter "mile" swum in international competition.

Simultaneously, the ornamental swimming so beloved by Benjamin Franklin and various nineteenth-century swimming "professors" was

---

set by Winn Aung in 2015. In the next chapter, we will get to why swimming times across time are not necessarily applicable.

interbreeding with gymnastics and dancing to produce synchronized swimming, which didn't become an established Olympic sport until 1984, and only settled into its current format—duet and team competitions, but no more solo performers—at the 2000 Games in Sydney, with the blessing, of course, of FINA, the powerful governing body of all Olympic aquatic sports.*

BY THEN, TOO, SWIMMING AND FINA HAD HAD A BRIEF AND, IN FINA's case, not altogether pretty star turn on the global diplomatic stage. "Ping-Pong diplomacy" is the phrase usually attached to the cultural interchanges hammered out by US Secretary of State Henry Kissinger and Chinese premier Zhou Enlai in Paris, back in 1973, but Chairman Mao was a swimmer, and the first group he wanted to have an exchange with was an American swimming and diving team, not Ping-Pong players. The US State Department got on board enthusiastically, but not FINA.

Even though the United Nations by then recognized the People's Republic of China, FINA and other sporting organizations still considered Taiwan the official Chinese government. Thus FINA announced that it would ban forever any participants in the proposed US-PRC competition—that is, goodbye Olympics dreams—but the matter didn't die there. Jim Gaughran, head coach at Stanford; Al Schoenfield, the founder and publisher of *Swimming World* magazine; and a few others recruited a team of recently retired top-tier swimmers and divers. Off they went to Beijing, where they were greeted warmly by Jiang Qing, aka Madame Mao herself, and from there on they went to a swim exhibition notable for its high spirits and quick camaraderie.

Back in the States, though, the reception was a bit different. Having done their bit to thaw the Cold War with China, returning team members were met by a representative of FINA, who handed them letters confirming that they had been kicked out of the organization.

---

* For reasons perhaps known only to itself, FINA now refers to the synchronized form as "artistic swimming" but still labels its two-person diving events as "synchronized" and "mixed synchronized." Maybe diving was already artistic.

Not only were strokes and aquatic competitions generally evolving and calving off from one another for the first half and more of modern Olympic history; basic understandings of competitive swimming itself needed to be worked out. Even more than Great Britain, Japan defines an island nation. The Japanese have been racing each other in swim competitions since before the time of Christ—that record is clear—but at least since the early seventeenth century the strokes used were based largely on Samurai warrior skills, which stressed crossing bodies of water with weaponry and under conditions of close-arms combat.

Tachi-Oyogi-Shageki requires mastering an egg-beater-type kick while keeping perfectly still otherwise—the better to handle a bow and arrow or fire a rifle with accuracy. *Inatobi* is a kind of swimming-jumping that allows warriors to see over incoming waves or disentangle themselves from underwater vegetation. *Katchu-Gozen-Oyogi* is often described as the most graceful and revered form of Samurai swimming, but it's no picnic in the park. Swimmers are expected to wear helmets and armor—maybe twenty-five pounds in all—while using a kind of overarm sidestroke.

To be sure, these and the other Samurai strokes have their Olympic uses. The egg-beater kick and jumping maneuver, for example, are tailor-made for water polo and artistic swimming. The Samurai strokes and challenges are also closely echoed in Western military swimming today. In the United Kingdom, Special Forces candidates must pass a fitness test that includes swimming five hundred meters in combat clothing and an underwater swim of ten meters while retrieving a small weight. Candidates for the US Navy SEALs are taught (and required to master as part of their Basic Underwater Demolition training) a low-profile, highly efficient combat sidestroke that closely resembles the Samurai *Katchu-Gozen-Oyogi*.

But the Japan of 1924 was still a mostly closed society, and the skeleton Japanese team (six men, no women) that showed up at the Paris Olympics that year steeped in Samurai notions of swimming had little idea what the sport was like in the rest of the world and was completely unprepared for what it found.

The Japanese, though, learned Western swimming quickly, in part by using underwater cameras to refine their strokes. In 1928, a railway worker, Yoshiyuki Tsuruta, won the 200-meter breaststroke—just the second Olympic gold in any sport for Japan. Four years later in Los Angeles, the Japanese dominated men's swimming: five golds in the eleven events contested, five silvers, two bronzes. The Japanese dominated again in Berlin in 1936—four golds and eleven medals in all, nearly half of all swimming medals awarded that year to both sexes.

The 1940 Olympics promised to be the golden moment for Japanese swimming: Not only was its program ascendant, but the Summer Games were to be staged in Tokyo. Home pool advantage! Then, as so often happens, sports collided with history—in this instance, Japan's undeclared war with China, increasing global uneasiness, and more locally, growing concern within the Japanese government that the nation simply could not afford to host the Olympics—and in July 1938, the Tokyo Summer Games scheduled for two years hence were canceled, never to be staged elsewhere as so many vectors converged on global war. As for Tokyo, it would have to wait another twenty-four years to host the Olympic Games.

Still, within two Olympic cycles, the Japanese had mastered Western swimming. One wonders if it could have happened the other way. Greece threw down the marker in 1896 for how Olympic swimming would develop: European strokes, Western understandings of competition. Had the first modern Games been held in Tokyo instead of Athens, Olympic swimmers today might be diving into the pool wearing armor, with swords sheathed on their backs. Actually, that might make a fun addition to the modern Olympics roster: must-watch TV!

Speaking of which . . .

15

THE FASTEST SWIMMER EVER

What's going to happen in another 100 years? Is the time for a 50-
yard free going to be 12 seconds? It wouldn't surprise me at all.
—Rowdy Gaines

Not to brag, but I once bettered the American record time for the 100-yard freestyle and didn't even finish in the top three. The date, I feel fairly certain, was Saturday, September 2, 1961—Labor Day weekend. The event I'm sure of: the annual Kipona Festival in Harrisburg, Pennsylvania. The venue wasn't exactly a pool: races took place between two floating docks anchored a hundred yards apart in the Susquehanna River. But the winning times were carefully measured and duly listed without further commentary in the local sports section. Steve Clark's American record in the 100-yard free stood then at 0:46.8, but even out-of-the-money runners-up like me smashed it. In fact, it was hard not to.

The river was running high that year, and we raced downstream with a powerful current pushing us on.*

Moral: Fast times and "fastest swimmers" often need to be seen in context.

Case in point, maybe: Back in 2000, during the Sydney Summer Olympics, Cadillac aired a virtual event to determine the best male swimmer of the twentieth century. The five contestants spanned eight decades of Olympics competition: Johnny Weissmuller from the 1924 and 1928 Games, holder of more than fifty world swimming records and later famous as Tarzan of the Apes; Buster Crabbe from the 1932 Games, who also played Tarzan on-screen and later added Flash Gordon and Buck Rogers to his credits; Santa Clara Swim Club and Yale University phenom Don Schollander, 1964's World Swimmer of the Year; Mark Spitz, who at the 1972 Olympics not only won all seven of his events but also set world records in each of them; and Matt Biondi, winner of eleven Olympic medals over three Games ending in 1992.

Blending old film clips and TV footage—and narrated by another Olympian, three-time gold medalist Rowdy Gaines—the "Cadillac Challenge" presents a stark contrast of styles, techniques, even body types and appearances. Schollander (an inch shy of 6 feet and 174 pounds) and Spitz (6 feet, 161 pounds) both look almost frail compared to the rugged Hollywood physique of Weissmuller (6 foot 3, 190) and the comparatively massive Biondi (6 foot 7, 209). Schollander's close-shaved head from the mid-1960s contrasts sharply with Spitz's floppy hair and fulsome moustache from less than a decade later. Biondi's arm positioning is ideal by modern standards: elbows high on recovery with a driving stroke below. Weissmuller's form looks impossible to duplicate: head literally out

---

* World record times are in meters only. Steve Clark also held the world 100-meters free record for almost three years, beginning with the 1964 Olympics. As for the Kipona meet, swimming the Susquehanna when the water was running high and fast might not have been the best idea in the world. In the early 1960s, the river at Harrisburg was a toxic mix of acids leaching from upstream coal mines, raw or poorly treated sewage, and agricultural runoff.

of the water; shoulders, even much of his upper chest raised high; arms pummeling ahead.*

Inevitably, the Cadillac promotional feels a little shopworn, even jingoistic. For decades, major swimming events have been held in eight-lane pools. This virtual pool uses only five lanes, all American occupied. Why not fill the unused three with Alexander Popov, the "Russian Rocket," who dominated international sprint racing in the mid-1990s; Michael Gross, the German "Albatross," who during the 1980s broke twelve world records in freestyle and butterfly; and Murray Rose, the telegenic Aussie from the 1950s? Rose might as well have been American born and bred: he starred for USC and spent the rest of his life in Southern California. Between the three of them, Popov, Gross, and Rose sport Olympic creds galore.

Or for ethnic diversity how about at least including the great Hawaiian swimmer of the early twentieth century, Duke Kahanamoku, who owned the world record in the 100-meters free for one day shy of ten years, from 1912 until Weissmuller dethroned him in 1922. Hawaii was a territory back then, not a state, but its swimmers competed under the US flag, as Puerto Rican swimmers do today. Throwing Kahanamoku into the mix would have been a nice nod to that other aquatic sport he introduced to the rest of the world: surfing.

"Virtual" was also far less virtual two decades ago. The challenge race covers 100 meters, two lengths of a standard 50-meter Olympic pool, but the film editors must make do with barely compatible footage. Splicing edges are so blurred that we seem to be looking at the contestants through a lens greased with Vaseline. Digital manipulation was also in its relative infancy back then. Buster Crabbe appeared in over one hundred movies and TV shows, but he must have left behind scant video evidence

---

* In his 1930 book, *Swimming the American Crawl*, Weissmuller likened his stroke to a speedboat hydroplaning ahead. Holding his head out of the water "facilitated a method of breathing that most closely approximates the natural, involuntary method of nature," while the hydroplaning drove his feet lower in the water, "where they maintain traction at all times. . . . Some say there is still room for improvement in this stroke. I do not see just where the improvement will come."

of his competitive swimming prowess because he all but disappears in this all-star race.

Real time has also overwhelmed this virtual event from five Summer Olympic cycles ago. The male athlete who has dominated swimming over the last two decades, Michael Phelps, did compete for the United States in 2000—at age fifteen, the youngest male to qualify for the team in sixty-eight years—but he failed to medal. Katie Ledecky, who owned women's swimming lock, stock, and barrel at the 2016 Olympics, was barely three when the Sydney Olympiad got under way. Neither, of course, belongs in a test of the best male swimmers of the last century, but their absences date a challenge that is only twenty years old.

All that said, though, the algorithm or whatever combination of forces determined the outcome keeps the race interesting. Matt Biondi, a breakaway sprinter with muscles on top of muscles, takes the early lead, trailed closely by Don Schollander. After the turn, Mark Spitz takes over as frontrunner and seems to be cruising to an easy win . . . until a fast-closing Johnny Weissmuller nearly touches him out at the end.

Accurate? At least virtually so? Biondi versus Schollander feels right. Schollander won gold in the 100-free at the 1964 Olympics, but 200 meters was clearly his best event. He held or shared the world record in the event almost continually for a decade, beginning in 1962, until Mark Spitz finally claimed it outright, by a tenth of a second. Matt Biondi, by contrast, was an early-speed machine, strongest at 50 and 100 meters.[*]

Biondi versus Spitz gets a little more complicated. In the real world, Biondi swam the 100-meter free 2.8 seconds faster than Mark Spitz, but that was sixteen years after Spitz posted his best time. On average, the 100-meter freestyle world record has improved by 0.1345 seconds per year over the eighty years between 1922, when Johnny Weissmuller first

---

[*] Two swimmers, the Australian Bob Windle and West Germany's Hans-Joachim Klein, briefly stole the 200-meter world record from Schollander during his long reign in the event—Windle for three months in 1963 and Klein for a few months the following year.

cracked the one-minute barrier, and 2002. Make that the handicap for these across-the-decades match-ups, and grant Spitz that same average improvement over sixteen years, and the race would have been a near dead heat, with Biondi perhaps winning by a whisker.

Spitz versus Weissmuller is equally complicated. Spitz's best time in the event was 6.84 seconds faster than Weissmuller's, but forty-eight years separate those marks. Applying the same across-time handicap lowers Weissmuller's best by a full 6.5 seconds and creates another near dead heat, even though Tarzan was using a swimming technique off-the-wall by modern standards.

IS SUCH HANDICAPPING FAIR? PERHAPS NOT. TIME IS TIME; THE STOP-watch doesn't lie. And time differences are surprisingly consistent over generations. The 6 plus seconds and forty-eight years that separate Mark Spitz and Johnny Weissmuller in the 100-meter free are closely paralleled by the 5.4 seconds and forty-eight years that separate Caeleb Dressel's sub-40-second 100-yard free at the 2018 NCAA championships and Zac Zorn's American record in the event as of 1970: 45.3. Ask any competitive swimmer: in a sprint, 5.4 seconds behind is an eternity. As John Updike once wrote in another context, "The kids keep coming, they keep crowding you up." And they keep getting faster, too. Lots faster. Almost exponentially faster and more adept depending on where you set the point of comparison.

George Breen, who twice set the world record in the 1,500 meters (in May and again in December 1956) told me that in the dozens upon dozens of 1,500s he swam in national and international competition, he only once used a flip turn—and got called a hot dog for doing so. Do age-group swimmers even know how to do an open turn anymore? If they did, is there one chance in a million they would dare use it in top-flight competition? I'm guessing: No.

Granted, that's over six decades ago—ancient days when mastodons still walked the Earth and swimmers carried clubs into the sea. But move closer to the current day, and the forward leaps can still be staggering. At the 2012 NCAA Division I Women's Championship, Stephanie Peacock of the University of North Carolina finally broke the most iconic record in women's college swimming, and one of the most notable in all of sports: Janet Evans's twenty-two-year-old NCAA record time for the 1,650-yard freestyle. Peacock's time, 15:38.79, topped Evans's mark by just about a full second. Five years later, Katie Ledecky bettered her own American record in the event with a time of 15:03.31—35 seconds faster than Peacock, more than a full 50-meter length ahead. Thirty years after Mark Spitz stunned the swimming world by becoming the first person to complete the 100-meter butterfly in under 55 seconds, his time—0:54.72—would not have made the cut for the US Olympic trials.

Dave Tanner was a classmate of Spitz at Indiana University. Both swam under the legendary Indiana coach James "Doc" Counsilman. After graduating in 1972, Tanner worked as an assistant to Counsilman for two years, then began a coaching and teaching career that took him to Spain, back to Indiana at Evansville, and eventually to Bloomington North High School. On the side he was a research associate for the Counsilman Center for the Science of Swimming, in Bloomington.

"Is it possible to compare swimmers over time?" I asked Tanner.

"Probably not," he answered. "Swimmers today are so much stronger. They train harder, and they train smarter. In the 1970s it was massive amounts of yardage. Today sprinters work very hard in very specific ways. We didn't do that back then. There's much more dry-land training."

And much more attention to diet, too, and to how diet, gym work, and pool training all interrelate. At the absolute top tier of competitive swimming, there's barely time for anything else. Consider Adam Peaty, the British breaststroke Olympic champion and world record holder. As *Men's Health* magazine reported in a March 2019 article, Peaty consumes on average about seventy-five hundred calories a day—Weetabix, lots of chicken and vegetables, brown rice, lean fish, and the like. He describes it as "active fueling," eating every few hours, and supplementing it all with buckets of sports nutrition products. Peaty cuts that calorie consumption in half as race days approach, but gradually and very carefully.*

"I've worked with nutritionists before where I've cut my calorie levels too quickly, and my testosterone levels have dropped," he told reporter Edward Cooper.

Then there's the gym work: barbell back squats, barbell bench presses, chin-ups, clap press-ups (push-ups where he basically throws himself into the air and claps his hands to mimic the power point of the breaststroke pull), extended crunches, and more. Finally, there's actual swimming—twice-a-day sessions, supplemented with three to four hydration tablets because "in the water you never know how much you are sweating. These tablets help replace the electrolytes."

Did the Apollo 11 astronauts train any harder than Adam Peaty does? Did NASA's scientists even know to worry about what Neil Armstrong's testosterone level was going to be when he took that one giant leap for mankind? Maybe the price of world records is eternal vigilance.

Top-shelf competitors are also, generally, far more big-boned than their peers from an earlier generation of swimming stars. Janet Evans owned distance freestyle in the late 1980s, just as Katie Ledecky does today. But Evans was only 5 feet 6 inches. To make up for her average stature, she used a stiff-arm stroke and rapid rotation—it looks almost as if she's trying to punish the water. In theory, that should have tired her out in longer races—her specialty—but she also had the heart of a lion and seemingly inexhaustible energy. Ledecky clearly has equal heart and stamina, but at 5 foot 10, she needs fewer strokes than Evans to cover the same ground. Over the course of an 800-meter or 1,500-meter race, those extra strokes can't help but take a toll.

---

* For comparison's sake, the Dietary Guidelines for Americans recommends a daily intake of 2,800 calories for a moderately active twenty-year-old male.

Or consider Michael Phelps, all 6 feet 4 of him. Off the blocks, he would have an automatic five-inch edge over Don Schollander, but the advantages don't end there—or maybe more accurately, the eccentricities of Phelps's physique just go on and on. Wingspan normally equals height, but Phelps has a wingspan of 6 feet 7 inches and an elongated upper torso such as you would usually find on someone 6 foot 8 inches tall. Together, the torso and wingspan, along with oversized hands, give him nearly unmatched reach and pulling power in the water. Meanwhile, Phelps's size 14 feet drive him steadily forward whatever stroke he happens to be doing. And, of course, he is—or very recently was—world caliber in all of them.[*]

And if that isn't enough, there's the lactic-acid edge. Strenuous exercise uses up glucose from the bloodstream and converts it to lactic acid, which then floods the muscles and saps energy. Michael Phelps isn't immune to that fact of nature, but studies have found that his body produces about 50 percent of the normal human quotient of lactic acid under similar stress conditions, and even that he tends to very carefully.[**]

If some mad scientist were to set out to create a perfect swimming physique, most likely the design would come out very like Michael Phelps's, but it all begins with height: a longer start, the extra reach, turns that begin further out from the wall, more power behind that undulating double-dolphin kick as he pushes off the wall. *Ka-ching. Ka-ching. Ka-ching.* When it comes to swimming times, all that is money in the bank.

Or maybe our mad scientist would come up with Caeleb Dressel instead. Dressel is an inch shorter than Phelps, with nothing like the latter's wingspan. (In fact, at 6 foot 3 and 190 pounds, Dressel is almost

---

[*] Body oddities and great swimming success often seem to go hand in hand. Australian Ian Thorpe—the "Thorpedo," who set a world record for the 400-meter freestyle at the 2000 Olympic Games—was roughly Phelps's height but was powered by size 17 feet.

[**] TV watchers of the 2016 Olympic swimming events might remember the round welts on Phelps's upper torso as he took the starting blocks in various events—the result of what's known as "cupping" to draw the remaining lactic acid out of the bloodstream. Other swimmers used cupping as well, but Phelps had less to extract.

an exact physical match with Johnny Weissmuller.) But what he lacks in reach, Dressel makes up in pure athleticism.

"Dressel isn't a body-freak like Phelps," University of Virginia head coach Todd DeSorbo explains; "he's an athletic-freak, one of the most athletic swimmers ever. Rumor has it that one day in the weight room at the University of Florida, he was doing box leaps, and the cornerbacks coach for the football team said 'Who's that kid? I want him!' Dressel doesn't move like a swimmer; he moves like a professional athlete. He's explosive off the starting block."

And he doesn't stop exploding once he's in the water. For those of us from an earlier swimming generation, Dressel's American record for the 50-yard freestyle—set at the 2018 NCAA Championships—is almost unbelievable: 17.63 seconds, the first sub-18-second 50 yards in history, eight-tenths of a second under the old record established in 2008, almost 5 percent faster than the event has ever been swum before in recorded history. For comparison, in August 2009 Usain Bolt became the "world's fastest man" by running the 100-meter dash in 9.58 seconds, 0.14 seconds better than the old world record set by Bolt's fellow Jamaican Asafa Powell eleven months earlier—a marginal improvement of 1.4 percent, less than a third of Dressel's record discounting. And Bolt breathed with every stride during his world's-best sprint. Dressel never breathed once during his.

SIZE COUNTS, OBVIOUSLY. ATHLETICISM, TOO. AND MUSCLE. AND SPRING. And lungs like a Louie Armstrong. All that is indisputable, but consider for a moment more nuanced issues having to do less with pure swimming talent, wingspan, and lactate buildup than with related technology and engineering and the simple march of time.

Let's start with the most basic item: swimsuits. When he set a new world record of 51.22 seconds in the 100-meter freestyle at the 1972 Berlin Games, Mark Spitz was wearing a barely decent racing suit spun of ultra-lightweight synthetic fibers incapable of absorbing water. Fifty years and one month earlier, when Johnny Weissmuller became the first person known to break the one-minute barrier for the 100-meter free, he wore a silk singlet that covered his chest and had none of the body-clinging elasticity of modern suits. Bruce Wigo, the retired CEO of the International Swimming Hall of Fame where Weissmuller's old suit is archived, speculates that it would have had the same retarding effect that mesh drag suits do today.

I asked UVa's Todd DeSorbo what difference that might make. "We have guys who wear drag suits in practice. They add the equivalent of a pound or two right around the middle, and that adds probably half a second, going full speed, to their 50-meter freestyle time. Over 100 meters, the difference is going to be greater."

How much greater? Two seconds? Three? These things can only be guesstimated, but remember: Mark Spitz's best time in the 100-meter free was less than seven seconds faster than Weissmuller's.

Until the early 1970s, female competitors had to deal with a drag issue all of their own: the so-called modesty panel, a second layer of nylon that assured breasts, lower body parts, and pubic hair didn't show through.

"The water ran right through the front of it, between the two layers," according to 1964 Olympic gold medalist Donna de Varona. "The American swimmers finally protested when the East Germans showed up at the 1973 World Games wearing form-fitting Lycra."

Swimmers from the de Varona/Spitz era—the sixties and seventies—have further reason to claim wardrobe foul when their top times are held up against modern world standards. Compare, for example, Mark Spitz's 1972 world-record time in the 100-free (51.22) to the world record in the event as I write: 46.91, set by César Cielo, of Brazil, in the 2009 World Championships. Spitz's record stood for almost three years. Cielo's has now lasted almost ten years, a monumental achievement in a constantly bettering event . . . except that César Cielo, rather than stripping down to almost nothing to swim, had covered himself up with a full-body technical suit that crammed the swimmer (along with trapped air) into a streamlined tube, thus increasing buoyancy, reducing drag, and launching a blizzard of new and very durable world records, especially among male swimmers, before the suits—Speedo LZR, Jaked, Arena X-Glide, and others—were banned from competition in 2010.[*]

That sounds like a no-brainer: the tech suit's impact on swimming records was much the same as steroids' impact on baseball homerun marks. Sports author and US Masters swimmer John Feinstein found that the tech suit reduced his stroke count by about 12 percent. Rich Burns, one of the great Masters swimmers of all time, says the tech suits are like "putting on a Superman costume. The suits rearrange your body. They tuck things in where they can't otherwise be tucked. I used to say they swam by themselves—you were just along for the ride. The tech-suit alone was worth two seconds in a hundred."

Two seconds in a 50-second swimming race is akin to adding 4 percent to a long fly-ball out in baseball—a 400-footer that stretches to 416 feet and clears the right-field fence in the corner. How can you trust such records, especially for comparative purposes? Throw 'em both out! Or at least mark them with an asterisk. Except that steroids had been outlawed in baseball, while the tech suits were perfectly legal in swimming until the moment they were not. And except that technological advances make comparisons challenging in almost any sport. How do you match up the speed of a serve with a space-age titanium tennis racket versus a serve with an old wood-framed one? How do you compare career points scored in the pre-three-point-line, pre-24-second-clock days of pro basketball with career points in the run-and-gun-from-anywhere NBA of today?[**]

---

[*] Of the twenty men's long-course world records recognized by FINA as of the summer of 2019, thirteen were set in the two years before the tech-suit technology was banned. Only three women's marks date back to that era. Why the difference? Quite possibly the longer standard woman's suit—shoulders to hips vs. hips only for men—already traps air. Women also have more adipose tissue than men, which makes them naturally more buoyant whatever they are wearing in the water.

[**] Not that swimming hasn't had its own steroid problems. Documents uncovered in the former East Germany after the Soviet Union collapsed confirmed what many had suspected: that the dominant East German female swimmers of the 1970s and 1980s had been taking performance-enhancing drugs. "If I were FINA, I would hold a healing ceremony," Donna de Varona told me recently. "A lot of athletes who competed against the East German machine are still bitter about it. And a lot of the swimmers who took those drugs feel terrible about it, too."

Besides, as John Craig pointed out in a 2012 guest editorial for *Swimming World* magazine, the tech-suit benefits were not uniformly distributed. Yes, the suits appear to have shaved off about seven-tenths of a second per hundred yards—but only for the first hundred yards. The benefit generally diminished the longer the race, and disappeared altogether by the 1,500-meter freestyle. Just as important, Craig writes, "Two different swimmers wearing the same tech-suit under the same conditions would benefit by different amounts, depending on their form and natural buoyancy." And not all the world records from the Tech-Suit Interregnum were set by swimmers in full suits. Some wore leggings only. How do we handicap those times? By seven-twentieths of a second per hundred? Is there such a thing as being just half pregnant?

Another challenge to comparing swimmers across generations, and even more basic: body hair. Johnny Weissmuller would have found it beyond weird if someone had suggested shaving his arms and legs before a big race. But at the Melbourne Olympics in 1956, the Australian men's swim team dominated the competition after "shaving down," and top-tier male swimmers have been doing it ever since. Spitz's moustache was much in evidence at the 1972 Games, but his body was shaved smooth as a baby's bottom, and that made a demonstrable difference.

No one knows for sure why—maybe shaving reduces drag or simply produces a temporary neurophysical sensation of "lightness" in the water—but doing so has been shown to enhance performance by as much as 4 percent. That alone might have lowered Weissmuller's best time by more than two seconds.[*]

Still another small item with big consequences: goggles. Until the late 1960s, almost no competitive swimmers wore them in practice. Unless you were training in a nonchlorinated medium like lake water, pool

---

[*] The Melbourne Olympics generally were a wake-up call for US swimming. The Americans sent the largest contingent to the Games, twenty-eight swimmers, two more than host Australia, but came away with only two individual golds and eleven medals in all. Australia, meanwhile, took eight of the thirteen golds awarded and fourteen medals overall.

time was limited to roughly three thousand yards at a pop. Eyes simply couldn't take more chlorine than that. Slim, form-fitting goggles changed training in a heartbeat. Many swimmers, Mark Spitz included, at first refused to use them in competition—the goggles too often shifted on impact after a racing dive or coming out of a turn—but suddenly, school-age swimmers could do lap after endless lap in the early morning and still see the blackboard in class, and practice again in the afternoon and do homework in the evening.

Competition pools have evolved, too, with pure speed in mind. In the next chapter, we'll get into the fluid dynamics of this. For now, just allow me to note that the Alameda, California, pool where Weissmuller swam the first sub-minute 100 meters was basically a watering tank. High sides guaranteed backwash as swimmers churned the water. If they were even used, lane markers would have been corks strung on ropes, just as they were at my YMCA pool in the 1950s. They did absolutely nothing to absorb agitation.

Top-tier swimmers today have none of these disadvantages. They compete on surfaces glass-like by comparison. They also take off from starting blocks pitched forward for greater spring and with adjustable handles and foot chocks for maximum thrust. On-screen, Johnny Weiss-muller got to leap into the water from swinging vines and dive out of trees. Poolside, though, he took off from a dull, flat surface race after race.

Tarzan also answered only to the rules of the jungle. Wherever top-flight competition is held today—Great Britain, China, Rio, or Timbuktu—swimmers, meet officials, and event organizers all have to answer to the same eighteen pages of FINA rules, including twenty-three regulations specifically applicable to the various strokes. And over the years, with the exception of the ban on tech suits, the rules changes have mostly favored speed, and common sense, too.

When I was a kid and later a coach, lane judges sometimes worked themselves into a lather over whether a breaststroker had taken a dol-phin kick out of the turn, or a semi-dolphin kick, or something that seemed to pertain more to a dolphin kick than to a frog or whip kick. The gradations of discernment were intense—disqualifications hung in the balance! That problem has disappeared. Breaststrokers are now allowed a single double-dolphin kick out of the turn, and they all use it because the dolphin kick is a demonstrably faster way to leave the wall and get on with the next length.[*]

How much faster? Who knows, but I would bet at least a half second, and with three turns in a 200-meter breaststroke race in a long-course pool, that adds up to a full second and a half. At the 2018 Commonwealth Games in Australia, the difference between first and third place in four of the five men's 200-meter races was less than a second. In the 200-free, it was a third of a second. On the women's side, 1.4 seconds separated all three medalists in the 200 breaststroke. In the 200 backstroke, the top three finishers—Canadians Tyler Masse (1) and Taylor Ruck (2) and Australian Emily Seebohm (3)—were separated by 0.44 seconds and 0.4 seconds, respectively. The takeaway: Small rules changes matter because small time differences matter greatly. This is also why swim meets get timed with electronic touchpads calibrated to the hundredth of a second.

But how much do they matter? Maybe not that much since comparing swimmers across time, even with state-of-the-art virtual reality, is virtually impossible given all the variables that have to be factored in. Not only do the kids keep coming. They keep getting stronger, and they practice smarter, and they explode off the blocks and out of turns. Caeleb Dressel's sub-17-second 50-yard free left me speechless. How can anyone swim that fast? Rowdy Gaines, who once was the fastest swimmer in the world, was less gobsmacked.

---

[*] To be exact, Regulation SW 7.1 of the FINA Swimming Rules for 2017–2021 reads: "After the start and after each turn, the swimmer may take one arm stroke completely back to the legs during which the swimmer may be submerged. At any time prior to the first breaststroke kick after the start and after each turn a single butterfly kick is permitted. The head must break the surface of the water before the hands turn inward at the widest part of the second stroke." Makes the Tax Code seem simple, doesn't it?

"What's going to happen in another hundred years? Is the time for a 50-yard-free going to be 12 seconds? It wouldn't surprise me at all."

Somehow, the thought of a future Caeleb Dressel coming close to halving my own best time ever for a 50-yard free is unsettling. But the more important measure might be how good a swimmer was (or is, or continues to be) within her or his potential and within the time frame and circumstances available to either sex—which brings us briefly back to the winner of the Cadillac Fastest Swimmer of the twentieth-century challenge: Mark Spitz. How did a skinny, six-foot-one kid manage to dominate swimming in so many ways throughout much of the 1970s? The answer, says his team- and classmate Dave Tanner, is something you can't teach and can barely describe.

> Mark had a really good feel for the water. It's hard to define what that is, but he made the maximum use of the strength that he had. Our coach, Doc Counsilman, would say it's the ability to pitch your hands in such a way to produce maximum propulsion.
>
> Certain laws of physics apply here. You're able to produce the maximum force if the hand is perpendicular to the direction of motion. Sensors in the hand and nerve endings feel that pressure and allow you to modify that pitch to maximize pressure. You don't think about it. You just do it by feel, and you can't really teach it.

Some people have it. Some don't. Of those who have it, a very few absolutely maximize the gift within the confines of the knowledge and training methods available to them and considering the body nature has endowed them with. We've had a glimpse of some of them in this chapter. For those of us devoted to swimming, they are our heroes, the competitive stars who light our night sky.

But rather than think of them as contesting forces lined up on a single string of timing clocks, we might try thinking of them as a continuum, each feeding off the others, and here one last piece of wisdom from Doc Counsilman, as relayed by Dave Tanner, pertains: "Back in the nineties, someone would ask Doc why swimmers are so much faster today than they were even in Mark's time, and he would say, 'the level of expectation.' If you expect to go that fast, you find a way to do it."

Peter Kennedy tells the story of sitting next to Murray Rose at the 1964 US Outdoor Nationals. After starring for Australia in the two previous Olympics, Rose had been left off the national team for the upcoming Games because his budding movie career had kept him away from the Olympic trials Down Under. Rose was hoping to reverse that decision by going under 17:20 at the US meet, then swimming a strong 880-yard freestyle in Canada, but times in the heats in front of him at the Outdoor Nationals were faster than expected, and the time he was planning to swim would have likely been unimpressive to the Australian Olympic committee.

"He had to re-plan his entire race on the spot," Kennedy told me. "When Murray touched the wall, the timer in his lane said to him, 'Wow, do you know what you did?' And Murray says, '17:02?' The actual time was 17:01.8. Murray was two-tenths of a second off—two-tenths!"

Talk about rising to your own expectations: Rose not only set a new world record that day; he also reclaimed the record he had set almost eight years earlier, with a time almost a minute faster.[*]

Sometimes world records go into holding patterns. Between the two of them, Duke Kahanamoku and Johnny Weissmuller held the 100-meter freestyle record for a collective twenty-two years. Other times, the advances are explosive. See Janet Evans and Katie Ledecky and Mary T. Meagher. On August 16, 1981, Meagher broke her own world record in the 100-meter butterfly by 1.33 seconds, an eternity in the event, establishing a new mark that held for eighteen years and one week before another American, Jenny Thompson, topped it by a more normal 0.05 seconds.

Most often, the change is incremental, sometimes barely visible. Most swim records are progress-by-committee. The heavily publicized

---

[*] World-record performance or not, Rose was still left off the 1964 Australian Olympic team.

At [left], Duke Kahanamoku, the Hawaiian swimming champion and godfather of surfing, and [right], Johnny Weissmuller, later famous as Tarzan of the Apes. Between them, the two held the 100-meter freestyle world record continuously for twenty-two years, beginning in 1912. Weissmuller's "starting blocks" look as if they might have been cobbled together in minutes by a one-armed carpenter. *(Library of Congress)*

barriers are the glitz moments of the sport, the show stoppers, but every small change in between, often by swimmers whose names are long forgotten, has made the next big breakthrough seem possible.[*]

That gets us to one more wrinkle, what sociologist Daniel Chambliss has termed "the mundanity of excellence." Just as world-record times drop incrementally, with every new standard refocusing the expectations of swimmers coming behind, so individual times are mostly lowered not by sudden bursts of glory (although they may look that way to the outside world) but by focus, discipline, and attention to detail.

---

[*] Sixty-three different men have held the 200-meter freestyle world record since reliable stats were first kept, beginning in 1902. Twenty-three women have held the world mark in the relatively new 200-meter butterfly since it was first set by American Nancy Ramey in 1958. A rising tide doesn't lift all swimmers, but it eggs on the highly motivated.

From January 1983 through August 1984, Chambliss attended virtually every major United States swimming competition—including Indoor and Outdoor National Championships, the 1984 Olympic Trials, and eventually the Games themselves—and interviewed some 120 national- and world-class swimmers and coaches. Most of that time he traveled with the California-based Mission Viejo Nadadores, then the National Team Champions. On the side, back home in New York State where he taught at Hamilton College, Chambliss coached a regional-level swim club, ages six to seventeen.

What he learned, basically, is that the little things count: "Superlative performance is really a confluence of dozens of small skills or activities, each one learned or stumbled upon, which have been carefully drilled into habit and then are fitted together in a synthesized whole. There is nothing extraordinary or superhuman in any of these actions; only the fact they are done consistently and correctly, and all together, produce excellence."

By way of illustration, Chambliss draws especially on his interviews with Mary T. Meagher. Meagher, he writes, was only thirteen when she first qualified for the National Championship and set a goal of breaking the world record in the 200-meter butterfly. Obviously, it was a big dream for a girl who had just reached her teenage years, but to get there, Meagher made qualitative, not quantitative, changes in her training routine. First, she began coming to practice on time, even encouraging her mother to speed through the streets of Louisville, Kentucky, on the way to after-school sessions: "That habit, that discipline, she now says, gave her the sense that every minute of practice time counted." Second, she concentrated on making *every* practice turn high quality, to accustom herself "to doing things one step better than those around her—always."

That was it, but that was also enough. Not yet fourteen and a half, Meagher broke the 200 fly world record at a meet in San Juan, Puerto Rico, and broke it three more times through 1981, leaving behind a mark that, like her 100 fly record time, lasted for almost two decades. Doing things the right way relentlessly, day after day, practice upon practice, may indeed be mundane, even boring, but doing so clearly counts.

Sportswriter John Feinstein said much the same thing when I asked him what makes swimming unique among competitive sports: "If you're really talented in golf, in tennis, in almost any other sport, you can fake it. Obviously, if you go out and shoot baskets on the driveway, you're going to become a better basketball player, but if you have a 44-inch vertical, you can play successfully whether you're a good shooter or not. But in swimming, there's no faking it."*

"People don't know how ordinary success is," Mary T. Meagher told Daniel Chambliss. True enough. Attention to detail counts enormously, but sometimes the Olympics gods intervene in even the best planned swimming careers in ways painful to behold.

Donna de Varona was probably the best-known swimmer in America, maybe in the world, in the first half of the 1960s—on the cover of *Sports Illustrated* when she was fourteen (and again at age seventeen), on the cover of the mass-circulation *Life* and *Saturday Evening Post* magazines, too. De Varona set the world record in the 400-meter individual medley in 1960 when she was only thirteen and broke it three more times over the next four years. She held the world record in the 200-meter IM as well. In fact, she was *never* beaten in the event, and she has exactly one individual Olympic gold medal to show for it all.

How can that be? Well, the women's 400-meter IM wasn't added to the Olympics until 1964—de Varona won that. The 200-meter event

---

* By way of illustration, Feinstein offered up his first Masters Swimming event, a 200-yard butterfly race in the forty to forty-four age group. "I'd gotten myself into what I believed was pretty good shape, and I thought I can handle this. My splits—and you'll need no further description of this event—were as follows: 30, 33, 37, and 59. I remember hitting the 150-yard wall, turning and thinking: I'm totally screwed. I can't possibly finish this race. A buddy of mine was walking on the deck the last length, next to the stroke-and-turn judge, who was of course watching me closely. My buddy says, 'He's still legal!' And the stroke-and-turn judge says to him, 'Don't worry. I'm not going to DQ him. He's already suffered enough.'"

didn't join the parade until 1968. De Varona covered that event as a paid sportscaster for ABC-TV, working alongside the legendary Jim McKay.

"I retired from competition at seventeen because there was no college swimming to speak of, no Title 9, certainly no scholarships for women," she explained. "If you wanted to go to college, you had to work to get the money. I was lucky. I was very visible, and I knew everyone in swimming. But once you started earning money in my era, you were banned from sports."

Then there's Rick DeMont. DeMont was a mere sixteen years old when he won the 400-meter freestyle at the 1972 Summer Olympics in Berlin, only to be disqualified when a postrace analysis found ephedrine in his urine, a banned substance that was also a basic ingredient of DeMont's asthma medication. As required, DeMont had included the medication on his pre-Olympics medical disclosure form, but the US Olympic committee failed to clear its use with the International Olympic Committee. That colossal snafu, in turn, cost DeMont a chance to compete in multiple other events, including the one in which he then held the world record: the 1,500-meter freestyle. In 1973, DeMont was named World Swimmer of the Year, but he never won an Olympic medal.

Eight years later, in 1980, Rowdy Gaines held the world record in the 200-meter freestyle and would soon set a new world mark in the 100-free. Add in anchoring two relays, and he was a heavy favorite to win four golds at the Moscow Olympics, but he never got the chance to compete after the entire US team was pulled from the Games by President Jimmy Carter.[*]

"It was pretty heartbreaking," Gaines told me, "and I wasn't alone. Three hundred sixty-three athletes made the US Olympic team in 1980 who hadn't made it in 1976 and wouldn't make it four years later. This was their only chance to compete, and it didn't happen. I at least got a

---

[*] The winning time in the 200 free at the 1980 Olympics was 0.65 seconds slower than Gaines's then world record. The winning time in the 100-free was more than a second slower than the record Gaines would set in April 1981. In swimming, a second translates to roughly a full body length.

chance to compete in the 100-free four years later in Montreal, but when I got up on the blocks in 1984, I was probably the fifth or sixth best swimmer in that final. There was no way physically I should have won." Gaines, though, timed his start perfectly, took the gold, and went to win two more in relay events. Occasionally, the Olympics gods can also be generous on the backside.

Swimming races, on the whole, tend to be highly predictable events. In big meets, the heats that precede the finals mostly separate the wheat from the chaff. By the time the finals arrive, lanes 4, 5, and 3—the top seeds, in that order—are the ones to watch. Probably 80 percent of the time, the winner will come from there.

Maybe that's why, when I asked long-time observers of the sport about the greatest performance they had ever witnessed, they tended to favor not the crowning achievements—Michael Phelps's eight golds in 2008, say—but the surprises.

Donna de Varona told me about being in the broadcast booth during the 1976 Olympics at Montreal as the women's 4×100-meter relay final was getting under way.

"Our women had been getting beat up in the press. The East German women had won eleven of the twelve gold medals already awarded, and they were favored in this event, too. Our women also knew that the East German women had been cheating [with performance-enhancing drugs]. But our team pulled it together. In the last relay on the last day of competition, they beat the East Germans [by 0.68 seconds] and broke the world record. That might have been the most incredible comeback I've ever seen."

Sportswriter John Feinstein recalled in particular a 200-meter butterfly final at the first Summer Olympics he covered, in 1984:

The 200-fly was a battle between Michael Gross—"The Albatross"—and our American guy, Pablo Morales. They'd finished one-two in the 100-fly. But in this race, they're in the middle of the pool at 150 meters, and they've wiped each other out. They start dying, and all of a sudden, there's this Aussie in Lane One, John Sieben, who starts to come out of nowhere. I had no awareness of him, none, until an Australian reporter sitting right behind me stands up and starts screaming, "Come on, John-o! Come on, John!" And this guy way out in Lane One shoots ahead of all the favorites and wins in a new world-record time.

Rowdy Gaines told a similar story of victory against long odds:

For me, the greatest performance I ever saw was Jason Lezak's anchor leg on the 400-free relay in 2008, only because of the dynamics behind the race. You're talking about a journeyman sprinter, basically a good relay guy. He'd made the team in 2008—in fact, tied for the bronze in the 100-free—but really his career was just ups and downs, He'd never broken 47 seconds in his life, and then he anchors the relay in :46.06, runs down the Frenchman Alain Bernard, the world-record holder in the 100, and our team wins. Jason never got close to that again.

I had a long conversation with him about this. He can't pinpoint exactly what it was except that he was tired of losing. He'd been part of that same relay in the 2000 and 2004 Olympics, and they'd been beaten both times—by the Australians in 2000 and by the South African and Dutch teams in 2004. When he took off this time, we were behind again, but he just said to himself, you know, I am sick of being in this position. He got angry, and the perfect storm was created.

Jason could have swum that race a thousand times, and he would have probably lost 999 of them, but that one magical moment in history is all that matters.

Of course, it also helped that Jason Lezak was swimming in the fastest pool that money and science could create. In Beijing, everyone was.

16

IS ENOUGH EVER ENOUGH?

When I'm in the groove during practice. I feel powerful but light, like I'm skimming across the surface of the water. My strokes are effortless and strong, and I start to get excited because I know I am going to swim fast.
—Lilli Croghan, age sixteen

We humans were destined to swim. We live, after all, on outcroppings of land surrounded by vast oceans, cut through with rivers, pockmarked with lakes and ponds. Water beckons us at every turn. Ten thousand years ago, it even beckoned the people of the Sahara.

Whether we were meant to swim the way we do now, at least in competition, is another matter. The intense training required to perform at high levels stresses the shoulders, knees, calves, and feet, depending on the stroke that consumes most of the workout, and stresses them in ways nature never intended. Freestyle and butterfly typically aggravate the shoulders. Breaststrokers know all too well the knee complaints that come with the whip kick. Backstrokers tend to get off the lightest, but not scot-free by any means.

"In reviewing the freestyle and butterfly stroke, it is clear that the supraspinatus tendon and biceps tendon are required to perform far more than they are designed to," according to New Zealand orthopedist Mary Holden. (The supraspinatus tendon is on top of the rotator cuff; the biceps tendon, below it.)

The medicine here gets complicated. The supraspinatus tendon is under constant pressure from the humeral head (the rounded head of the humerus, where it fits into the shoulder socket) when the arms are outstretched to their maximum point, while the underwater pull in both strokes can irritate the avascular area of both tendons (the so-called critical zone near where they meet bone), leading to localized cell death and subsequent inflammation. Bottom line, and no surprise to top competitors: freestylers and butterflyers especially are at risk of tendonitis, bursitis, rotator cuff tears, and more.

Breaststrokers long ago migrated from the stately frog kick to a whip kick that produces far more power with less disruption, but at a much greater anatomical cost. Ligaments are strained as the knee moves rapidly from flexion to extension; further tension comes from rotating the tibia, ankle, and foot. One day, you're winning the 200-meter breaststroke; the next day, you're on crutches.

Before the rules were altered to allow backstrokers to roll over on their turns, broken wrists and shoulder dislocations were not uncommon. Leveraging and pivoting on the outstretched arm could produce tremendous torque on the shoulder, and swimming hard into a wall you couldn't see was a crapshoot. Today, according to Mary Holden, backstrokers are at greatest orthopedic risk from the kick, which positions the foot in an extreme plantar flexion. Stretching the exterior tendons in that way (and freestylers are also at risk of this) can lead to edema, inflammation, and adhesions.

Happily (at least for kids), these issues are more likely to plague Masters swimmers than age-group competitors. The young have greener and more supple everything—bones, joints, tendons, the whole works. But youth and college-age swimmers are not immune to the dangers of over-working their pivot points.

In an article for the *British Medical Journal* on musculoskeletal injuries in child athletes, Leslie Klenerman, a professor of orthopedic surgery at the University of Liverpool, notes that impingement of the tendons of the rotator cuff can be indicative of general shoulder instability, especially in age-group butterflyers. Simply put, at some point the shoulder can no longer take it. Another article, this one for *Public Health Reports*, suggests that 50 percent of competitive swimmers will end up dealing, at some point in their sports career, with shoulder injuries. Some of the best will never get over them.

In April 2016, Missy Franklin was a five-time Olympic gold medalist in backstroke and freestyle, holder of the world record in the 200-meter backstroke—a swimming natural. Then the unnaturalness of her sport caught up with her at the Mesa Pro Series event.

"I had to be pulled from the meet due to intense shoulder pain from an injury suffered in warm-up," she wrote in a retirement announcement made public in December 2018. "I had never experienced that kind of pain before and I began to completely unravel. The Olympic Games were just four months away and many expected it to be the greatest moment of my athletic career. After the success I saw at my first Olympics in London, the expectations for my second Olympic appearance only felt greater."

Franklin did make it to the Rio Olympics but performed well short of her best times. Early the next year, 2017, she had surgery on both shoulders. By that fall, although far from pain free, she was back in training again, alternating practices with multiple weekly physical therapy sessions. Frustrated with her progress, Franklin shifted her training venue from Northern California to Athens, Georgia, where she began working under Jack Bauerle at the University of Georgia. The coaching, she wrote, was excellent; the vibe, just right. But her shoulder pain just got worse and worse.

"Every moment I wasn't training was spent recovering with ice and rest, as I tried to heal and prepare myself for the next practice—but nothing was working. I went through three different rounds of cortisone shots . . . and also had an ultrasound biceps tendon injection at the end of September. . . . After the failure of my last round of shots, I had only one other option: another surgery, and even that was a long shot."

And with that, Missy Franklin called it quits. Hers is a cautionary tale probably out of all proportion to the danger posed to high-level swimmers as a whole, but it does tend to confirm the obvious: that the miles and miles of swimming and the months and months in the weight room can wear down even the best-trained body, especially when it is performing at high speeds a repetitive motion that the human skeleton wasn't exactly designed for.

A far more common problem for swimmers is what I've come to think of as the Curse of the Rounded Shoulders. As the team physician at University of North Carolina at Wilmington, now-retired orthopedic surgeon James Hundley spent decades looking after swimmers and other athletes. He explained to me how those distinct swimming shoulders come to be:

> The problem is overstrengthening the pectoralis muscles, the front-of-the chest muscles, relative to those on the back of the chest. If you're swimming the crawl or butterfly, you build those up over the other muscles, so a lot of swimmers develop rounded shoulders. The muscles are out of balance. Those that pull your shoulder blades forward become bigger and stronger than the ones that pull the shoulder blades backward.

The rounded shoulders, Hundley says, are more than cosmetic:

> If you run your hand out the clavicle to the tip of the shoulder, you can feel the acromion, an extension of the scapula that forms a roof over the top of the humerus. The normal position of the acromion is tilted

backward so that it's more open in the front than the back. That leaves room for the outward projection at the top of the humerus, to which much of the rotator cuff is attached, to move underneath the acromion as you sweep your arm upward. If your pectoralis muscles have positioned the scapula toward the front, it flattens the position of the acromion, decreasing the available space and thus increasing the likelihood of impinging soft tissues between the two bones. To counteract this in swimmers, we had the trainers help them strengthen the muscles that pull the shoulders backward, to balance out the forces and functionally reposition the acromion.

Back in the fall of 2017, at the funeral service for my long-ago college coach, I could tell nothing about the tendon impingements of the hundreds of people in attendance. Ralph "Sonny" Law lived into his eighties, a much-loved man around Charlottesville, Virginia, as coach, school principal, swim-meet official, football referee, and father, but even though I couldn't find anyone else I knew in the sprawling church, I could tell without fail every serious swimmer who walked in to pay last respects. They were to a person, male and female, every bit as round-shouldered as I am.

Round shoulders, of course, are a small price to pay for robust health in later life. Swimming seems to be especially kind to the aging human body, and the more swimming, the better. For nearly four decades, Rich Burns has been a one-man longitudinal study of how serious swimming can sustain strength and performance.

A college swimmer at Indiana University in the early 1960s, Burns returned to competition for good in 1981, in his mid-thirties, competing at the US Masters Outdoor Championship in Santa Clara, California. He has competed in the same meet every year since, training under the same coach, Marie McSweeney; doing roughly the same training regimen; and tapering off before championships in nearly identical fashion each time. The almost four decades of consistency has allowed him to measure his physical decline "in hundredths of a second, then tenths of a second, and now in seconds" . . . but not many seconds.

"For the first ten years when I got back into swimming, I would swim three 50-yard backstrokes at every one of these short-course nationals, two relays and one individual event. That was thirty backstrokes in all, and they were all within half a second of each other. Every one of them. Over almost forty years, the total fall-off for me has been about three seconds in a 50-yard race, probably six or seven seconds in a 100"—about an 11 percent decline over four decades. A golfer who regularly shot 70 for eighteen holes as a thirty-five-year-old might conceivably still play in the high 70s forty years later, but it's hard to imagine any high-energy-output sport other than swimming where Rich Burns's longitudinal consistency is even possible. Then again, Burns is an exceptional case.

In the fall of 2014, he had his cancerous bladder removed and replaced with a new bladder constructed of a length of his own intestine. In all, he was out of the water for six weeks and lost twenty pounds. The next summer, he was back at the Nationals and winning again. Over the course of his forty years of Masters Swimming, he set 111 US age-group records and, as of spring 2019, still held 23 of them.

With swimming as with so many other things, though, there's no free lunch. Although everyone agrees that exercise is vital to long-term health, new research from the Medical University of South Carolina suggests there might be limits as to how much. A survey of more than seventy elite US Masters swimmers age sixty and older—men and women who averaged seven miles of training per week, including Rich Burns—found that 26 percent of participants had documented incidents of atrial fibrillation, nearly five times the AFib rate in the general population. Further study is under way, but the survey results are in line with other data on top-notch endurance athletes generally.

Damned-if-you-do and damned-if-you-don't, in short, but the endorphin high of sustained exercise in a virtually weightless environment is such that dedicated aging swimmers are often willing to endure the inconveniences, even threats of AFib, in pursuit of steady times and total laps swum. I'm one of them.

"When I'm in the groove during practice, I feel powerful but light, like I'm skimming across the surface of the water," sixteen-year-old age-group swimmer Lilli Croghan told me. "My strokes are effortless and strong, and I start to get excited because I know I am going to swim fast."

We serious lap swimmers all want to feel that way, whether we're teenagers like Lilli; careening through our sixties and seventies (me, on the backside); like Tom Maine heading into our mid-nineties with a passel of US Masters Swimming records under his belt; or to cite the near impossible, England's John Harrison, who in 2014 broke the Masters age 100–104 world record for the 50-meter backstroke by a full 15 seconds.[*]

If we started swimming early enough, most of us also retain some muscle memory of those water-spider-like moments. But somehow we seem to get heavier in the water as we age along. The skimming sensation becomes more a matter of plowing through a medium eight hundred times more dense than air and almost four times as resistant. And all of that is before we even stop to consider the structural and morphological deficiencies of humans when it comes to moving quickly or even efficiently through the water.[**]

Mammals that can swim really, really fast—bottlenose dolphins, for example—have been streamlined by evolution for the purpose. They

---

[*] US Masters Swimming lists eighteen records for swimmers age 90 to 94. As I write, Tom Maine accounts for exactly one-third of them, including the 200-yard breaststroke, the 100- and 200-yard butterfly, and the 100-, 200-, and 400-yard individual medleys. John Harrison's age-100-plus backstroke record of 1:29.78 was set using the "old English backstroke," basically, elementary backstroke using an overarm recovery.

[**] The "almost four-times" theory is courtesy of Howard Wainer, a swimmer and renowned statistician. Wainer calculated that the actual differential is 3.75 for men, meaning that a man equally adept at both sports can theoretically run 3.75 times farther than he can swim over a set period of time, and 3.5 for women. Over the same period of time, a male or female swimmer will also burn 25 percent more calories.

move by what's known as lift-based propulsion, that is, undulating, and they have tremendous aerobic efficiency, which allows them to stay underwater for long periods of time. Living essentially underwater also dramatically reduces "transport costs," another charming phrase that gets at the energy expended to get from point A to point B.

Human swimmers can—and do—mimic dolphins at the start of races and off the turns, but FINA rules and oxygen depletion require them to come to the surface after fifteen meters. And on the surface of the water, transport costs are considerably higher, energy depletion far greater, and aerobic efficiency much lower. Why? Because propelling yourself by essentially paddling with arms and feet is what's known as "drag-based swimming"—the phrase says it all—and because on the surface as opposed to beneath it, "hull speed" comes into play. Hull speed, more commonly applied to shipping, is achieved when the wavelength of the bow wave equals the length of the entire ship, and the vessel can go no faster. The same applies to humans swimming on the surface of a body of water. When their bow wave equals the length of their body, they get trapped inside it, and that becomes their maximum speed—they would have to swim uphill to get out of the wave—and thus they remain until, say, a turn disrupts the wave, and the whole process starts over again.

Nonetheless, we persist at trying to swim like the dolphins, and maybe someday we will get there. As the appropriately named Frank E. Fish points out in an article on the subject for *American Zoologist*, "Only slight modification to the neuromotor pattern used for terrestrial locomotion is required to allow for a change to lift-based propulsion."

Charts tracking the world record progression in the four competitive strokes, by women and by men, are remarkably consistent between roughly 1960 and just before 2010, at which point the extra-fast full-body LZR racing suits and their imitators rendered world records basically useless for longitudinal comparisons. Whether it's 1975, 1985, 1995, or 2005, the difference between the men's and women's world records in the 100-meter breaststroke holds steady at just about 7 seconds.

Same for the 100-meter freestyle (steady at 5.6 seconds) and backstroke (6.5 seconds). Stretch the race out to 200 meters, and the differential grows but remains startlingly constant over time. Tighten the race to 50 meters, and the gap narrows but again stays consistent across the decades.

But here, to me at least, is the really interesting part of this: not only are the male and female curves consistent with each other; they are also both consistently flattening out as they move toward the present day. During Don Schollander's remarkable reign through the 1960s as the international 200-meter freestyle champ, he broke the world record eleven times in almost seven years and lowered his best time more than six seconds. As of the summer of 2019, Britain's Adam Peaty had broken the world record for the 100-meter breaststroke five times in four years— another remarkable reign—but he has lowered the record by only 1.04 seconds, twenty-six hundredths of a second (a couple of eye blinks) per year. Is Peaty less of a champion than Schollander was because of that? Obviously not. He's clearly the number one sprint breaststroker of all time, but the margins for improvement become tighter and tighter.

Another way to look at this: British swimmers have won two Olympic gold medals in the 200-meter breaststroke: the first gold ever awarded in the event, in 1908, to Frederick Holman with a time of 3:09.2; and the 1976 gold to David Wilkie, in a then-world-record time of 2:15.11. Clearly, the stately turn-of-the-century breaststroke became a speed-breaststroke over those sixty-eight years, with an average annual improvement of 0.8 seconds. Another forty years later, in 2016 at the Rio games, Kazakhstan's Dmitriy Balandin won the same event in a time of 2:07.46, almost 8 seconds faster than Wilkie. The 200-meter breaststroke, like other events, had gone turbo-charged, but the average annual improvement between Wilkie and Balandin was only 0.19 seconds, a quarter of the improvement between Holman and Wilkie.

Swimming, in short, is becoming a mature sport, or maybe it's a case of an unstoppable force (ever-improving best times) meeting an irresistible object (the resistance and flow dynamics of water). For world records

A tale of three British breaststrokers and the evolving body types of champion-ship swimmers. Top left, with his coach, is Frederick Holman, gold medalist in the 200-meter breaststroke at the 1908 Olympics. Holman stood 5 foot 10 and was a sturdy 175 pounds. Top right is David Wilkie, the next British gold medalist in the same event, in 1976. At 6 feet, Wilkie was 2 inches taller than Holman, but relatively slight, at 168 pounds. At bottom is the newest British breaststroke gold medalist, Adam Peaty, who took gold at the 2016 Games in Rio at 100 meters. Peaty stands 6 foot 3, weighs 190 pounds, and, as this photo suggests, is all well-honed and infinitely worked-on muscle. *(Peaty photograph: Fernando Frazão/Agéncia Brasil, altered to black & white)*

to continue falling, something is going to have to give, or the sport will have to continue to evolve and swimmers to innovate.

UNTIL THE LATE 1980s, NO ONE SEEMS TO HAVE GIVEN MUCH THOUGHT TO avoiding the surface resistance of water by swimming as long as possible under it. Then a 5-foot-10-inch, 150-pound Harvard backstroker named David Berkoff revolutionized the event with an upside-down double-dolphin kick that carried him more than 30 meters underwater before breaking the surface, and by the 1988 Olympics five of the eight finalists in the 100-meter backstroke—and all the top finishers—were doing the same.

FINA's rule writers put an end to that, capping the "Berkoff Blast-Off" at a maximum 15 meters underwater (or yards, in a pool so calibrated), and did the same with the freestyle and butterfly events, but that still means that in a short-course pool, only 40 percent of the distance is being contested on the surface of the pool. One top-ranked Masters swimmer told me about seeing Tom Shields, who won a silver medal in butterfly at the 2016 Olympics, compete in a 200-yard fly at a 2019 meet in California.

"This was short course, eight lengths, and it took him 32 strokes total—underwater, then three strokes for the first length; underwater and four for the second. By the last length, he might have needed six strokes, but in this regard, it's a totally different sport."

And more innovation is sure to follow. Swimming is an ancient activity but a relatively young competitive sport. There's plenty of room left for creativity.*

---

* I remember seeing Dick Fosbury in the early summer of 1968, maybe in San Francisco, approach the high-jump bar, and then turn and arch over it backward. A backward high jump? That's whacky, I thought. A month or so later, Fosbury flopped his way to a gold medal at the Mexico City Olympics and changed high-jumping forever. Innovations happen all the time in sports.

Scientists and engineers are also working overtime to make increased speed under these conditions as attainable as possible.

Take pool depth. For years, top competition pools, Olympic venues and the like, were a uniform seven feet deep. Everyone agreed: that was just right. Then along came the 2008 Summer Games in Beijing, and records fell like autumn leaves in the brand-new Water Cube. Why? Well, the full-body tech suits certainly played a role, but pool depth (10 feet instead of 7) and pool width were also important. The ten-lane Cube pool wasted a lane on either side—only eight swimmers competed at a time—but that allowed surface agitation to dissipate to the unoccupied extremes of the pool, while also not penalizing the swimmers assigned to the outside lanes.

Just as important, wave-mechanics analysis had shown that a ten-foot-deep pool would more effectively absorb the turbulence caused by the downward thrusts of kicking, both with the stroke and with the now universal practice of doing the double-dolphin kick out of a turn. But the fine-tuning didn't have to stop there. If ten feet, why not twelve? Why not twenty? Because, as Rowdy Gaines explained to one reporter, swimmers need to see a bottom to know where they are in the pool, and below ten feet, markings tend to fade out of vision.

Or take lane markers. As noted earlier, they once served no purpose other than to separate lanes and keep swimmers from slamming into each other. Now, they are designed with baffles that almost literally eat waves. (In fact, Kiefer, one of the main US suppliers of swimming and pool equipment, calls its top-of-the-line markers exactly that—the Wave Eater—and charges $1,000 or more for each 50-meter length of them.) And they are constantly being refined based on hydrodynamic studies thick with coefficients, physics exotica like the Froude number (swimming speed divided by the square root of gravity times the length of the swimming body in the direction of the flow), and other measurements breathtaking in their complexity and depth.

One such study, by Nadim-Pierre Rizk of Sweden's Lund University, analyzed two different grades of lane markers manufactured by the Malmsten Company, a Swedish supplier to an almost endless list of Olympic competitions and world and regional championships. Using cameras, wave analysis, and multiple swimmers doing all four competitive strokes under lab conditions, the study compared Malmsten's standard marker and its "gold" one. The gold one—the "standard" of international meets—won, of course, but there's a lot to be learned by wading into the details.

For example, water's viscosity at 20 degrees Centigrade is fifty-five times that of air at the same temperature. Or that "skin drag" is separated into two regions: the boundary layer, where (because of that higher viscosity) the water actually tries to stick to the body and moves roughly at the same speed as a swimmer, and a more distant layer where waves are generated and a second layer of resistance is created.

The bottom line to all this, though, is fairly simple:

- The "gold" lane markers are worth the money. They dampen the wave creation of elite competitive swimmers twice as effectively as the everyday markers.
- The tension of the lane markers matters, too, and inversely to swimming skill. The better the swimmer, the more slack is needed to allow all those baffles to do their job and eat the waves. Slower swimmers, by contrast, get tossed around in their own wake if the lane tension is too slack.
- Stroke matters, too. The highest waves are produced by the stroke that requires the most energy: butterfly. Thus, butterflyers benefit the most by the highest-grade lane markers. Next in order are crawl and backstroke, tailed by breaststroke. But velocity also matters because of the frequency of wave peaks and troughs. Measured that way, crawl wins the lane-marker derby, followed by butterfly and backstroke, with breaststroke still bringing up the rear.
- And finally, circumference is king. The fatter the lane marker, the more wave eating it can do.

Not much surprise there, maybe, but lots to anticipate. Look for lane markers the size of mini-oil drums in the years to come. And look probably for a growing list of FINA rules governing them. For now, the few lane marker regulations have mostly to do with coloring and minimum and maximum diameters. The future might well resemble the rules for starting blocks, which have become so heavily engineered that FINA ladens them with parameters stretching to almost three hundred words.

Goggles also get a light pass from swimming's ruling councils. "Goggles have the function to protect the eyes against water and ensure visibility," FINA regulations conclude. "Their design or construction shall serve these functions and especially shall not seek to obtain aquadynamic advantages (e.g. through extended shapes not related to the above functions)." But such bland language masks some phenomenal efforts to engineer goggles that will actually increase human speed in the water.

US Patent No. 7475435 B2, issued to four Oregon swim goggle inventors and assigned to Nike, Inc., in January 2009 provides a window into the process. At issue are swim goggles that aren't really goggles in any conventional sense. There's no nosepiece connecting the two eyepieces; no strap holding them to the head (and eye sockets) either. Instead, these goggles are basically two separate, form-fitting monocles, shaped to individual eye orbits and held in place by an adhesive backing or, alternatively, to quote the patent application, by the swimmer's "contracting the orbicularis oculi muscles [the muscles surrounding the eye sockets] against the frame portions."

And why would a swimmer want to add contracting her or his orbicularis oculi muscles to all the other muscle motions necessary to compete at a top level? Easy: speed.

The dual-monocle design reduces hydrodynamic drag by eliminating the nosepiece and head strap. The absence of any connective protrusions also allows for the frame portions to form a smooth and continuous surface over and around which water can more easily pass. Third and maybe most important, as freestanding pieces, the monocles can more easily be shaped to totally eliminate the drag caused by the sunken human eye orbits. In

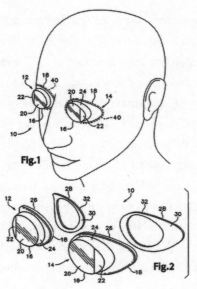

The wonderful world of swimming science: Part of Nike's patent application for a new line of strapless goggles, basically twin monocles. The patent application contends that the goggles will shave 0.146 seconds off a swimmer's time in the 100-meter freestyle.

effect, the monocle goggles move the eye to the streamlined surface of the head, just as in, say, a bottlenose dolphin.

To test their new goggle design, Nike's inventors positioned a life-size mannequin facedown, with arms fully extended forward, in a tank and ran water past it at various velocities. The baseline for the testing was the mannequin without goggles. Compared to that, the mannequin with "goggles B" (a commercially available Swedish set) produced 0.408 kilograms more drag, likely to add 0.816 seconds to the time for a 100-meter freestyle. "Goggles A"—a commercially available racing model, also with traditional nosepiece and strap—reduced drag to 0.266 kilograms but were still estimated to add more than half a second to the 100-free time. The strapless goggles, by contrast, produced less drag than the bare mannequin and were estimated to save 0.146 seconds in the 100-meter sprint.

Again, for perspective's sake, the difference between the first- and second-place men's 100-meter times at the 2016 Rio Olympics was 0.22 seconds. The difference between first and third for women was 0.29 seconds. Fourteen-hundredths of a second can make or break dreams in competitive swimming, but maybe not enough to overcome the sheer oddity of the concept or the difficulty of holding strapless disconnected monocle goggles in place when you are self-propelling in a resistant environment at an average speed of about 5 miles per hour. Or maybe the problem has simply been FINA's requirement that any aquadynamic advantages that might accrue to new goggle design be related to protecting eyes or improving vision. (Nike's patent application claims specifically that it does the latter.) Whatever the cause, so near as I can discover, the monocle goggles have never gone into production, but the patent for them is patiently waiting.

And so it goes in the Wonderful World of Swimming speed research.

Current projects under way at the highly regarded Counsilman Center for the Science of Swimming at Indiana University include using leg-mounted omnidirectional accelerometers to measure swimming energy expenditure as a path to quantifying optimal swim-training distance and speed; the relationship between drag forces and velocity for all four competitive strokes; the impact of shaving down on the perception of cutaneous sensation, including whether such altered input can actually increase muscle output; and to throw a little fun into the mix (but not exhaust by any means the topics under study) whether chocolate milk can be just as effective as modern fluid-replacement and carbohydrate-replacement drinks for post-workout recovery, not to mention better tasting. Spoiler alert on the last item: chocolate milk definitely held its own.

All of which raises this question: Is enough ever enough?* When do swimmers cease being competitors and start serving instead as

---

* When the billionaire John D. Rockefeller was asked "How much money is enough?" he famously replied, "Just a little bit more."

mannequins of a sort—test dummies in a scientific and engineering quest to squeeze out ever-lower times from a sport inevitably pressing up against elemental limits on speed? The answer to that, I suppose, is never, so long as there is more joy in the competition than exhaustion in the training and disappointment in not meeting expectations. People grow by challenging themselves—on land, in school, at work, and in the water.

But not all great swimming accomplishments have to do with times, per se, or with ramping up swim-related technology or, for that matter, with crossing daunting channels or swimming near impossible seas. Sometimes the best swimming stories are about what all best stories ultimately invoke: the indomitable human spirit. Three examples, two of which I know about only by talking to the principals, one of which I was closer to.

Jeff Farrell arrived in Detroit in the summer of 1960 as the odds-on favorite to win the 100-meter freestyle. He'd taken gold earlier in the AAU Short-Course Nationals and seemed a mortal lock for the Games the following month in Rome. Then, six days before the trials opened, he was operated on for appendicitis.

Farrell was through with college by then but training under Yale coach Bob Kiphuth, who advised the surgeon to cut with the abdominal muscles, not across them. Good advice, but still Farrell had a five-inch incision and little time to recover. The first day post-surgery he spent walking the hospital corridors. Day 3 he tried to swim in a small pool in the hospital basement but couldn't even manage a doggy paddle. He mastered that on day 4 and even took some regular strokes. Day 5, the evening before his first time trial, he found himself back in the hospital pool almost pleading with Kiphuth to let him compete the next day even though he had no idea if he would be able to do a diving start.

Kiphuth eventually gave the go-ahead after watching Farrell swim a 50 free the next morning—"the most memorable swim of my life," Farrell calls it—and that set the stage for some high swimming drama accented by the sight of Jeff Farrell standing on the starting blocks with a good inch of plastic-wrapped gauze sticking out of the top of his racing suit.

A profile in courage: Six days before the 1960 Olympic trials, speed specialist Jeff Farrell was operated on for appendicitis. Here he is, less than a week later, taking the blocks in the 100-yard freestyle. The plastic-wrapped gauze bandaging his wound is sticking out of the top of his racing suit. *(Courtesy of Jeff Farrell)*

"I'm well beyond bragging about anything, but the next day I was the second fastest qualifier in the preliminaries going into the semifinals. When I stepped up on the block for the semis, three thousand people at Brennan Pool seemed to be cheering. I think the roar went on for five minutes. That must have inspired me because I was the fastest qualifier in the semifinals going into the finals, the number-one seed."

"And then?" I asked.

"And then in the finals I hit the lane marker. I was careless. It was just stupid negligence. I've never swum all that straight. But hitting the lane marker almost stopped me for a second. . . ."

As demonstrated earlier, swimming is a sport measurable in hundredths of a second and tiny miscalculations. The lane-marker collision cost Jeff Farrell his place on the team and his dream of an individual Olympic gold, but this story has not one but two happy endings. The morning after Farrell's disappointing finish, Bruce Hunter, who had passed him for second place, told Farrell that he had somehow injured his foot the night before and offered Farrell his place on the team. Farrell turned that offer down—there seemed to be no substance to it other than bottomless kindness—but he did qualify for the relay teams before the Detroit trials were over and returned from Rome with two well-deserved gold medals.

Brad Snyder got a gold medal, too, but via a much harder route. In September 2011, Snyder was a US Navy lieutenant serving as an Explosive Ordnance Disposal officer with SEAL Team Ten in Afghanistan, when he was blinded by an IED, an improvised explosive device.

That fall, he returned to the States, to a series of VA facilities, which eventually brought him to Tampa, near where he had grown up in St. Pete. Not long after he arrived, his swim coach from earlier days, Fred Lewis, showed up for a visit and asked Snyder if he wanted to practice with his former team. Snyder, who had been swim team captain at the US Naval Academy, accepted, and he and Lewis began innovating.

The end of the pool was impossible to anticipate exactly, so Lewis put a tennis ball on a stick and began slapping Snyder on the back when it was time to initiate a turn. For many of the same reasons—a swimmer is always leading with his or her head at some point—Snyder learned to delay his front-arm stroke until the opposite arm had passed beyond his head.

Slowly, it all pulled together, and then what seems like a miracle happened.

Not long after I started back swimming, someone said, "Hey, how about the Paralympics? They have a blind category." The Olympics had always been a dream for me. As a kid, I had the Olympic qualifying time in my events written on the bill of my cap. So we looked into it—they were going to be held in the fall of 2012, in London, but there was a deadline. This was January, and I had to qualify by February. It seemed impossible, but then a lot of things came together.

The Association of Blind Athletes offered to pay my travel if I would go to this Olympic Training Center to see if I could make the team, and I did. By virtue of having been a competitive able-bodied swimmer, I came into the blind world like a hurricane and rapidly rose to the top, and before I knew it, we were in London, and I had won a Paralympics gold medal on the exact one-year anniversary of the day I lost my vision.

Such coincidences really happen, in swimming and the real world, sometimes simultaneously.

Mary (Brundage) DeLashmutt never won an Olympic medal or competed for one, but as a high-schooler in 1962, she was part of a Vesper Boat Club 400-meter freestyle relay team that set a new American record. Her story, though, is a lesson in perseverance. It picks up three years later when she transferred from Mary Washington College to the nursing program at the nearly all-male University of Virginia.

Mary Brundage, as she was then, was still competing in the summers for the Vesper team, but her previous school had no swim squad and few opportunities to practice. UVa at least had a team, but it was all-male. What to do? With the encouragement of Virginia coach Ralph Law, Brundage joined the men's team, which inevitably led to a cascade of problems:

First was the clothing issue. Locker-room facilities for women in Memorial Gymnasium were nonexistent. Rather than use a small nook covered by a shower curtain for my changing room, I simply wore my tank suit under an overcoat to and from workout. Cold winter days, I could almost feel icicles forming on my back as I crossed The Lawn to my nursing-school dorm.

Then there was the matter of routing. There was no possible way to get to the pool without passing through a shower room often occupied by unclothed men. Happily (in this instance) I have had severe myopia since I was age six. That didn't prevent some embarrassing encounters, but nurses, I told myself, have to get used to these things.

Finally came the "freak factor." This was well before feminism, and I was the only woman on the bench—sometimes, it turned out, with little meaningful to do. More than one coach refused to allow me to compete at all; other times, I swam "exhibition."

Truth told, I never knew how my teammates felt about me swimming with them.

I do. In the yearbook photo of the 1965–1966 University of Virginia's "men's" swim team, Mary Brundage is second from the right, in row 2. I'm in that photo, too.

Mary's chance to compete officially in the Atlantic Coast Conference came during a road trip of meets in North Carolina. Offered the chance to make history, Duke's coach said no, but the Wake Forest coach agreed, and thus "Brundage, M.," as the results roster records it, became the first woman to ever compete in men's swimming in the ACC—and so far as I know, the last to do so, too. I should add that she was barred that year from the Conference championships.

Finally, there's also something to the critique of modern swimming culture that Irish architect Eva Cantwell offers up in an article titled "Swimming and the Senses."

Swimming pools today have developed into machines merely for physical fitness rather than sensual enjoyment. . . . Clocks adorn the interior of the pool, and rope lanes are laid down. The object is to cover the greatest distance and to do it in the shortest space of time. For efficient use of space, swimmers are organized into continually moving lines. This ensures nobody is able to stop and socialize.

This more industrialized model of swimming, Cantwell argues, has divorced even (or maybe especially) those of us who are ardent swimmers from what drew us to the activity in the first place: the tactile sensation of swimming, the sheer joy of contact between flesh and water, the sensual kick of sunshine on nearly naked bodies (or completely naked ones, depending).

What Cantwell calls "inanimate swimming environments" might also explain the rising popularity of open-water sea swimming. "Unlike the unchanging environment of the indoor pool," she writes, "an understanding of tides, climate and local condition is necessary to organize and compete in these swims." Afterward, too, the chatter is less likely to be about times and more about water temperature and tidal swings.

But open-water swimming, Cantwell told me, is about much more than that:

I live in Dublin, between the city and the sea. I bike twenty minutes to these Martian-looking bathing shelters from the 1920s. You can change in the shelter, go straight into the water, and wherever I am in my life—whether I have just had a baby or whatever—it's a complete transition.

The Irish Sea is always cold. It's part of the charm. Colder water is cleaner water. It's got less bacteria in it. But you're also keenly aware of nature and of your own body. Your feet are numb. You can feel each paddle with them.

Where I swim, you very quickly cannot touch bottom. You are out there with nothing below you. There's fear. It's like the thrill of facing death in a way. It's the closest you get to it, especially in Irish water. It's like getting into a washing machine sometimes. You often can't see because the waves around you are so high. You can't even tell where the shore is, so it can be very terrifying. But it's also kind of thrilling. It's like waking up in a different house and not even knowing where you are. You're at the mercy of the water, but you are also completely reliant on it, and you are viewing things from a different perspective. Space and time are different. It's almost like the power to be a bird. It's just supernatural.[*]

Events are plentiful, in salt and freshwater: the annual Hellespont swim, properly known as the Bosphorus International Swim; the Chesapeake Bay crossing that tracks the bridge of the same name connecting Annapolis with Kent Island and Maryland's Eastern Shore; international races across the Caribbean, in Australia and South Africa, across Lake Zurich in the Alps, through Copenhagen's canals; at various venues in England and many spots elsewhere; and at the Olympic Games since 2008.

The oldest open-water swim of them all, at least on a continuing basis, is one Eva Cantwell has taken part in many times, the Liffey Swim in Dublin, which has tracked the same route continuously since 1920, from the Guinness factory, where the city began, down the Liffey to the Irish Sea. The Liffey Swim can even claim an Olympic gold medal, not for a competitor but for the man who painted it. Jack B. Yeats, brother of the famous poet, won the top painting medal for *The Liffey Swim* back in 1924 when the Olympic committee was still awarding gold, silver, and bronze in five nonsport categories: architecture, literature, music, sculpture, and painting.

Could those days possibly seem more innocent, or any further away?

---

[*] Cold water would seem important in other ways as well. One of America's most successful and admired open-water swimmers, Fran Crippen, a former college star at the University of Virginia, died during an open-water swim in the United Arab Emirates in 2010, at age twenty-six. Water in the Persian Gulf that day reached a temperature of 31 degrees Celsius, almost 88 degrees Fahrenheit.

EPILOGUE

MY WATERY LIFE

This book didn't come about by chance. Swimming has been central to my life. I swam in, and won, my first race at age five. (Speed mattered less than skill set: I was able to dive in, while my competitors had to jump in and get started as best they could.) The summer I was eight, I completed my first nonstop mile, in a little over an hour, and received a hot fudge sundae for my troubles. From ages nine to twelve, I competed for my local YMCA team. We practiced naked but suited up for meets.

Summers in my early teens, I swam for a local club on the AAU circuit—the Amateur Athletic Union, which then controlled national swimming. In the mid-Atlantic states, meets were often held at sprawling suburban country clubs, a sharp contrast to the dingy, inner-city Ys I had become so accustomed to. Baltimore stands out in memory: In earlier winters, I had competed at a Y in desperately poor Dundalk, a building and community that seemed ready to fall down around us. Then, I was warming up six miles away in a stainless steel pool at Sparrows Point Country Club, built for the executives at the nearby massive Bethlehem

Steel plant. (The pool, by the way, made for nearly impossible turns. There seemed to be no way to plant your feet before pushing off.)

Swimming can be an education if you let it. I didn't always do that.

I always thought the pools I practiced in or lifeguarded were open-admission, public pools. You paid your money at the front gate or you flashed a season's pass. It may reflect nothing more than the self-absorption of a sixteen-year-old handed a whistle and a lifeguard chair to lord over the summer long, but I was shocked to learn just recently that both pools had been the subject of black protests and attempted legal action while I sat in that chair. White and black protesters would line up for entry in an alternating pattern. First, a white "customer" would buy an entry ticket. Then a would-be black swimmer would put down his money, only to be told that he needed to fill out an application and would hear back from the pool at an appropriate time, which was, of course, never. Then the next white, and the next black.

Did I notice this going on? No. Nor did I pay much attention to the fact that the country club where I had learned to swim and where I spent six days a week every summer until I began lifeguarding didn't allow even black caddies or kitchen help.

I was co-captain of my high school team, co-captain of my freshman team at the University of Virginia (back when freshmen were barred from varsity competition), co-captain of my varsity team, and holder, when I graduated, of every freestyle school record for 200 yards and up—the proverbial big fish in a very little pond. UVa was a swimming backwater in the very competitive Atlantic Coast Conference back then. That's no longer the case, and those records have long since been ground into dust.

My most crowd-pleasing win ever came in my junior year in high school but had little to do with me. The event was the 200-yard freestyle. I was matched against a senior from Coatesville High School, Tom Snyder. My team was sure to win the meet—we were loaded with talent—but Tom was faster than I was. Not that day, though.

As I followed him into our flip turns after the first hundred yards, I couldn't help but notice a patch of snow-white flesh where his racing suit should have been. The flesh became more prominent on the next two turns, and by the final turn even I—no goggles then, and not great vision generally—could see that Tom's suit was sliding down his thighs. I left him behind me in that last length as his kick became tangled in his departing garment. Afterward, his teammates draped him with a towel as he climbed out of the pool. One of them must also have dived in to retrieve his suit. The small but robust home crowd our meets attracted, cheerleaders included, was in an uproar, and I was happy to have scored five points for our team, no matter how I got them.

Among those cheerleaders was my senior prom date, recently deceased. With part of her graduation money, she bought a two-piece powder-blue swimsuit with a tiny vee along the top that revealed just the hint of a cleavage. Before we could even get the suit wet—at an abandoned quarry north of town that had long since filled with spring water— my girlfriend's mother made her close the vee with a patch of terry cloth. We thought of that quarry as being bottomless. It was one of the great dating sites of all time.

During the summers, transitioning from high school to college, I migrated from a hometown lifeguard chair to managing a community swimming pool west of Charlottesville, in the foothills of the picture-perfect Blue Ridge Mountains. The town, Crozet, was then a rural Virginia village full of wonderful, friendly people. I gave lessons, taught junior and senior lifesaving, put on a summer water show (think crude floats and lots of dry ice, a pale shadow of Bob Kiphuth's Yale Water Carnivals), coached the club team, and generally had a blast. One mother who was short of funds to pay for her three daughters' swimming lessons rewarded me instead with meatloaf dinners and pickled watermelon rind. Today, I make my own pickled rind, just like hers.

I did that job two years running. The next summer, the good local citizens closed the pool rather than bow to a court order to integrate. For decades now it has been open again, on the same site. The story of swimming is inseparable from the changing world around it.

After graduate school, I taught English and coached for eight years, all but one at St. Albans School in Washington, DC, on the grounds of the National Cathedral, a den of great privilege. We had a relatively new six-lane pool that opened to a sunny deck, with an observation platform for the coaches. Two DC public high schools also had pools—Cardozo and Dunbar. Cardozo had been the elite white high school, Dunbar the elite black one back in the days of segregation and theoretical separate-but-equal. Now both schools were integrated and almost entirely black. The one time I took my team to Dunbar, we had to descend four floors to the pool. At each landing, we waited for guards to unlock and remove the chain that secured the fire door leading to the next level down. Crime was rife at the high school, and Dunbar's team was terrible.

A family triple-decker from the later half of the 1980s: the author at bottom, son (Nathan), and daughter (Ihrie) on top. *(Candy Means)*

So was Cardozo's. We swam the kids who never got in the closer meets and still trounced them. No one felt good about it.

The sole African American swimmer on my team over those years was the son of two doctors and is now a doctor himself. In addition to his own practice, he has been team physician and orthopedic surgeon for the Oakland Raiders of the NFL since the mid-1990s.

My coaching days are well behind me, but my swimming days go on and on. Summers and winters I'm in the pool several times a week, and I swim hard when I'm there, or as hard as aging will let me. Until I busted a shoulder bodysurfing a few years back, I made sure to swim a 500-yard butterfly several times a year. It was never pretty, or easy, but for reasons obscure even to me, it seemed important to make the effort. Now, 100 yards of butterfly maxes my shoulder out. *Tempus fugit.*

Collectively over the years, I'm sure I have swum the equivalent of halfway around the world, probably the whole way, maybe more or much more. The math gets hard when I try to factor in all those practices and all the places I've swum—pools, oceans, seas, rivers, lakes, ponds, quarries; any place that didn't look like it was hosting a snake convention, or had gators sunning on the banks, or harbored snapping turtles if I had to walk out through the muck, or ill-disposed sharks.

Once, years ago, I was in Cooperstown, New York, covering an induction ceremony at the National Baseball Hall of Fame. (This was 1983. The great Brooks Robinson was being honored, along with Juan Marichal, George Kell, and the former Dodgers manager Walter Alston.) Driving south out of town the next morning, I saw a road sign marking the very beginning of the Susquehanna River, just at the southern tip of Lake Otsego. As high school kids, one of our rites of spring had been to go racing off cliffs into the Susquehanna, far downriver from where I now was, near to what is now the site of a nuclear power plant. Unable to let the opportunity pass, I pulled off the road, slipped into the woods, stripped to my skivvies, and waded in. There was barely enough water to lie down.

Far more recently, I was walking with a dear friend along the banks of the Serpentine—the central London artificial lake that was the scene of some of the earliest English purse races—when we came to a roped-off area a hundred yards long, by my quick measurement, and open to public swimming. This was mid-May, a sunny day and the water temperature seemed swimmable, but I had no suit with me and, under the circumstances, skivvies seemed an unsatisfactory solution. Still, I regret staying dry.

I used to have a wonderful course marked out on the North Carolina coast, a mile each way between fishing piers. Then I swam smack into a jellyfish that shouldn't have been there that early in the summer. The next year, one of the piers disappeared in a hurricane, another likely effect of climate change. The upside to a hotter planet is that I got in a decent swim a decade ago in the North Sea.

During the twenty-one years my wife and I lived in the close-in Maryland suburbs of Washington, DC, I swam winters in a heated outdoor pool at the Bethesda YMCA. Access was closed only if ice was on the deck. Otherwise, you could swim back and forth with snow settling briefly on your arms with each recovery, even sleet pelting your cheek as you turned to breathe. Sometime back in the 1970s, Denver's Stapleton International Airport was shut down with a white-out when I pushed off in a heated indoor pool atop of one of the surrounding hotels, slipped under a glass panel to go outside, and swam for half an hour in what was pretty much a blizzard.

Another swim that leaps out of memory, from my earliest twenties, back when I was managing that community pool in rural Virginia: one lovely, sunny morning about half an hour before the club was to open, I jumped in the pool, pushed off the wall, and swam three lengths underwater—75 meters in all, 25 percent longer than the winning distance in the sole Olympics underwater swim, and 65 years later. These are the things you can do when you are one with water, when you work with it instead of against it. I stopped not because I was out of breath but because

I worried that I might pass out if I kept on going. Water is the wrong medium for fainting.

Small lakes are my favorites now, especially being out in the middle with a hundred feet of water beneath me. Two summers ago, on Christine Lake in far northern New Hampshire, a loon whooped maniacally as I swam from shore to shore and back again. The sun was hot; the water almost cold enough to make my teeth hurt. I was utterly by myself out there, and completely connected to where I was. Perfect.

Christine Lake in northern New Hampshire, an ideal watery expanse for swimming shore to shore and back again. Depth at the center is estimated to be about 100 feet. *(Courtesy of author)*

ACKNOWLEDGMENTS

This book has been a collaboration in ways almost impossible to tally, over more than two decades. I first conceived of an informal "history" of swimming in the mid-1990s, after reading Charles Sprawson's mesmerizing *Haunts of the Black Masseur*. A jumble of articles and random notes followed until my son, Nathan, helped organize them into a tentative outline. Swim teammates from long ago—Jeff Alexander, Mary (Brundage) DeLashmutt, and others—helped clarify memories of high school and college days. Nick Andes, my great swimming pal almost from the cradle, appointed himself a one-man clipping service, to my immense benefit. Ben Lamberton and Dick Victory were, as ever, encouraging, as were Winslow McCagg, Joe Johnston, my brother Tom, sister Mary Ellen, daughter Ihrie and her late husband, Jon London.

Ralph "Sonny" Law, my college coach, died as I was just beginning to write, but his voice kept circling me as I sat at the keyboard. Bruce Wigo, now retired as CEO of the International Swimming Hall of Fame, went far out of his way to be helpful. Extraordinarily generous people took time from busy schedules to share their experiences and expertise: John Feinstein, Donna de Varona, Rowdy Gaines, Todd DeSorbo, Lynne Cox, Dave Tanner, Peter Kennedy, George Breen, Suzie Holubek, Rich Burns, Lilli Croghan, Jeff Farrell, Jim Hundley, Jeff Harris, Brad Snyder, Tom Kenyon, Eva Cantwell, Jack Howett, and so many others. The problem with such a list is the inadvertent omissions, not the inclusions: I'm grateful to you all, named and unnamed.

I also benefited immensely from the work of other authors, and I hope I have given them proper credit. Of particular note: Nicholas Orme and Christopher Love, meticulous historians both. Julie Checkoway's *The Three-Year Swim Club* reminded me that swimming is inseparable from the world around it. Lynn Sherr's *Swim* convinced me that I could mix the historical and personal without doing harm to either. Kate Edgar, executive director of the Oliver Sacks Foundation, generously allowed me to begin this book with a quote that in some ways captures the essence of what I have been trying to say from the very first page.

Thanks to my agent, David Patterson, for having faith in *Splash!* through many delays, and to my editor, Bob Pigeon, for once again making my thinking clearer and prose better at every turn. I own the mistakes in these pages, but Bob and the team at Hachette Books and the Hachette Book Group have done all they could to save me from myself.

Finally, and as ever, thanks and love to my wife, Candy. Writing a book is never easy. Suffering a mate who is writing a book borders on the recklessly heroic.

Howard Means
Millwood, Virginia

SOURCES

Prologue: Once Upon a Time in Egypt . . .

2 *The cave and its pictographs:* For general information on László Almásy and the rock art of Gilf Kebir, see http://www.bradshawfoundation.com/africa/gilf_kebir _cave_of_swimmers/index.php.

5 *Recent excavations led by the National Geographic Society:* "Stone Age Graveyard Reveals Lifestyles of a 'Green Sahara': Two Successive Cultures Thrived Lakeside," uchicago news, August 14, 2008, https://news.uchicago.edu/story /stone-age-graveyard-reveals-lifestyles-green-sahara-two-successive-cultures -thrived-lakeside. For a more scientific limning of the Gobero site, go to the *PLoS ONE* article "Lakeside Cemeteries in the Sahara: 5000 Years of Holocene Population and Environmental Change" at http://dx.plos.org/10.1371/journal.pone.000 2995.

5 *Skeletal evidence was also found:* An overview of the Tassili site is available at http:// www.thesalmons.org/lynn/wh-wcmc/Algeria%20-%20Tassili%20n'Ajjer.pdf.

5 *What's known is that about twelve thousand years ago:* For more on the Green Sahara and African Humid Period, see B. Damnati, "Holocene Lake Records in the Northern Hemisphere of Africa," *Journal of African Earth Sciences* 31, no. 2 (August 2000): 253–262.

6 *And then? Maybe it was just the Earth:* Lorraine Boissoneault, "What Really Turned the Sahara Desert from a Green Oasis into a Wasteland," Smithsonian .com, March 24, 2017, https://www.smithsonianmag.com/science-nature/what -really-turned-sahara-desert-green-oasis-wasteland-180962668/. And David K. Wright, "Humans as Agents in the Termination of the African Humid Period," *Frontiers of Earth Science*, January 26, 2017, https://www.frontiersin.org /articles/10.3389/feart.2017.00004/full.

7 *In his novel, Ondaatje:* Michael Ondaatje, *The English Patient* (New York: Alfred A. Knopf, 1992). Specific quotes are from the following pages: "boat of sticks" (5), "I had information" (18), "These were water people" (19), "Even today caravans" (19), "In the desert" (19).

9　*One adventure travel outfit:* See Adventure Safari at http://adventuresafari.nl/Silica_Wadi_Hamra_Wadi_Sura_E.htm.

9　*Another guidebook:* Dan Richardson, *The Rough Guide to Egypt* (London: Rough Guides, 2003), 550–551.

9　*And then there's Wadi Sura itself:* Richardson, *Rough Guide,* 550.

10　*No one can say exactly:* Jiri Svoboda, "Action, Ritual, and Myth in the Rock Art of Egyptian Western Desert," *Anthropologie* 47, nos. 1/2 (2009): 159–167, http://www.jstor.org/stable/26292865. See also the Q&A with David Coulson, founder of TARA (Trust for African Rock Art), at https://www.reddit.com/r/IAmA/comments/3apamh/i_am_david_coulson_in_20_years_ive_travelled_the/.

10　*Other scholars have suggested:* Pauline de Flers, Philippe de Flers, and Jean-Loïc Le Quellec, "Prehistoric Swimmers in the Sahara," *Arts & Culture* (2006): 46–61, http://rupestre.on-rev.com/page76/assets/AC_GB.pdf.

1. Gods, Humans, and the Aquatic Ape

14　*As Brian Switek wrote:* Brian Switek, "I'm an Ape, and I'm Also a Fish," *Wired,* March 21, 2012, https://www.wired.com/2012/03/im-an-ape-and-im-also-a-fish/.

15　*Spend an hour up to your head in water:* A. Mooventhan and L. Nivethitha, "Scientific Evidence-Based Effects of Hydrotherapy on Various Systems of the Body," *North American Journal of Medical Science* 6 (May 2014): 199–209.

15　*One more piece of evidence reinforces:* https://www.breatheology.com/mammalian-dive-response/.

16　*And then there's sound:* Helen Czerski, "The Calm of the Underwater Soundscape," *Wall Street Journal,* May 18–19, 2019, C4.

16　*Combine the embedded human:* For more, see Robin McKie, "First Human Learned to Swim Before She Walked," *The Guardian,* December 10, 2000, https://www.theguardian.com/science/2000/dec/10/evolution.uknews. Also, Erin Wayman, "A New Aquatic Ape Theory," smithsonian.com, April 16, 2012, https://www.smithsonianmag.com/science-nature/a-new-aquatic-ape-theory-67868308/.

20　*As Alan Isles and John Pearn:* Alan F. Isles and John H. Pearn, "Swimming and Survival: Two Lessons from History," *International Journal of Aquatic Research and Education* 7, no. 2 (2013): 163–166.

20　*Swimming exists only by inference:* Dorothy W. Phillips, "Cosmetic Spoons in the Form of Swimming Girls," *Metropolitan Museum of Art Bulletin* 36, no. 8 (August 1941): 173–175.

22　*In a 1942 essay:* James Hornell, "Floats: A Study in Primitive Water-Transport," *Journal of the Royal Anthropological Institute of Great Britain and Ireland* 72, nos. 1–2 (1942): 33–44.

24　*In a 2009 study:* Stathis Avramidis, "Drowning in Ancient Greek History and Mythology," *International Journal of Aquatic Research and Education* 3, no. 4 (2009): 1–10.

2. Swimming's Golden Age

27 *"A man is not learned until":* Cited in https://www.azquotes.com/quote/865602 and elsewhere.

27 *For swimmers and swimming:* Savary's praise for Egyptian swimming is found in Herodotus, *The Ancient History of Herodotus,* trans. Rev. William Beloe (New York: Derby & Jackson, 1859), 402n3.

27 *The Greeks of antiquity:* E. Albanidis and V. Kassaris, "Swimming and Rowing in Ancient Greece," Pre-Olympic Congress, Athens (2004). See http://cev.org .br/biblioteca/swimming-and-rowing-in-ancient-greece/.

28 *The Romans treasured swimming, too:* Horace's quote comes from his *Satire* II, 1, 8.

28 *As Frances Norwood noted:* Frances Norwood, "Hero and Leander," *Phoenix* IV, no. 1 (1950): 9–20.

28 *In 480 BCE, during the great naval clash:* Herodotus's account (from VIII, viii, 1–3 of his *Histories*) is cited in H. N. Couch, "Swimming Among the Greeks and Barbarians," *Classical Journal* 29, no. 8 (1934): 609–612. See also Sir William Smith, *A New Classical Dictionary of Greek and Roman Biography, Mythology, and Geography* (New York: Harper & Brothers, 1851), 792.

29 *Even with the use of a reed snorkel:* Couch, "Swimming Among the Greeks and Romans," 609–612.

30 *As much as swimming benefited the Athenian:* Herodotus, *Ancient History of Herodotus,* 402.

33 *The Romans were a practical people:* For more on Titus's one hundred days of aquatic merriment, see K. M. Coleman, "Launching into History: Aquatic Displays in the Early Empire," *Journal of Roman Studies* 83 (1993): 48–74.

33 *Early attitudes eventually eased:* Don Kyle, "Direction in Ancient Sports History," *Journal of Sports History* 10, no. 1 (Spring 1983): 7–34.

33 *The Republic was still forming:* Titus Livius (Livy), *The History of Rome, Book 2,* trans. Benjamin Oliver Foster (Cambridge, MA: Harvard University Press, 1919), 2–11, http://www.perseus.tufts.edu/hopper/text?doc=Perseus%3Atext %3A1999.02.0151%3Abook%3D2%3Achapter%3D13.

34 *The standard ending (Livy's) has Porsinna:* The rogue version is recounted in a December 7, 1986, travel piece for the *New York Times* (p. 55). Writer Paul Hofmann, however, heavily discounts the story.

34 *Near-mythical claims have attached:* Suetonius, it should be noted, was writing a century and a half after the Alexandria battle, but Caesar's strength as a swimmer is well rooted in his own time.

34 *The* Commentary on the Alexandrian War: Gaius Julius Caesar, *Commentary on the Alexandrian War,* trans. W. A. McDevitte and W. S. Bohn (New York: Harper & Brothers, 1869), http://www.forumromanum.org/literature/caesar/alexe.html.

35 *"The torrent roar'd, and we did buffet it":* The quoted passage is from William Shakespeare's *The Tragedy of Julius Caesar,* Act 1, Scene 2, lines 190–191*ff.*

36 *In a 1925 article for the* Classical Journal: H. A. Sanders, "Swimming Among the Greeks and Romans," *Classical Journal* 20, no. 9 (June 1925): 566–568.

37 *I would offer one additional piece of evidence:* The coins cited can be viewed at http://ancientcoinage.org/other-interesting-ancient-myths.html.

3. First There Was Swimming; Then There Was None

40 *"At the seventh hour, my mother":* Pliny the Younger's letter can be found in Robert I. Curtis, "Archaeological Evidence for Economic Life at Pompeii: A Survey," *Classical Outlook* 57, no. 5 (1980): 98–99, http://www.jstor.org/stable/43934163.

40 *It wouldn't end there:* Curtis, "Archeological Evidence," 99.

42 *In a 1980 article for the* Classical Outlook: Curtis, "Archaeological Evidence," 99–102. An excellent, user-friendly online guide to Pompeii can be found at https://sites.google.com/site/ad79eruption/home.

43 *Nor did I have trouble imagining:* Seneca, *Seneca ad Lucilium Epistulae Morales,* trans. Richard M. Gummere (London: William Heinemann, 1917), LVI: On Quiet and Study, https://en.wikisource.org/wiki/Moral_letters_to_Lucilius/Letter_56.

47 *Hadrian gummed up the works:* James Gerrard, "The End of Roman Bath," *Current Archaeology,* March 4, 2008. Also summarized at https://www.archaeology.co.uk/articles/features/the-end-of-roman-bath.htm.

48 *The breakdown of civil authority:* For a comprehensive view of Roman waterworks, see A. Trevor Hodge, *Roman Aqueducts and Water Supply,* 2nd ed. (London: Bristol Classical Press, 2002).

50 *Sixteen-hundred-year-old wall paintings:* International Swimming Hall of Fame, Fort Lauderdale, Florida, multiple displays.

51 *There were, of course, pockets of resistance:* Chrétien de Troyes, *Lancelot, the Knight of the Cart,* trans. W. W. Comfort, Vv., 3021, downloadable at http://mcllibrary.org/Lancelot/lancelot2.html.

51 *Among the European ruling classes:* Einhard, *The Life of Charlemagne,* trans. Samuel Epes Turner (New York: Harper & Brothers, 1980), 22: Personal Appearance, https://sourcebooks.fordham.edu/basis/einhard.asp#Personal%20Appearance.

52 *In a 1999 piece for the* Journal: Jill Caskey, "Steam and *Sanitas* in the Domestic Realm: Baths and Bathing in Southern Italy in the Middle Ages," *Journal of the Society of Architectural Historians* 58, no. 2 (1999): 170. doi:10.2307/991483.

53 *Witches and water were another often fatal combination:* Russell Zguta, "The Ordeal by Water (Swimming of Witches) in the East Slavic World," *Slavic Review* 36, no. 2 (1977): 220–230. doi:10.2307/2495037.

53 *Imagine witnessing that:* The Boulton quote is found in Scott Cleary, "The Ethos Aquatic: Benjamin Franklin and the Art of Swimming," *Early American Literature* 46, no. 1 (2011): 54, http://www.jstor.org/stable/25800131.

54 *That story gets told in the great Anglo-Saxon epic:* The quoted material comes from Frances B. Grummere's translation, available in print from *Harvard Classics,* volume 49 (1910), or online at https://www.poetryfoundation.org/poems/50114/beowulf-modern-english-translation.

54 *Perhaps Beowulf is the model:* Peter A. Jorgensen, "Beowulf's Swimming Contest with Breca: Old Norse Parallels," *Folklore* 89, no. 1 (1978): 52–59.

4. Rediscovering a Lost Art

58 *Musaeus was a swimmer himself:* Musaeus, *Hero & Leander,* trans. E. E. Sikes (London: Methuen & Co.), 25, https://archive.org/stream/heroandleander 00musauoft/heroandleander00musauoft_djvu.txt.

59 *"Leander, being up, began to swim":* Christopher Marlowe, *Hero and Leander,* http://www.gutenberg.org/cache/epub/18781/pg18781.txt. The quoted material is from the Second Sestiad.

60 *To which Michael West adds (fn.):* Michael West, "Early British Swimming 55 B.C.–A.D. 1719 with the First Swimming Treatise in English, 1595, by Nicholas Orme," *Renaissance Quarterly* 37, no. 3 (1984): 457–460. doi:10.2307/2860971.

61 *As the head of the Merchant Taylors' School in London:* West, "Early British Swimming," 458.

61 *As the author writes near the beginning:* Sir Thomas Elyot, *The Boke Named the Governour,* ed. Henry Herbert Stephen Croft (London: Kegan Paul, Trench & Co., 1883). Quoted material is from the following pages: "In the first [book] shall be comprehended" (24), "There is an exercise" (46), "what great advantage is in the feat of swimming" (49). The bulleted military examples and accompanying quotes are from pp. 47–49.

64 *But as Nicholas Orme notes:* Nicholas Orme, *Early British Swimming 55 BC–AD 1719* (Exeter, England: University of Exeter Press, 1993), 70.

65 *By 1587, when* The Art of Swimming *was first published:* Orme, *Early British Swimming.* Orme devotes pp. 71–81 to Digby's life.

66 *That seems more than a little exaggerated:* Orme, *Early British Swimming,* 71.

67 *In the opening pages, Digby himself makes:* The complete text of Christopher Middleton's shortened English translation of *De Arte Natandi* is included in the back of Nicholas Orme's *Early British Swimming.* Quoted material from Digby and Middleton is from the following pages of Orme's book, the most convenient source for the curious reader: "If medicine be worthy of commendations" (117), "[Humans] above all fouls of the air" (117), "The fishes in the sea" (119), "[Men] have not had some practice" (120).

70 *One more note on Everard Digby:* West, "Early British Swimming," 457–460.

5. Swimming 2.0

73 *In a ghostly way, Everard Digby:* I'm indebted throughout these middle chapters to Ralph Thomas's exhaustive and erudite bibliography: *Swimming with List of Books Published in English, German, French and Other European Languages . . .* (London: S. Low Marston & Co., 1904), https://openlibrary.org/books/OL7103794M /Swimming.

75 *In a 1771 letter to his son:* Benjamin Franklin, *The Autobiography of Benjamin Franklin* (The Harvard Classics, Vol. 1) (New York: P. F. Collier & Son, 1909), 10–11.

75 *"I taught him, and a Friend of his, to swim":* Franklin, *Autobiography,* 47.

76 *Word of Franklin's escapades:* Franklin, *Autobiography*, 49.

76 *At the other end of the broad spectrum of his interests:* Benjamin Franklin, *Proposals Relating to the Education of Youth in Pensilvania* (Philadelphia: University of Pennsylvania Press, 1749), 8–10, https://archive.org/details/ProposalsRelatingToTheEducationOfYouthInPensilvaniaBenjaminFranklin/page/n31.

77 *"These imbibing Pores":* Franklin Papers, "From Benjamin Franklin to Mary Stevenson, 10 August 1761," *Founders Online,* National Archives, https://founders.archives.gov/documents/Franklin/01-09-02-0140. [Original source: *The Papers of Benjamin Franklin,* Vol. 9, *January 1, 1760, through December 31, 1761,* ed. Leonard W. Labaree (New Haven, CT: Yale University Press, 1966), 338–339.]

78 *"Travelling in our severe Winters":* Franklin Papers, "From Benjamin Franklin to Benjamin Rush, 14 July 1773," *Founders Online,* National Archives, https://founders.archives.gov/documents/Franklin/01-20-02-0167. [Original source: *The Papers of Benjamin Franklin,* Vol. 20, *January 1 through December 31, 1773,* ed. William B. Willcox (New Haven, CT: Yale University Press, 1976), 314–316.]

79 *"Learn fairly to swim":* Franklin Papers, "From Benjamin Franklin to O[liver] N[eave, before 1769]," *Founders Online,* National Archives, https://founders.archives.gov/documents/Franklin/01-15-02-0169. [Original source: *The Papers of Benjamin Franklin,* Vol. 15, *January 1 through December 31, 1768,* ed. William B. Willcox (New Haven, CT: Yale University Press, 1972), 295–298.]

80 *Russell was born in Lewes:* L. W. Lauste, "Dr. Richard Russell, 1687–1759," *Proceedings of the Royal Society of Medicine* 67 (May 1974): 327–330.

80 *"That great Body of Water therefore, which we call the Sea":* Richard Russell, *A Dissertation Concerning the Use of Sea Water . . .* (Oxford, England: Printed at the Theatre and sold by James Fletcher . . . and J. Rivington, 1753), vii.

83 *Byron's family history is dotted:* Vybarr Cregan-Reid, "Water Defences: 'The Arts of Swimming' in Nineteenth-Century Culture," *Critical Survey* 16, no. 3 (2004): 34–35, http://www.jstor.org/stable/41557287.

84 *Byron was only twenty-two in late April 1810:* Alex Preston, "Swimming the Turkish Hellespont: Alex Preston Follows in Lord Byron's Wake," *The Telegraph* (London), August 11, 2018, https://www.telegraph.co.uk/health-fitness/body/swimming-turkish-hellespont-alex-preston-follows-lord-byrons/.

84 *Vybarr Cregan-Reid suggests that Byron's "disability" (fn.):* Cregan-Reid, "Water Defences," 46n10.

84 *Back on shore, he fired off letter after letter:* The various letters are cited in Cregan-Reid, "Water Defences," 35–36.

85 *On another Venetian occasion, Byron gladly: The Globe: An Illustrated Magazine,* Vol. III (Buffalo, NY: 1876), 55.

86 *"According to Mark Spitz, swimming is perfect":* Willard Spiegelman, "Buoyancy: In Literature, as in Life, the Art of Swimming Isn't Hard to Master," *American Scholar* 77, no. 3 (2008): 105–106, http://www.jstor.org/stable/41221906.

86 *"There can be no comparison between them":* Cited in John H. Ingram's introduction to *Edgar Allen Poe's Complete Poetical Works,* http://www.fullbooks.com/Edgar-Allan-Poe-s-Complete-Poetical-Works1.html.

6. A Frog in Every Tub

90 *In 1832, the* Penny *magazine reprinted:* Again, readers interested in pursuing further the bibliography of swimming are referred to Ralph Thomas, *Swimming with List of Books Published in English, German, French and Other European Languages* . . . (London: S. Low Marston & Co., 1904).

91 *"There is but one well known exception":* Cited in Thomas, *Swimming with List,* 92.

91 *"Swimming is not encouraged":* Cited in Vybarr Cregan-Reid, "Water Defences: 'The Arts of Swimming' in Nineteenth-Century Culture," *Critical Survey* 16, no. 3 (2004): 37.

92 *"Lady Gimcrack: The truth on't is":* Cited in Thomas, *Swimming with List,* 82.

94 *As Christopher Love shows:* Christopher Love, *A Social History of Swimming in England, 1800–1918* (London: Routledge, 2008).

96 *In a 2006 article for the* Journal of American History: Kevin Dawson, "Enslaved Swimmers and Divers in the Atlantic World," *Journal of American History* 92, no. 4 (2006): 1327–1355. doi:10.2307/4485894.

98 *"The Indian, instead of parting his hands":* George Catlin, *North American Indians: Being Letters and Notes on Their Manners* . . . , Vol. 1 (London: Published by the Author at the Egyptian Hall, Piccadilly, 1880), 109–110.

98 *"We were soon surrounded by a dozen ":* Catlin, *North American Indians,* 220–221.

99 *"At a signal, the Indians jumped in to the Bath":* The *Times* (of London), April 22, 1844. Cited in Mr. H. Kenworthy, *A Treatise on the Utility of Swimming* (London: 1846), 17. It should be noted that this is the same "Mr. Kenworthy" who claims to have later beaten the Ojibway "with the greatest of ease."

100 *An 1866 compilation of articles:* London Society: An Illustrated Magazine, Volume X (London: London Society, 1866), 49–53.

100 *Besting upstart foreigners (fn.):* Kenworthy, *A Treatise,* 18.

101 *John Leahy could not have agreed more:* John Leahy, *The Art of Swimming in the Eton Style* (London: Macmillan & Co., 1875), 1.

102 *The book does contain some practical advice*: Leahy, *Art of Swimming,* 4.

102 *He also has some harsh words for older boys:* Leahy, *Art of Swimming,* 5.

103 *To give Leahy a bit of credit:* Leahy, *Art of Swimming,* 52.

103 *Just to add to the general condescending tone:* Leahy, *Art of Swimming,* 82.

103 *American swimmers seem to have been less wedded:* "How to Swim," *New York Times—Illustrated Magazine,* July 23, 1899, 10–11.

104 *"Few persons know how to swim":* "How to Swim," *New York Times—Illustrated Magazine,* July 23, 1899, 10.

7. Diving In for Dollars and Pounds

108 *Back in April 2019*: Cited in Zoe Zaczek, "More Than Bill Gates: Australian Swimmer Cate Campbell's Outrageous Pay Cheque from a Chinese Tournament Is Revealed After Athletes Demanded Better Pay," *Daily Mail* (Australia), April 29, 2019.

109 *One of the earliest accounts of a swimming race:* Christopher Love, *A Social History of Swimming in England, 1800–1918* (London: Routledge, 2008), 37. And Ralph Thomas, *Swimming with List of Books Published in English, German, French*

and Other European Languages . . . (London: S. Low Marston & Co., 1904), 268.

109   London Society *magazine reported on an 1866 race: London Society: An Illustrated Magazine,* 10 (London: 1866): 50.

110   *One other report from that same time:* Love, *A Social History,* 41.

111   *In his 1875 contribution to the swimming bookshelf:* John Leahy, *The Art of Swimming in the Eton Style* (London: Macmillan & Co., 1875), 16.

111   *Captain Stevens offers an early example*: Thomas, *Swimming with List,* 267.

113   *Stevens also seems to have been among the first:* Love, *A Social History,* 37.

113   *"I once accompanied Fred Beckwith":* London Society, 49.

114   *As one enraptured spectator put it:* London Society, 52.

114   *Beckwith, it should be noted, had his imitators (fn.):* "Hints to Swimmers," *New York Times,* April 3, 1880, 3.

115   THE LATE CHALLENGE FROM THE BOY BECKWITH: Love, *A Social History,* 39.

117   *Nineteenth- and early-twentieth-century America:* H. Roy Kaplan, "The Convergence of Work, Sport, and Gambling in America," *Annals of the American Academy of Political and Social Science* 445 (1979): 24–38, http://www.jstor.org /stable/1042952.

118   *But there were countervailing trends, too:* "Background Books: Sports in America," *Wilson Quarterly* 3, no. 3 (1979): 85–87, http://www.jstor.org/stable /40255663.

118   *Baby betting steps, of course:* "Boat Race Scandal," Potomac Boat Club history, https://www.potomacboatclub.org/about/potomac-boat-club-history/.

119   *Almost forgotten among such wonders:* Penny Lee Dean, *A History of the Catalina Channel Swims Since 1927,* 5–18, https://swimcatalina.org/wp-content /uploads/2017/02/catalinachannelhistory-1.pdf. Dr. Dean is herself a world-class distance swimmer. In 1978, she swam the English Channel in 7 hours and 40 minutes, a record that stood for seventeen years. She was inducted into the International Swimming Hall of Fame in 1996.

8. Climb Every Mountain, Swim Every Sea . . .

124   *"Our soldiers in places unknown to them":* Cited in Bill Yenne, *Julius Caesar: Lessons in Leadership from the Great Conqueror* (New York: St. Martin's Press, 2012), 98.

125   *Every endeavor has its acme accomplishment:* Frances Klemperer and Emily Simon Thomas, "Captain Webb's Legacy: The Perils of Swimming the English Channel," *BMJ* 349 (2014), https://www.jstor.org/stable/26519139.

128   *Webb's swim was an astounding achievement:* Vybarr Cregan-Reid, "Water Defences: 'The Arts of Swimming' in Nineteenth-Century Culture," *Critical Survey* 16, no. 3 (2004): 44.

130   *"Capt. Webb started nearly in the middle of the stream": New York Times,* July 25, 1883, 1.

131   *Matthew Webb may have suffered a violent death (fn.):* Cregan-Reid, "Water Defences," 45.

132 *Clarabelle Barrett entered the channel at Dover:* "Miss Barrett Fails to Swim Channel," *New York Times,* August 3, 1926, 1, 3.

132 *Only nineteen years old, Gertrude Ederle:* General biographical details can be found at Richard Severo, "Gertrude Ederle, the First Woman to Swim Across the English Channel, Dies at 98," *New York Times,* December 1, 2003, B7.

133 *"I will swim another fourteen hours anywhere":* T. G. Middleton, "Miss Ederle Happy, Won't Try It Again, Hailed in France," *New York Times,* August 8, 1926, 1.

134 *"Traveling the great circle route":* Paul Gallico, *The Golden People* (Garden City, NY: Doubleday & Company, 1965), 61.

135 *Eventually, though, the crush got to her:* "Gertrude Ederle Freed," *New York Times,* March 23, 1929, 9.

137 *"I had a lifelong fear of the water":* Susan Sheehan and Howard Means, *The Banana Sculptor, the Purple Lady, and the All-Night Swimmer* (New York: Simon & Schuster, 2002), 92.

137 *Still in her early teens:* Details on Cox's swims are available at http://www.lynnecox.com/.

138 *Before her first channel swim in 1972 (fn.):* Lynne Cox, interview with author, May 29, 2019.

139 *"I've spent a lot of time before I take a swim":* Cox, interview with author, May 29, 2019.

140 *"I was able to do swims that no one had ever done before":* Cox, interview with author, May 29, 2019.

9. The Great Swimming Cover-Up

141 *The Dark and Middle Ages put an end to that:* The Oscar Wilde quote is from Oscar Wilde, "A Few Maxims for the Instruction of the Over-Educated," in I. Murray, ed., *Oscar Wilde* (Oxford: Oxford University Press, 1989), 570. Cited in Randall C. Griffin, "Thomas Eakins' Construction of the Male Body, or 'Men Get to Know Each Other Across the Space of Time.'" *Oxford Art Journal* 18, no. 2 (1995): fn. 8, 78.

142 *"It is Ordered Established and Decreed":* Cited in Penelope Byrde, "'That Frightful Unbecoming Dress': Clothes for Spa Bathing at Bath," *Costume* 21, no. 1 (1987): 44–56.

143 *"Though Margate, in summer, is a pleasant":* Thomas Fisher, *The Kentish Traveller's Companion* (Rochester, England: T. Fisher; and Canterbury, England: Simmons & Kirkby; 1776), 118–119.

145 *"Such screaming and splashing about has not been heard":* "The Public Baths," *New York Times,* July 2, 1870, 2.

145 *Then there's John Leahy's 1875 manual:* John Leahy, *The Art of Swimming in the Eton Style* (London: Macmillan & Co., 1875), closing two pages (unnumbered).

146 *As to the bathing dresses the ladies are expected to wear:* Vybarr Cregan-Reid, "Water Defences: 'The Arts of Swimming' in Nineteenth-Century Culture," *Critical Survey* 16, no. 3 (2004): 40.

146 *Men got off easier:* Ralph Thomas, *Swimming with List of Books Published in English, German, French and Other European Languages* . . . (London: S. Low Marston & Co., 1904), 265.

147 *The Jane Austen Society of Australia (fn.):* "The Bathing This Morning Was So Delightful," Jane Austen Society of Australia. Self-published.

147 *"Imagine to yourself a small, snug wooden chamber":* Tobias Smollett, *The Expedition of Humphry Clinker,* ed. Thomas R. Preston and O. M. Brack (Athens: University of Georgia Press, 1990), 213, http://www.jstor.org/stable/j.ctt46n9xh.

148 *"Those bathers that belong to the royal dippers":* Fanny Burney (aka Madame d'Arblay), "Letter from Fanny Burney to Dr. Burney sent from Weymouth July 13, 1789," in *Diary and Letters of Madame d'Arblay,* https://ebooks.adelaide.edu.au/b/burney/fanny/diary-and-letters-of-madame-darblay/complete.html#chapter15.

149 *"There is to be no bathing":* Cited in Bonnie S. Ledbetter, "Sports and Games of the American Revolution," *Journal of Sport History* 6, no. 3 (1979): 35, http://www.jstor.org/stable/43609001.

149 *That's a scene to cheer any naturist:* Thomas, *Swimming with List,* 270.

150 *The all–male, mostly all–East Coast and WASP:* John A. Lucas and Ian Jobling, "Troubled Waters: Fanny Durack's 1919 Swimming Tour of America . . ." *OLYMPKA IV* (1995): 93–112.

151 *"I think it is disgusting that men should be allowed":* Lucas and Jobling, "Troubled Waters," 95.

152 *In a 1995 article for the* Oxford Art Journal: Randall C. Griffin, "Thomas Eakins' Construction of the Male Body, or 'Men Get to Know Each Other Across the Space of Time.'" *Oxford Art Journal* 18, no. 2 (1995): 70–80, http://www.jstor.org/stable/1360554.

152 *Ironically, though, it might have been those overclothed:* Cartriona M. Parratt, "Athletic 'Womanhood': Exploring Sources for Female Sport in Victorian and Edwardian England," *Journal of Sport History* 16, no. 2 (1989): 140–157, http://www.jstor.org/stable/43609444.

153 *In part, this was the popular doctrine of muscular Christianity:* Griffin, "Thomas Eakins' Construction," 73. Also Lucas and Jobling, "Troubled Waters," 100.

153 *On May 30, 1919:* "Women Deputies Sworn In," *New York Times,* May 30, 1919, 7. And "Judge Reprimands Police," *New York Times,* June 26, 1919, 3.

155 *"Believing that the request made by certain entrants":* Penny Lee Dean, *A History of the Catalina Channel Swims Since 1927,* 5.

155 *The photographic record confirms what news accounts tell us:* For the photos mentioned, see https://rarehistoricalphotos.com/women-arrested-bathing-suits-1920s/.

10. An Aussie Wrecking Ball Goes Rogue

158 *Born in Sydney, Australia, in 1886:* John Lucas, "Making a Statement: Annette Kellerman Advances the Worlds of Swimming, Diving, and Entertainment," *Sporting Traditions* 14, no. 2 (May 1998): 25–35.

159 *As dynastic as they were, the Cavills (fn.):* J. G. Williams, "Cavill, Frederick (1839–1927)," *Australian Dictionary of Biography,* Vol. 7 (1979), http://adb.anu.edu.au/biography/cavill-frederick-5536.

162 *Audiences oohed and aahed at the daring feats:* Paul Gallico, *The Golden People* (Garden City, NY: Doubleday & Co., 1965), 56.

163 *At her trial, Kellerman admitted:* "From Bloomer's to Bikini's: How the Sport of Swimming Changed Western Culture in the 20th Century," International Swimming Hall of Fame, 59–60, https://www.ishof.org/assets/history_swimwear.pdf.

164 *In New York she won a popularity contest:* Meyer Berger, "About New York," *New York Times,* October 9, 1953, 29.

164 *"At the time of the worship of the beautiful":* "Modern Women Getting Near the Perfect Figure," *New York Times,* December 4, 1910, section 5, 4.

165 *Kellerman herself couldn't have agreed more:* Annette Kellerman, "The Girl Who Wants to Swim," *Ladies' Home Journal* 32 (1915): 513.

166 *Back home in Peru, Indiana, in the summer of 1912:* Robert Barlow, "Some Unpublished Cole Porter Lyrics," *Yale University Library Gazette* 30, no. 1 (1955): 38, http://www.jstor.org/stable/40857690.

167 *Kellerman seems to have suffered for about six seconds:* Clarice M. Butkus, "Annette Kellerman," Women Film Pioneers Project, https://wfpp.cdrs.columbia.edu /pioneer/ccp-annette-kellerman/.

167 *In his book* Players *(fn.):* Tim Harris, *Players: 250 Men, Women, and Animals Who Created Modern Sport* (New York: Random House, 2009).

168 *"When I die," she told one reporter:* Isabel Johns, "Boston Arrest a Mistake, Says Annette," *Boston Globe,* October 11, 1953, 67.

169 *In her later years, Annette Kellerman:* Lucas, "Making a Statement," 32. Also Berger, "About New York," 29.

169 *For an epitaph, though:* Cited in Butkus, "Annette Kellerman."

11. Nylon, WWII, James Bond, and the G-String

174 *Carl Jantzen and John Zehntbauer would go on to dominate:* For a pictorial and text history of Jantzen, see https://www.jantzen.com/through-the-decades/. Excerpts from the *Jantzen Yarns* newsletter are available at https://en.wikipedia.org /wiki/Jantzen#cite_note-5.

177 *Swimming was hot—as sport, recreation, and mass entertainment:* For more on the Cleveland Aquacade, see "The Rose on the Water," *New York Times,* February 28, 1937, section 11, 2. For more on the World's Fair version of Rose's show, see "Dive Right In! Billy Rose's Sensational Aquacade," New York Public Library, at exhibitions.nypl.org/biblion/worldsfair/gallery/gallery-aquacade.

178 *By then, too, college swimming had a Billy Rose:* I'm indebted to Peter Kennedy for alerting me to the Yale carnivals and the footage of the 1935 installment and for providing a program from his own participation in the late 1950s.

179 *Meanwhile, and interrelated, swimwear was becoming:* For general information on the evolution of swimsuit technology, see http://www.madehow.com/Volume-7 /Swimsuit.html.

180 *Two-piece women's swimsuits were not invented:* *Elle* magazine provides a nice photographic tour through a century of women's swimwear, beginning in 1913, at https://www.elle.com/fashion/g2906/the-history-of-the-bikini-654900/. Wikipedia does likewise with extensive citations at https://en.wikipedia.org

/wiki/Bikini. Also see, from the Metropolitan Museum of Art in New York: https://www.metmuseum.org/toah/hd/biki/hd_biki.htm.

181   *When bikinis first surfaced, news outlets (fn.):* For more on the etymological journey of *bikini,* see Neville Hoad, "World Piece: What the Miss World Pageant Can Teach About Globalization," *Cultural Critique* no. 58 (Autumn 2004): 56–81.

182   *Shock value aside, reception of Réard's creation:* Pope Pius XI, "A Papal Decree Concerning Modesty," January 12, 1930, http://www.olvrc.com/reference /documents/Modesty.Pius.XI.pdf. Also, the Cardinal Vicar of Pope Pius XI, "The Marylike Standards for Modesty in Dress," http://www.salvemariaregina .info/Modesty.html.

182   *Yesteryear's beauty icons didn't all fall in line either:* Isabel Johns, "Boston Arrest a Mistake, Says Annette," *Boston Globe,* October 11, 1953, 67.

183   *In the 1953 film* From Here to Eternity: Samuel Wigley, "The Most Famous Beach Scene in the Movies Turns 60," https://www.bfi.org.uk/news-opinion/news-bfi /features/most-famous-beach-scene-movies-turns-60.

183   *Ex–Disney Mouseketeer Annette Funicello:* Full lyrics of "Itsy Bitsy Teenie Weenie Yellow Polkadot Bikini" are available at https://www.songfacts.com/lyrics /brian-hyland/itsy-bitsy-teeny-weeny-yellow-polka-dot-bikini.

12. Swimming Together, Swimming Alone

188   *The English, as we've seen:* Archibald Sinclair and William Henry, *Swimming* (London: Longman, Green, and Co., 1893), 337–338.

189   *Following the British model of providing sanitary bathing:* "Taking the Plunge: Pools of New York City," New-York Historical Society, http://blog.nyhistory.org /taking-the-plunge/. Includes the *Harper's Weekly* illustration from August 20, 1870.

190   *A 1900 survey found a total of sixty-seven public pools:* Frank R. Shaw "Trends in Bathing Beach and Swimming Pool Sanitation," *Canadian Public Health Journal* 23, no. 4 (1932): 153–158, http://www.jstor.org/stable/41979122.

191   *The numbers defy easy imagination:* "The Best of 1928," *Beach & Pool Magazine,* 1928, 67–83.

193   *If you build it, they will come:* Shaw, "Trends," 156.

194   *The list goes on and on:* For the entire list, see "New Deal Category: Swimming Pools," Living New Deal, https://livingnewdeal.org/?s=swimming+pools.

194   *In New York City alone, in the single summer of 1936:* For a lengthy account of the "miracle" NYC pool boom of 1936, see Marta Gutman, "Race, Place, and Play: Robert Moses and the WPA Swimming Pools in New York City," *Journal of the Society of Architectural Historians* 67, no. 4 (December 2008): 532–561.

196   *Let's start with the country club movement:* James M. Mayo, "The American Country Club: An Evolving Elite Landscape," *Journal of Architectural and Planning Research* 15, no. 1 (1998): 24–44, http://www.jstor.org/stable/43030441.

198   *That thinking was, in fact, wrong on multiple levels:* "Polio and Swimming Pools: Historical Connections," June 28, 2012, https://www.historyofvaccines.org /content/blog/polio-and-swimming-pools-historical-connections.

201 *Cheever's masterful short story, "The Swimmer":* John Cheever, "The Swimmer," *New Yorker,* July 18, 1964, 28–34.

202 *One more word on swimming alone:* Susie Scott, "Reclothing the Emperor: The Swimming Pool as a Negotiated Order," *Symbolic Interaction* 32, no. 2 (2009): 123–145. doi:10.1525/si.2009.32.2.123. And Scott, "How to Look Good (Nearly) Naked: The Performative Regulation of the Swimmer's Body," *Body & Society* 16, no. 2 (2010): 143–168.

13. The Last Taboo

206 *In a number of these cities—Wilmington, Delaware, for example:* For the opening pages of this chapter, I'm generally indebted to Jeff Wiltse, *Contested Waters: A Social History of Swimming Pools in America* (Chapel Hill: University of North Carolina Press, 2007).

207 *Leap forward another decade:* Niraj Chokshi, "Racism at American Pools Isn't New: A Look at a Long History," *New York Times,* August 5, 2018, section SP, 2. The online version is richly illustrated with photographs: https://www.nytimes .com/2018/08/01/sports/black-people-pools-racism.html?searchResultPosition=1.

208 *Give Fred Rogers credit for trying to ease the taboo (fn.):* The online version of Chokshi, "Racism at American Pools," links to the *Mr. Rogers* segment.

209 *One 1935 survey found that swimming:* Wiltse, *Contested Waters.*

209 *As Caleb Smith writes in a 2012 article:* P. Caleb Smith, "Reflections in the Water: Society and Recreational Facilities, a Case Study of Public Swimming Pools in Mississippi," *Southeastern Geographer* 52, no. 1 (2012): 39–54, http://www.jstor .org/stable/26228994.

211 *"Sometimes," she wrote, "I feel like I'm alone":* Simone Manuel, "A Letter to My Younger Self," https://theundefeated.com/features/simone-manuel-no-ceilings-a -letter-to-my-younger-self/.

213 *In an article for the* International Journal: Adrian Bean, Edward C. Jones, and Jordan D. Charles, "The Evolution of Speed in Athletics: Why the Fastest Runners Are Black and Swimmers White," *International Journal of Design & Nature and Ecodynamics* 5, no. 3 (2010): 199–211.

213 *Besides, history argues in the opposite direction:* Kevin Dawson, "Enslaved Swimmers and Divers in the Atlantic World," *Journal of American History* 92, no. 4 (2006): 1327–1355. doi:10.2307/4485894.

216 *Simone Manuel and a few others notwithstanding:* Samuel L. Myers Jr., Ana M. Cuesta, and Yufeng Lai, "Competitive Swimming and Racial Disparities in Drowning," *Review of Black Political Economy* 44 (2017): 77–97. https://doi.org /10.1007/s12114-017-9248-y.

216 *In 2003, an article in the* British Medical Journal: Deborah Lehmann, Mary T. Tennant, Desiree T. Silva, Daniel McAullay, Francis Lannigan, Harvey Coates, and Fiona J. Stanley, "Benefits of Swimming Pools in Two Remote Aboriginal Communities in Western Australia: Intervention Study," *BMJ* 327, no. 7412 (2003): 415–419, http://www.jstor.org/stable/25455325.

218 *The practical effects of this lethal stew:* "Six Teens Drown in Louisiana River,"

Salon (via Associated Press), August 3, 2010, https://www.salon.com/2010/08/03
/us_teens_drown_louisiana/.

219 *My WPA high school:* Jim Dwyer, "Survival Skill Abandoned by Schools," *New York Times,* June 15, 2012, A30.

220 *What to do? In my hometown:* Suzie Holubek, interview with author, April 8, 2019.

221 *"To be a successful swimmer, you have to be disciplined":* John Feinstein, interview with author, May 23, 2019.

14. Growing Pains

223 *People who earned their living on and from the water:* Ralph Thomas, *Swimming with List of Books Published in English, German, French and Other European Languages . . .* (London: S. Low Marston & Co., 1904), 337 and elsewhere.

224 *On September 3, 1878, the* Princess Alice: Alice Evans, "Princess Alice Disaster: The Thames' 650 Forgotten Dead," BBC News, https://www.bbc.com/news/uk-england-london-44800309.

225 *Many of the same factors were in play a quarter century later:* Valerie Wingfield, "The General Slocum Disaster of June 15, 1904," New York Public Library Archives Unit, June 13, 2011, https://www.nypl.org/blog/2011/06/13/great-slocum-disaster-june-15-1904.

225 *The sole female to survive, an eighteen-year-old (fn.):* Thomas, *Swimming with List,* 347.

225 *That questionable honor belongs to a little-remembered moment:* See my website—www.howardmeans.com—for more on the Sultana tragedy.

227 *Sweden's Uppsala Swimming Society:* Elaine K. Howley, "Uppsala Swimming Society," *Swimmer,* September–October 2016, 48.

228 *Competitive swimming, by contrast:* https://marydonahue.org/history-of-swimming-section.

229 *The dolphin kick of butterfly has a more exact father:* Marie Doezema, "The Murky History of the Butterfly Stroke," *New Yorker,* August 11, 2016, https://www.newyorker.com/sports/sporting-scene/the-murky-history-of-the-butterfly-stroke.

236 *By then, too, swimming and FINA had had a brief:* Bruce Wigo, former CEO of International Swimming Hall of Fame, interview with author, April 2019. In 2013, Wigo and ISHOF staged a fortieth reunion for the US and Chinese swimmers and divers who took part in the cultural exchange.

237 *Not only were strokes and aquatic competitions generally evolving:* "The History of Swimming in Japan," based on archival materials at the Henning Library at the International Swimming Hall of Fame, including *Swimming in Japan* (1935). A video demonstration of the Navy SEAL combat sidestroke is available at https://www.sealswcc.com/navy-seal-combat-side-stroke-guide.html.

238 *The 1940 Olympics promised to be:* For more on the human cost of canceling the 1940 Summer Olympics, see Julie Checkoway, *The Three-Year Swim Club : The Untold Story of Maui's Sugar Ditch Kids and Their Quest for Olympic Glory* (New York: Grand Central Publishing, 2015).

15. The Fastest Swimmer Ever

240 *Case in point, maybe:* Footage of the "world's fastest swimmer" Cadillac Challenge is available at https://www.swimmingworldmagazine.com/news/watch-virtual-race-between-tarzan-matt-biondi-buster-crabb-mark-spitz-and-don-schollander/.

241 *In his 1930 book,* Swimming the American Crawl *(fn.):* Johnny Weissmuller, *Swimming the American Crawl* (Boston: Houghton Mifflin, 1930), 45.

243 *Is such handicapping fair:* John Updike, *Rabbit, Run* (New York: Alfred A. Knopf, 1960), 5.

243 *George Breen, who twice set the world record:* George Breen, interview with author, June 2019.

244 *Dave Tanner was a classmate of Spitz:* Dave Tanner, interview with author, April 1, 2019.

244 *And much more attention to diet, too:* Edward Cooper, "Olympic Swimmer Adam Peaty Shares His Exact Workout and Training Tips," *Men's Health,* March 6, 2019, https://www.menshealth.com/uk/fitness/a27625842/adam-peaty-workout-diet/.

247 *"Dressel isn't a body-freak like Phelps":* Todd DeSorbo, interview with author, April 16, 2019.

248 *I asked UVa's Todd DeSorbo:* DeSorbo, interview with author, April 16, 2019.

248 *"The water ran right through the front of it":* Donna de Varona, interview with author, June 2019.

249 *That sounds like a no-brainer:* Rich Burns, interview with author, May 21, 2019.

249 *Not that swimming hasn't had its own steroid problems (fn.):* De Varona, interview with author, June 2019.

250 *Besides, as John Craig pointed out in a 2012 guest editorial:* John Craig, "Guest Editorial," *Swimming World,* April 10, 2012, https://www.swimmingworldmagazine.com/news/a-comparison-of-textile-bests-to-world-records/.

253 *"What's going to happen in another hundred years":* Rowdy Gaines, interview with author, May 28, 2019.

253 *"Mark had a really good feel for the water":* Tanner, interview with author, April 1, 2019.

254 *"He had to re-plan his entire race on the spot":* Peter Kennedy, interview with author, May 25, 2019.

255 *That gets us to one more wrinkle:* Daniel F. Chambliss, "The Mundanity of Excellence: An Ethnographic Report on Stratification and Olympic Swimmers," *Sociological Theory* 7, no. 1 (1989): 70–86. doi:10.2307/202063.

258 *"I retired from competition at seventeen":* De Varona, interview with author, June 2019.

258 *"It was pretty heartbreaking":* Gaines, interview with author, May 28, 2019.

259 *"Our women had been getting beat up in the press":* De Varona, interview with author, June 2019.

259 *"The 200-fly was a battle between Michael Gross":* John Feinstein, interview with author, May 23, 2019.

260 *"For me, the greatest performance I ever saw":* Gaines, interview with author, May 28, 2019.

16. Is Enough Ever Enough?

262 *"In reviewing the freestyle and butterfly stroke":* Mary Holden, "Swimming—the Orthopaedic Manifestations," *GP* (New Zealand), August 5, 1992, 24–25.

263 *In an article for the* British Medical Journal: Leslie Klenerman, "Musculoskeletal Injuries in Child Athletes," *BMJ* 308, no. 6943 (1994): 1556–1559, http://www .jstor.org/stable/29723814. And Jeffrey P. Koplan, David S. Siscovick, and Gary M. Goldbaum, "The Risks of Exercise: A Public Health View of Injuries and Hazards," *Public Health Reports* 100, no. 2 (1985): 189–195, http://www.jstor.org /stable/20056435.

263 *"I had to be pulled from the meet":* Missy Franklin, "It Took Me a Long Time to Say 'I Am Retiring,' but Now I'm Ready," ESPN.com, December 19, 2018, http://www.espn.com/espnw/voices/article/25568406/missy-franklin-explains -why-now-time-retire-competitive-swimming.

264 *"The problem is overstrengthening the pectoralis muscles":* James Hundley, interview with author, March 30, 2019.

266 *"For the first ten years when I got back into swimming":* Rich Burns, interview with author, May 21, 2019.

267 *"When I'm in the groove during practice":* Lillian Croghan, interview with author, April 2019.

267 *The "almost four-times" theory (fn.):* Howard Wainer, "How Much More Efficiently Can Humans Run Than Swim?" *Chance* 6 (1993): 17–21. In an email communication, Wainer qualified his findings as follows: "I would guess that the advantage of running over swimming has shrunk in the twenty-five years since we did that because swimming times have improved much more than running."

267 *Mammals that can swim really, really fast:* Frank E. Fish, "Transitions from Drag-Based to Lift-Based Propulsion in Mammalian Swimming," *American Zoologist* 36, no. 6 (1996): 628–641.

272 *Take pool depth. For years, top competition pools:* Howard Berkes (interviewer), "China's Olympic Swimming Pool: Redefining Fast," NPR, August 10, 2008, https:// www.npr.org/templates/transcript/transcript.php?storyId=93478073.

272 *Or take lane markers:* Nadim-Pierre Rizk, "Wave-Dampening Properties of Swimming Lines" (master's thesis, Division of Water Resources Engineering, Department of Building and Environmental Technology, Lund University, 2013), 1–75, http://lup.lub.lu.se/student-papers/record/4406822.

274 *US Patent No. 7475435 B2, issued to four Oregon swim goggle inventors:* Patent No. 7,475,435 B2 was assigned to Nike, Inc., on January 13, 2009. Listed inventors are Dylan S. Van Atta, Alan W. Reichow, Karl M. Citek, and Robert M. Bruce.

276 *Current projects under way at the highly regarded:* For a current look at research under way at the Counsilman Center for the Science of Swimming, see http://www .indiana.edu/~ccss/research/index.php.

277 *Jeff Farrell arrived in Detroit in the summer of 1960:* Jeff Farrell, interview with author, April 29, 2019.

279 *Brad Snyder got a gold medal, too:* Brad Snyder, interview with author, May 2019.

280 *Mary (Brundage) DeLashmutt never won an Olympic medal:* Mary Brundage DeLashmutt, multiple interviews with author, January–June 2019.

281 *"Swimming pools today have developed into machines":* Eva Cantwell, "Swimming and the Senses," *Building Material* 8 (Spring 2002): 48–51. doi:10.2307/29791455.

282 *"I live in Dublin, between the city and the sea":* Eva Cantwell, interview with author, April 17, 2019.

INDEX

Aachen (aka Aix-la-Chapelle), 51–52
acromion, 264
Adams, John Quincy, 118, 149
Aegeus, 24
African Americans
    access to pools, 205–216, *206*
        (photo), 214, 219
    drowning rate, 214
    as lifeguards, 216
    near-total absence of in
        competitions, 212–213
    racial discrimination at pools, 208
    racial diversity in Philadelphia pools,
        207
    swimming pools for blacks in
        Washington, DC, 206
    in top tiers of American swimmers,
        216
Africans, swimming prowess of, 96,
    213–214
Agesilaus, 31
Akhenaten, 20
Albee, Edward, 166
Albee, Edward (playright), *166*
    (footnote)
Alcyone, 25
Alexander, James Edward, 97
Alexander the Great, 63
Allan, Sir William, *85* (footnote)
Almásy, László, 2, 3, 7
Alvey, Henry, 65
Amateur Athletic Union of the United
    States (AAU), 150

Amateur Swimming Association, 117,
    153
American Scholar, on Mark Spitz, 86
American Zoologist, on changing from
    terrestrial movement to lift-
    based propulsion, 268
Andreescu, Bianca, 107
Andress, Ursula, 184, *184* (photo and
    footnote)
Anthropologie, on swimming figures at
    Wadi Sura, 10
Aphrodite, 25
Aqua Augusta aqueduct, 41
Aquae Sulis, 45–47, *46* (footnote), *47*
    (photo)
aqueducts, 40, 41
aridity index, 9
Aristotle, 28
Armbruster, David, 229
L'Art de Nager (Thévenot), 74
The Art of Swimming//De Arte Natandi
    (Digby)
    influence on Spenser's *Faerie Queen,*
        70–71
    reintroduction of swimming to
        Renaissance world, 64–65, *67*
        (footnote)
    seriousness of swimming, 67
    woodcuts in, 68–70, *69* (illustrations)
The Art of Swimming in the Eton Style
    (Leahy), 101, 145–146
The Art of Swimming (Webb), 129
Ashurnasirpal II, king of Assyrians, 22

Athenian naval attack on Syracuse, 29–30
atrial fibrillation (AFib), 266
Aung, Winn, *235* (footnote)
Australian aboriginal communities use of
        swimming pools, 216
Australian crawl. *See* strokes
Avalon, Frankie, 183
Avramidis, Stathis, 24

backstroke. *See* strokes
backswimming, 110
Balandin, Dmitriy, 269
Bannister, Roger, 128–129
Barbot, Jean, 96
Bardot, Brigitte, 182
Barillet, Louis, 188
Barrett, Clarabelle, 121–122, 131–132
Bath, England, 47
"The Bath House" woodcut by Durer, 143
bath houses, 142–143
bathing machines, 143–144, *144*
        (illustration), 147–148
baths, Roman, 28, 39–40, 42–48, 52
Bauerle, Jack, 263
Beale, Benjamin, 143
Beckwith, Agnes, 116
Beckwith, Charles, 116
Beckwith, Frederick, 113–115
Beckwith, Willy, 114, 115
Bejan, Adrian, 213
Beowulf, 54
Berger, Meyer, 169
Berkoff, David, 271
Bernard, Alain, 260
Bernardi, Oronzio de', 90
Bernardi Method of Upright Swimming
        (Bernardi), 90
Bernardini, Micheline, 181, *181*
        (footnote)
Bibbers, Marquis, *114* (footnote)
biceps tendon, 262
bikini, 180–181, *181* (footnote)
Billy Rose's Aquacade, 177
Biondi, Matt, 240, 242–243
Black Death, *49* (footnote)
blacks. *See* African Americans
Blondin, Charles, *129* (footnote)
Boerhaave, Herman, 80

The Boke Named the Governour (Elyot), 61
Bolt, Usain, *213* (footnote), 247
bone conduction of sound, 24, 79
Booker Prize, 8
Booth, John Wilkes, 227
Boston Globe, on Kellerman's opinion of
        bikinis, 182
Boston Post, on Annette Kellerman, 169
Boulton, Richard, 39, 53–54
breaststroke. *See* strokes
Breen, George, 243
Brennan, E. C., 150
Briffault, Eugene, 147
British Manly Exercises (Walker), 90, *90*
        (footnote)
British Medical Journal
        challenges of swimming the English
            Channel, 125
        musculoskeletal injuries in child
            athletes, 263
        sociological effects of learning to
            swim, 216
Brown, Stanley, 217
Buddhist caves, Kizil, 50
Burney, Frances, 148
Burns, Rich, 249, 265–266
Bursk, Daniel S., 189
Bursk, John Howard, 171
Busby, Berkeley, 168
Bush, Douglas, 60
butterfly. *See* strokes
butterflying breaststroke. *See* strokes
Byrd, William II, 97
Byron, Lord. *See* Gordon, George

Cadillac Challenge, 240–243
Caesar Augustus, 41
Campbell, Cate, 108
Cantwell, Eva, 281–283
Captain Stevens, 111–113, *112*
        (illustration)
Captain Stevens' System of Swimming
        (Stevens), 111
Carter, Jimmy, 258
Caserta Vecchia bath, 52–53
Caskey, Jill, 52
Catalina Island marathon. *See* Wrigley
        Ocean Marathon

Catlin, George, 97
Cato the Elder, 28
Cave of the Beasts, 9
Cave of the Swimmers
    aridity of, 9–10
    discovery of, 2 (footnote), 3, 4
        (photo)
    The English Patient (film and book),
        7–8
    location of, 2, 4 (photo), 8 (photo)
    as possible depiction of afterlife hell,
        10
    tourism, 8–9
Cavill, Frederick, 105
Cavill, Sydney, 229
Ceyx, 25
Ceyx, 25 (footnote)
Chadwick, Florence, 138 (footnote), 158
Chambliss, Daniel, 255–257
Chaplin, Charlie, 168
Charlemagne, 51–52
Charles, Jordan, 213
Cheever, John, 187, 201, 201 (footnote)
Chinese Book of Odes, 21
Christy, Nicholas, 154
Cielo, César, 248
Clark, Steve, 239, 240 (footnote)
Clark, William (aka Ebenezer
        Cullchickweed), 91
Classical Journal
    on ancient Greek and Roman
        swimming style, 36
    examples of swimming in battle, 29
Classical Outlook, on businesses in
        Pompeii, 42
Cavill, Arthur "Tums," 159, 159
        (footnote)
Cavill, Charles, 159, 159 (footnote)
Cavill, Ernest, 158–159
Cavill, Frederick, 158, 159 (footnote)
Cavill, Percy, 159
Cavill, Sydney, 159
Cavill's Floating Baths, 158
Clayton, Dorothea, 7
Clayton, Patrick, 3
Clayton-East-Clayton, Robert, 3, 7
Cloelia, 33–34, 62 (footnote)
Cocles, Horatius, 62

Colymbetes (Wynman), 64
Commentary on the Alexandrian War
        (Julius Caesar or Hirtius), 34
Compleat History of Magick, Sorcery, and
        Witchcraft (Boulton), 54
The Compleat Swimmer (Percey), 73–74
Cone, Edward A., 228
Connaught, Duke and Duchess of, 153,
        160 (footnote)
Contested Waters (Wiltse), 206
Coolidge, Calvin, 134
Cooper, Edward, 245
Correia, Maritza, 210
corsets, 164–165
Corson, Amelia Gade, 121, 134–135
        (footnote)
Couch, H. N., 29
Coulson, Douglas, 10
Counsilman, James "Doc," 244,
        253–254
Counsilman Center for the Science of
        Swimming, Indiana University,
        1, 276
country club movement, 196–198
Courtney, Charles, 118
Cox, Lynne
    body density of, 138
    distance swimming feats, 18,
        137–138
    English Channel swims, 137
    protection by dolphins, 138–139, 138
        (footnote)
Crabbe, Buster, 178, 240, 241
Craig, John, 250
creationism vs. evolution, 13–14
Creator Varicocha, 24
Cregan-Reid, Vybarr, 83, 84 (footnote),
        146
Crippen, Fran, 283 (footnote)
Critical Survey (journal), on Lord Byron's
        family history, 83
Croghan, Lilli, 261, 267
Crozet, Virginia, 11, 287
Cullchickweed, Ebenezer (aka William
        Clark), 91
Curtis, Robert I., 42, 44 (footnote)
Cyana, 29, 29 (footnote)
Czerski, Helen, 16

Daily Mail, on hourly rate of Cate Campbell's win at a FINA event, 108

Daily Mirror, on payment per mile to Annette Kellerman for English Channel swim, 160

Daily Telegraph, on Matthew Webb, 123, 128

Daley, Richard, 208

Dalton, Davis, 103

Dand, Hilda, 233

Daniels, Charlie, 234, *234* (photo)

Darst, Joseph, 208

Darwin, Charles, 94

Davies, Georgia, 212

Dawson, Kevin, 96, 213–214

De Arte Natandi//The Art of Swimming (Digby), 65, *67* (footnote), 73

De Re Militari (Vegetius), 33

de Varona, Donna, 248, *249* (footnote), 257–259

Deakin, Roger, *201* (footnote)

del Toro, Guillermo, 25

DeLashmutt, Mary Brundage, 280–281

DeMont, Rick, 258

The Descent of Woman (Morgan), 18

DeSorbo, Todd, 247, 248

Deucalion, 24

Devendeville, Charles, 231

Dickey, William, 233

Digby, Everard, 64–67, 73, 74, 92

Dine Hussein, Kamal el, 3

dippers, 144, 148

A Dissertation Concerning the Use of Sea Water in Diseases of the Glands, Etc, (Russell), 80

diving

    diving girl as logo for Portland Knitting Company swimsuits, 176, *176* (footnote)

    free, *16* (footnote)

    reflex, mammalian, 16, *16* (footnote)

    technique, *172* (photo), *173* (footnote)

Doezema, Marie, 229

dolphin kick, 229–230, 252, 271

Don Juan (Byron), 85

Dr. No (film), 184

Dressel, Caeleb, 243, 246–247, 252

Dreyer, Jim, 136–137, *139* (footnote)

drowning/near drowning

    African-Americans, 214

    Alaska natives, 215

    American Indians, 215

    black teenagers in Red River, 218

    incidents in Greek literature, 24–25

    rates in United Kingdom, 219

    teenage boys, *215* (footnote)

    William Percey's experience, 73–74

Drury, Henry, 84

Dudgeon, R. E., 95–96

DuPont's invention of elastic synthetic fibers, 179

Durack, Fanny, 153

Durer, Albrecht, 143

Dwyer, Jim, 219

Eakins, Thomas, 152

Early British Swimming (Orme), *50* (footnote), 64

Eckenhead, Lieutenant, 84

Ederle, Gertrude

    in *Billy Rose's Aquacade,* 178

    Brighton Beach, NY, 500-meter performance, 132

    English Channel swim, 132–133

    Olympic gold medal, 132

    opinions on swimming attire, 155–156

    as swimming instructor, 135–136

    use of crawl stroke, 133, *135* (photo)

    Wrigley's offers for swim to Catalina Island, 120

Edgley, Ross, 137

Edward II, King of England, 52, *52* (footnote)

Egyptians, swimming ability of, 27

Einhard, 51–52

Elyot, Sir Thomas, 57, 61–63

English Channel

    Allied assault on Normandy in 1944, 124

    Calais-Dover crossing, 124

    challenges for swimmers, 125–127

Julius Caesar's conquest of Britannia, 123–124
most successful day for crossing, *136* (footnote)
English Channel swimmers
Barrett, Clarabelle, 121–122, 131–132
Chadwick, Florence, 158
Corson, Amelia Gade, 121, *134–135* (footnote)
Cox, Lynne, 137
Ederle, Gertrude, 132–133
Grimsey, Trent, 125
Thomas, Sarah, *140* (footnote)
Tirabocchi, Enrique, 133
Webb, Matthew, 125
The English Patient (book by Ondaatje), 7–8
The English Patient (film), 7
Environmental Health Perspectives, on chlorinated indoor pools, *198* (footnote)
Epic of Gilgamesh, 23
Etruscan tombs, depiction of swimming on, 21
Evans, Janet, 158, 244, 245, 254
evolution and swimming, 18
The Expedition of Humphry Clinker (Smollet), 147

Faerie Queene (Spenser), 70–71
Fairbanks, Douglas, 168
Farrell, Jeff, 277–279, *278* (photo)
Feinstein, John, 221, 249, 257, *257* (footnote), 259
FINA (Fédération internationale natation/International Swimming Federation), 108, 236, *236* (footnote), 271
Firth, Barbara, 168
fish, anatomical resemblances to humans, 14
Fish, Frank E., 268
flood myths, 23–24
flotation devices, ancient, 20–23
Flying Gull, 99
Folklore journal, on swimming as heroic activity, 54

Fosbury, Dick, *271* (footnote)
Fox, Stanley, 189
Franklin, Benjamin
on causes of colds, 78
educational academies, 77
hand and foot paddles, 76
idea for a swimming school, 76
illustration of, *83*
on importance of learning to swim, 79–80
interests, 76
life-saving tip for mariners, 78
observation about sound traveling under water, 78–79
on overcoming fear of water, 79
quote, 73
swimming in Thames River, 76, 148, 214
teaching friends to swim, 75
theory of "imbibing" and "discharging" pores, 77–78
youthful attraction to sea and swimming, 75
Franklin, Missy, shoulder injury, 263–264
freestyle. *See* strokes
frogs, 91
From Here to Eternity (film), 183
Funicello, Annette, 183

Gaines, Rowdy, 239, 240, 252, 258–259, *258* (footnote), 260
Galaup, Jean-François de, Count de Lapérouse, 97, *97* (footnote)
Gallico, Paul, 133–134, 162
Gaughran, Jim, 236
General Slocum's eruption in flames, 225
George III, King of England, 148
Gernreich, Rudi, *181* (footnote)
GI Bill (Servicemen's Readjustment Act of 1944), 198
Gibson, Althea, 211
Gibson, Emily, 168
Gilbert, Cass, 190
Gilf Kebir plateau, Egypt, 2, *2* (footnote), 7
Giraffe Rock, 3
Glorifying the American Girl (film), 177
Go-Yozei, Emperor of Japan, 219

Gobero, Niger, 5
goggles, 274–276, *275* (illustration)
The Golden People (Gallico), 133–134
Goldman, Anna, 154
golf, 196–197
Gordon, George, Lord Byron
    club foot, 84, *84* (footnote)
    family drownings, 83
    illustration of, *83*
    as most famous swimmer of
        Romantic movement, 86
    mother's fortune, 83–84, *84*
        (footnote)
    swimming race in Venice, 85–86, *85*
        (footnote)
    swimming the Hellespont, 84, *85*
        (illustration)
Gorée Island, 96
"Grace of Wapping," 53
Greeks, 27, 31, 187
Griffin, Randall, 152
Griswold, Larry, 178
Gross, Michael, 241, 259
gunite, 199
Gurr, Harry, 100, 102, 110
Guy, James, 212

Hadrian, 47
Halcyonidae, 25 (footnote)
Halfdanar saga, 54
Halmay, Zoltán, 234
Hammurabi, 19–20
Handy, Jamison "Jam," 228–229, *229*
    (footnote)
Hanlan, Ned, 118
Hardy, Sir Alister, on advantages of living
    near water, 17
Harper's Weekly, swimming bath
    illustration in, 189
Harris, Tim, 167
Harrison, John, 267
Haspel, Judith, *230* (footnote)
Hassanein, Ahmed, 2, *3* (footnote)
Hawkins, Sally, 25
Hays Code, 180
Heim, Jacques, 180
Hellespont, 28, 36, 58, 84, 85, 136,
    283

Helsten, Eric, 228
Henry Frederick, Prince of Wales, 71
Henry VIII, King of England, 63
Henry VIII (play by Shakespeare), 52
Herculaneum, 41
Hero, 28, *36* (illustration)
Hero and Leander myth, 58–59
Herodotus, 29, 49–50
Hillary, Edmund, 128
Hirtius, 34
Hitler, Adolf, 195
Holden, Mary, 262
Holm, Eleanor, 177–178, *177* (footnote)
Holman, Frederick, 233, 269, *270*
    (photo)
Holubek, Suzie, 220–221
Homer, 24
Hoover, Herbert, 193
Horace, 28
Hornell, James, 22
horses, swimming, 63
Houser, Margaret, 122
How to Swim (Dalton), 103
hull speed, 268
humans
    ape-human differentiations, 18
    aquatic heritage of, 14–16
    involuntary responses, 15–16
    relationship with water, 26
Humboldt, Alexander von, *104*
    (illustration)
Hundley, James, 264
Hunter, Bruce, 279
Hyland, Brian, 183
Hynes, Michael, 127

Icarus, 24
*International Journal of Circumpolar
    Health,* on winter swimming,
    15
*International Journal of Design & Nature
    and Ecodynamics,* on center of
    mass and sports performance,
    213
International Swimming Hall of Fame,
    230
Isacescu, Walpurga von, 161
Isles, Alan, 20

James, LeBron, 108
Jantzen
    diving girl as logo for, 176, *176*
        (footnote)
    "The Suit That Changed Bathing to
        Swimming," 176
    wartime products of, 180
Jantzen, Carl, 174
Japanese competitive swimming skills,
    237–238
jellyfish, 127, *127* (footnote)
Jesus, 25
Jiang Qing, 236
Johnson, J. B., 115, *115* (footnote)
Jones, Cullen, 218
Jones, Edward, 213
Jones, James, 183
Jorgensen, Peter A., 54
Journal of American History, on swimming
        prowess of Africans, 96
*Journal of the Royal Anthropological
        Institute of Great Britain and
        Ireland,* on historical use of
        flotation devices by soldiers, 22
*Journal of the Society of Architectural
        Historians,* on bathing in
        Middle Ages, 52
Joyner, Florence "Flo-Jo" Griffith, 211
Julius Caesar, 22, 34–35
Julius Caesar (play by Shakespeare), 35

Kafka, Franz, 93
Kahanamoku, Duke, 177, 241, 254, *255*
        (photo)
Kaplan, H. Roy, 118
Kearns, Daniel, on sanitation issues in
        Philadelphia pools, 206
Keith, B. F., 166
Kellerman, Annette
    in aquatic entertainment business,
        159–162
    arrest for indecent exposure, 162–163
    born with weak and deformed legs,
        158
    as branding genius, 168
    competition at Ladies' Amateur
        Swimming Association, 161
    Danube River race, 161

in *A Daughter of the Gods* (film), 167,
        167 (footnote)
    diving exhibitions, 161
    on greatest moments of career, 169
    international performances of, 164
    in *Neptune's Daughter* (film), 167
    New York Hippodrome
        performances, 161–162
    one-piece bathing suit, 160, 162
    opinion of bikini bathing suit, 182
    payment per mile by *Daily Mirror* to
        swim English Channel, 160
    as perfectly proportioned woman,
        162 (photo), 165
    performance for King and Queen of
        England, 160, *160* (footnote)
    Seine River race, 161
    swimsuit line inauguration, 163–164,
        163 (photo)
    on swimwear, 157
    Thames River swim, 159–160
    underwater ballet at London
        Hippodrome, 161
    on women's physical suitability for
        swimming, 165–166
    world records, 159
Kennedy, Peter, 254
The Kentish Traveller's Companion, on
        bathing machines, 143
Kerr, Deborah, 183
Khan, Kublai, 188
Kiernan, Barney, 234
King's Bath in Bath, England, 52
Kiphuth, Bob, 178, 277
Kissinger, Henry, 236
Klein, Hans-Joachim, *242* (footnote)
Klemperer, Frances, 125–126
Klenerman, Leslie, 263
Komjádi, Béla, 232

La France, on number of nudists at Île du
        Levant, 182
Ladies Home Journal, on suitability of
        women for swimming, 165–166
Lamour, Dorothy, 180
Lancaster, Burt, 183, 202
Lancaster, Pennsylvania, swimming
        instruction in, 220

Lancelot (de Troyes), 51
Lane, Frederick, 159, 231
lane markers on water surface,
    272–273
lane markings on pool bottom, 272
Law, Ralph "Sonny," 265, 280
Leahy, John
    ad for Ladies' Swimming and
        Bathing Saloon, 145–146
    boasting of accomplishments,
        101–102
    caution about swimming instructors,
        111
    quote, 89
    view of women learning to swim,
        103
Leander, 28, *36* (illustration)
Lecomte, Benoît, *139* (footnote)
Ledbetter, Bonnie, 148
Ledecky, Katie, 108, 242, 245, 254
Letters on Egypt (Claude-Étienne Savary),
    27
Lewis, Fred, 279
Lezak, Jason, 260
Lhasa, Tibet, 51
lifeboat men, swimming instruction for,
    224
The Liffey Swim (painting by Yeats), 283
Lissberger, Walter, *135* (footnote)
Livy, 33
logs, sawing through underwater, 30, *30*
    (footnote)
logs as flotation devices, 22–23
London Society magazine
    on Frederick Beckwith, 113–114
    as indication of state of swimming in
        mid-1800s, 100, 107
London *Times,* on swimming race in
    1844, 99–100, *100* (footnote)
lorica hamate, 34
lotteries in America, 118
Love, Christopher, 94, 116–117
"The Love Elegies" (Sextus Propertius),
    36
Lucas, John, 163
Lusitanians' use of inflated bladders,
    22

Magellan, Ferdinand, 97
mailman, aquatic Peruvian, *104*
    (illustration)
Maine, Tom, 267, *267* (footnote)
Manchester United football first-team
    average annual salary, 108–109
Mandan tribe smallpox epidemic, 99
Manu, 24
Manuel, Simone, 205, 210, *211* (photo)
Mao Zedong, *210* (footnote)
Marees, Pieter de, 96
Margate, Kent, England, 143
Marlowe, Christopher "Kit," 57–60, *60*
    (footnote)
Mason, Theodorus Bailey Myers, 224
Masse, Tyler, 252
Matsya, 24
Mature, Victor, *168* (footnote)
McKay, Jim, 258
McSweeney, Marie, 265
Meagher, Mary T., 254, 256–257
Means, Howard
    Amateur Athletic Union club
        member, 285
    Bethesda YMCA, 290
    Christine Lake, New Hampshire,
        291, *291* (photo)
    co-captain of high school and
        university teams, 286
    community pool manager, 287
    competitor's wardrobe malfunction,
        287
    English teacher and coach at St.
        Albans School in Washington,
        DC, 288
    family, 288, *288* (photo)
    girlfriend's bathing suit
        modification, 287
    lifeguard, 286
    regret at not swimming in London's
        Serpentine, 290
    in rooftop pool in Denver, 290
    at Susquehanna River source, 289
    swimming three lengths underwater
        in community pool in Virginia,
        290
    YMCA team, 285

medley relay, 235
Men's Health magazine, on Adam Peaty's
    diet, 244–245
Merrick, George, 192
Merryman, Alfred Thomas, 224
Messi, Lionel, 108
Metamorphosis (Ovid), 36
Metropolitan Swimming Association, 110
Middleton, Christopher, 66
Million Dollar Mermaid (film), *168*
    (footnote)
Minghella, Anthony, 7
Mitchell, Samuel, 154
Moab, *21* (footnote)
Mogao Caves, China, 50
Morales, Pablo, 259
Morgan, Edmund S., 76
Morgan, Elaine, 18
Morris, William, 166
moviegoing and swimming comparison,
    209
Mulcaster, Richard, 61
Musaeus, 57–58
Myers, Henry, 229

Nagasawa, Jiro, 230
Narcissus, 25
National Basketball Association players'
    median annual salary, 108
National Geographic Society, 5
National Swimming Pool Foundation,
    202
Neave, Oliver, 78, 79
Neptune's Daughter (film), 167
Nero, 29
New South Wales Ladies Swimming
    Association, 150
New York City, swimming instruction,
    219–220, *220* (footnote)
New York City Department of Parks
    poster for "Learn to Swim
    Campaign," 207, *207* (footnote)
New York Daily News campaign to fund
    White House indoor pool, 194
New York Times
    on appointment of women as Special
    Deputy Sheriffs 154, 154

interview with Gertrude Ederle, 133
on "Ladies Day" at bathing house,
    145
on Webb's attempt to swim the
    Niagara River, 130
Niagara Falls, *129* (footnote)
1927 national events, 119
Nitsch, Herbert, *16* (footnote)
North American Indians (Catlin), 98
Norwood, Frances, 28
nudity, effect of, 31–32
nudity while swimming
    Bath Corporation official notice, 142
    by Benjamin Franklin, 148
    enforced modesty, 142
    by George Washington's soldiers,
        148–149
    by Henry David Thoreau, 151
    in "I Sing the Body Electric," poem
        by Whitman, 152
    by John Quincy Adams, 149
    by male swimmers, 146–148
    The Swimming Hole (painting by
        Thomas Eakins), 152
Nyad, Diana, *140* (footnote)

O'Connor, Siobhan-Marie, 212
Odyssey (Homer), 24
Oleksiak, Penny, 210, *211* (photo)
Olympic Games
    changes in swimming events,
        235–236
    pullout of entire US team by
        President Carter in 1980, 258
Olympic Games swimming events
    1896 Athens, 231
    1936 Berlin, 230, *230* (footnote),
        238
    1908 London, 233–234, *234*
        (photos), *270* (footnote)
    1932 Los Angeles, 238
    1956 Melbourne, 250, *250* (footnote)
    1976 Montreal, 269
    1984 Montreal, 259–260
    1980 Moscow, 258, *258* (footnote)
    1900 Paris, 231
    2016 Rio de Janeiro, 269

Olympic Games swimming events
        (*continued*)
    1960 Rome, 278, 279
    1904 St. Louis, 231–232
    1912 Stockholm, 235
    2000 Sydney, 236, 240
    1940 Tokyo cancelled, 238
Ondaatje, Michael, as author of *The
        English Patient*, 1, 7
One Million Years B.C. (film), 184
open-water events, *163* (photo), 235, *235*,
        282, 283, *283* (footnote)
Orme, Nicholas, *50* (footnote), 64, 65, 74
*Orr's Book of Swimming as practiced and
        taught in civilized nations* (J. W.
        Orr and N. Orr), 149
Oxford Art Journal, on Eakin's painting,
        152

Paralympics, London 2012, 280
Paris dans l'eau (Briffault), 147
Parrington, Francis, 233
Pausanias, 29
Peacock, Leslie, 167
Peacock, Stephanie, 244
Pearn, John, 20
Peaty, Adam, 212, 244, 269, *270* (photo)
pectoralis muscles, 264
Peerless Pool, London, 89
Peloponnesian War, 30
Penny magazine, on Franklin's egg
        exercise, 90
Percey, William, 73–74
Persia, naked girls swimming, 51
Persians' inability to swim, 30
Phelps, Michael, 108, 213, 242, 246
Philadelphia swimming pools, racial
        diversity in, 207
Phoenix (classical journal), 28
Pickford, Mary, 168
Pidgeon, Walter, *168* (footnote)
Pinckard, George, 213
pirates, capital punishment for, 53
Plato, quote from, 27
*Players: 250 Men, Women, and Animals
        Who Created Modern Sport*
        (Harris), *167* (footnote)
Pliny the Younger, 40

the plunge, 232–233, *233* (footnote)
Plutarch, 31
Poe, Edgar Allan, 86
polio scares, 197
Pollet, Lucien, 188
Pompeii
    ancient location, *44* (footnote)
    Aqua Augusta aqueduct, 41
    baths, 42–45
    as commercial center, 42
    description of, 42
    the Forum, 42
    Great Palaestra, 44, *45* (photo)
    laconium, 43
    pools, 43
    water features in, 41
pools
    African Americans' access to,
        205–216
    Ambassador Hotel, 190–191
    amenities in, 196
    attempted desegregation of St. Louis
        pools in 1949, 207–208
    backyard pools, 199, *200* (photo)
    as barometer of economic health, 201
    Brockwell Lido, London, 195, *200*
        (photo)
    Brown University, second collegiate
        pool at, 190
    Casino Pool at Las Olas Casino, Fort
        Lauderdale, Florida, 192, *192*
        (footnote)
    chlorinated water in, 198, *198*
        (footnote)
    as communal exercise in self-
        governance, 203
    community swimming pools in
        suburbs, 199
    competition pool depth, 272
    Derby Baths, Blackpool, England,
        195
    diseases in, 190
    Earls Court Exhibition Center,
        London, 195
    effect of country club movement,
        196–198
    Fleishhacker Pool, San Francisco,
        191, *191* (footnote), *200* (photo)

floating pools along Hudson and East Rivers, 190

floating pools in Thames River, 188

Great Bath at Mohenjo-daro, Pakistan, 187

infrastructure introduction by Swedes and English, 188

Lake Norconian Club, Riverside, California, 192

Lakeside Pool, Salem, Virginia, 192

lane markers on water surface, 272–273

lane markings on pool bottom, 272

large-sized, 191, 196

muddy-water ditch at Harrow School, 188

Musée La Piscine, Roubaix, France, 188

New York state legislature bill mandating free bathhouses, 189

Piscine Molitor, France, 188, *201* (footnote)

polio scares, 197

Price Run Pool, Wilmington, Delaware, 192

Raven Hall Baths, Coney Island, 191

resistance pools, *200* (photo), 201

Stadtbad Mitte, Berlin, *200* (photo)

Stadtbad Neukölln, Berlin, 195

surveys of, 190, 202

Taiye Pond in Imperial City, China, 188

Teachers College, New York City, 190

University of Pennsylvania, first collegiate pool at, 190

Venetian Pool, Coral Gables, Florida, 192

White House indoor pool, 194

Woolworth Building, New York, 190

Young Men's Christian Association (YMCA), 189

Pope Pius' Decree on Modesty, 182

Popov, Alexander, 241

Porsinna, 33–34

Porter, Cole, 166

Portland Knitting Company, 174–175

Portsmouth Ladies Swimming Club, 153

Potomac River, 149, *149* (footnote)

Powell, Asafa, 247

Pride & Prejudice (TV program), *147* (footnote)

Princess Alice's collision with coal boat, 224, *225* (footnote)

prisoners, stripping of, 31, *31* (footnote)

Ptolemy, 34–35

Public Health Reports, on shoulder injuries of competitive swimmers, 263

Pyrrha, 24

racial violence

Biloxi Beach "wade-in," 208

"dive-in" in St. Augustine, Florida, 208

Fairgrounds Park pool, St. Louis, Missouri, 208

Rademacher, Erich, 229

Ramey, Nancy, *255* (footnote)

Réard, Louis, 180–181

Red Sea, parting of, 23

Reed, Patrick, 107

Renaissance Quarterly, 60 (footnote), 61, 70

"A Report to an Academy" (Kafka), *93* (footnote)

Riggin, Aileen, 157

Rizk, Nadim-Pierre, 272–273

Robinson, Marilyn, 218

Robinson, William, 233

rock art sites, 9

Rockefeller, John D., *276* (footnote)

Roger Bannister Memorial Sub-4-Minute-Mile Club, 136

Rogers, Fred, *208* (footnote)

role in evolution, 18

Romans

appreciation of military value of swimming, 33, 47

as builders of municipal baths, 28, 188

construction of Great Bath, 45–47, *46* (footnote), *47* (photo)

glorification of water, 39–47

Romans (*continued*)
    interest in humanities and the arts, 32
    practical qualities of, 33
    water system, 48
Roosevelt, Franklin, 193–194
Rose, Billy, 177
Rose, Murray, 241, 254, *254* (footnote)
Ross, Norman, 120, 121, *121* (footnote)
Royall, Anne Newport, 149
Ruck, Taylor, 252
Rudolph, Wilma, 211
Rush, Dr. Benjamin, 78
Russell, Richard
    characteristics of seawater, 81
    interest in medicinal properties of
        seawater, 80
    popularity of dissertation, 81
    portrait of, *83*
    praise for seawater quality near
        Brighton, 82
    as saltwater cure promoter, 143
Rutilius Claudius Manatianus, 37

Sahara
    effect of northward shift of
        monsoons, 5
    regreening and desertification, 6
    skeletal evidence of aquatic life in,
        4–5
Saigeman, Laura, 116
Sailor's Magazine, on importance of
    learning to swim, 224
Salamis, Battle of, 30
Salamis, Straits of, 28
Salk, Jonas, 197
Sanders, H. A.., 36, 37
Santa Catalina marathon, 136
Sargent, Dudley A., 164–165
Savery, Claude-Étienne, 27
Schoemmell, Charlotte Moore, 154, 155
Schoenfield, Al, 236
Schollander, Don, 240, 242, 269
Scott, Alexander, 85
Scott, Rose, 150
Scott, Susie, 203, *203* (footnote)
sculling race on Potomac River, 118–119
Scyllis, 28–29, *29* (footnote)
seahorses, 91

Seebohm, Emily, 252
Seneca, 43
Serpentine, 102, 115, *115* (photo), 290
Sertorius, 62
Shadwell, Thomas, 92
Shakespeare, William, 35–36
The Shape of Water (del Toro), 25
"She Was a Fair Young Mermaid"
    (Porter), 166–167
Shields, Tom, 271
sidestroke. *See* strokes
Sieben, John, 260
Silk Road, China, 50
skateboarding in abandoned pools, 201,
    201 (footnote)
skin drag, 273
smallpox epidemic among Mandan tribe,
    99
Smith, Caleb, 209–210
Smollet, Tobias, 147
Snyder, Brad, 279
Snyder, Tom, 286–287
A Social History of Swimming in England
    (Love), 94, 116
Society of Directors of Physical
    Education, 193
Southern Geographer, on mixed races in
    pools, 209
Spartan army *vs.* Athenians on
    Sphacteria, 29
Spenser, Edmund, 70–71
"Spenser, Everard Digby, and the
    Renaissance Art of Swimming"
    (West), 70–71
Spiegelman, Willard, 86
Spitz, Mark, 240, 242–243, 244, 247,
    248, 251, 253
Spock, Benjamin, 132
spoons, swimmer-girl, 20
"Sports and Games of the American
    Revolution" (Ledbetter),
    148–149
Sports Illustrated, first swimsuit cover,
    184–185
St. Louis auditorium's conversion to pool,
    191–192
Stager, Martha, 122
Stanton, Edwin, 227

Steedman, Charles, 91
steroids, *249* (footnote)
Stevens, Captain, 111–113
Stewart, LaDairus, 218
Stewart, Latevin, 218
Stewart, Literelle, 218
strokes
    backstroke, 101, 104, 107, 110, 231,
        262, *267* (footnote)
    breaststroke, 93–94, *93* (illustration),
        96, 101, 104, 229–231, 233,
        261, 269
    butterfly, 159, *230* (footnote), *231*
        (footnote), 261–262, 264, 273
    butterflying breaststroke, 229–230
    crawl, 96, 101, 105, 133, *135* (photo),
        157, 264
    freestyle, *96* (footnote), 150, *151*
        (photo)
    sidestroke, 100, 104, 228, 245
Sullivan, Henry, 120, 122
Sullivan, James, 168
Sullivan, James Edward, 150
Sultana, explosion of boilers in, 226
supraspinatus tendon, 262
Svoboda, Jiri, 10
The Swimmer (film), 202
swimmer-girl spoons, 20
"The Swimmer" (short story by Cheever),
    201
swimming
    African American competitors, near-
        total absence of, 212–213
    in America, *117* (footnote)
    ancient representations of, 2
    Armenians, 27
    Assyrian warriors, 21–22, *21*(photo)
    bathing machines, 143–145, *144*
        (illustration), 147–148
    benefits of, 193, 216
    betting on swim races, 109–110, 117
    Biblical references, 20–21
    body types of champions, *270*
        (photos)
    bone conduction of sound, 24, *79*
        (footnote)
    Cambridge and Oxford students
        banned from, 64, 147

    competitive, 221–222, 228 (*See also*
        training)
    depictions of, 50–51
    diving, *16* (footnote), *172* (photo),
        173 (footnote)
    drag-based, 268
    endurance feats, 131
    as entertainment, 113–114, 116,
        177–179
    gender and, 139
    Golden Age of Swimming, 141
    heroes, 33–34
    illiteracy rates, 215
    indomitable spirit examples,
        277–281
    instruction, importance of, 219–221,
        223–228
    long-course (footnote), *139*
    marathon, 136–140
    meanings of, 1
    as military art, 28–30, 62–63, 79
    monetary-prize events, 107–122
    open-water racing (*See* open-water
        events)
    perfect physique for, 245–247, *246*
        (footnote)
    as racial issue, 209
    records, 268–269
    short-course (footnote), *139*
    speed, 272–276
    style, of Romans and Greeks, 35–37
    superlative performance components,
        256
    synchronized, 235–236
    in U. S. public schools, 217
    See also Olympic Games; pools;
        strokes; swimwear; training
swimming, decline of in Europe
    collapse of infrastructure, 48
    drowning as punishment for pirates,
        53
    fate of the damned, *50* (footnote)
    fear of demons, 49–50
    as guilt of witchcraft, 53
    during Middle Ages, 48–55, 61–62
    prudery, 49
    rising insularity, 48–49
    sanitation, 49

swimming, revival of in Western world
  bathing and recreational
    opportunities, 94
  Baths and Washing-Houses Act
    (1846), 94–95
  Cregan-Reid, Vybarr, 83
  De Arte Natandi (Digby), 73
  Don Juan (Byron), 85
  Drury, Henry, 84
  Eckenhead, Lieutenant, 84
  improved sanitation, 94
  Poe, Edgar Allan, 86
  public baths in London, 95
  Scott, Alexander, 85
  Spiegelman, Willard, 86
  Spitz, Mark, 86
  swimming professors' promotion of,
    111
  See also Franklin, Benjamin; Gordon,
    George, Lord Byron; Russell,
    Richard
"Swimming and Survival: Two Lessons
    from History" (Isles and Pearn),
    20
"Swimming and the Senses" (Cantwell),
    281–282
swimming styles
  Easter Island inhabitants, 97
  Hawaiians, 103, *103* (footnote)
  Mandan tribe, 97–98
  Micronesian Islanders, 97
  Native Americans, 97
  Ojibway, 99
Swimming the American Crawl
    (Weissmuller), *241* (footnote)
Swimming World, on tech suits, 250
swimwear
  bikini, 182
  G-string, 183
  history of, 174–175
  influences on, 174
  for men, 146–150, *147* (footnote),
    155, 172–173, *172* (photos), 185
  modesty panels, 248
  in mosaic in Villa Romana del
    Casale, Sicily, 174
  tech suits, 248–250, *249*
    (footnote)

Victorian era, 174
  for women, 144, *144* (photo), 146,
    151 (photo), 154–155, 248
Switek, Brian, comparison of humans and
    fish, 13, 14
Syracuse, 29–30

Tacitus, 40
Tane, 23
Tangaroa, 23
Tanner, Dave, 244, 253
TARA (Trust for African Rock Art), 10
Tassili n'Ajjer, 5
T'en'er'e Desert, 5
Thévenot, Melchisédech, 74, 146
Thomas, Emily Simon, 125–126
Thomas, Ralph, 92, 112
Thomas, Sarah, *140* (footnote)
Thompson, Jenny, 254
Thoreau, Henry David, 151
Thorpe, Ian, *246* (footnote)
Thorpe, Miss, sole female survivor of
    Princess Alice sinking, *225* (footnote)
Thucydides, 31
Tinirau, 14
Tirabocchi, Enrique, 133
Tobacco, 99
Tomb of the Diver, 31, *32* (photo)
training
  anatomical effects of intense
    training, 261–265
  competition pools, 251
  cupping, 246, *246* (footnote)
  diet, 244, *245* (footnote)
  FINA regulations, 251–252, *252*
    (footnote)
  goggles, 250–251
  gym work, 245
  removal of body hair, 150, 250
  swimsuits, 247–250
Troyes, Chrétien de, 51
Trudgen, John Arthur, 105
Twelve Maxims (Cullchickweed), 91

Una Pachakuti, 24
Updike, John, 243
Uppsala Swimming Society, 227–228,
    227 (footnote)

upright swimming, 90–91
US Navy SEALS' use of combat
    sidestroke, 237
USA Swimming Foundation, 108, 215,
    218

Val, Laura, *132* (footnote)
Valéry, Paul, 152
Valley of the Pictures, 3, *4* (photo)
Varuna, 23
Vegetius, 33
Vesuvius, Mount, 40–41
Viking children, learning to swim, 51
Virgil, 28
The Virtuoso (Shadwell), 92
Vishnu, 24
Voutis, 25

Wadi Sura, Egypt, 2, 3, 8–9
Wainer, Howard, *267* (footnote)
Walker, Donald, 90
Walker, Jimmy, 134
"walking catfish," 14
Wall Street Journal, on underwater sound
    waves, 16
Wallace, Alfred Russell, 94
Wanamaker, John, 189
Warner, DeKendrix, 218
Warner, JaMarcus, 218
Warner, JaTavious, 218
Warner, Takeitha, 218
Washington, George, 148–149
Washington, Martha, 144–145
water
    bone conduction of sound in, 24, *79*
        (footnote)
    demon forces in, 23
    fear of, 23, 51
    involuntary responses of humans
        when submerged in, 15–16
    pirates' punishment, 53
    quality of in Thames and
        Serpentine, 102, *102* (footnote)
    removal of sin, 31
    resistance compared to air, 267, *267*
        (footnote)
    role of in human existence, 14
    Romans' enjoyment of, 39–47

temperature, 282, *283* (footnote)
    walking on, 25
    as witchcraft punishment, 39,
        53–54
water polo, 231–232, *232* (footnote), *234*
    (photo)
Waterlog (Deakin), 201 (footnote)
Watermarks (documentary), *230*
    (footnote)
Webb, Matthew
    attempt to save cruise-ship
        passenger, 127
    as author of *The Art of Swimming*,
        129
    choice of date for crossing English
        Channel, 126, *136* (footnote)
    death in Niagara River, 129–131
    paid appearances, 129
    photo, *128*
Weissmuller, Johnny, 132, 177–178, *177*
    (footnote), 240, *241* (footnote),
    243, 247–248, 251, 254, *255*
    (photo)
Welch, Raquel, 184
West, Michael, *60* (footnote), 61, 70
Weymouth, England, 82
Whitaker, William, 65
White House indoor pool, 194
Whitman, Walt, 152
Wigo, Bruce, 248
Wilde, Oscar, quote, 141
Wilkie, David, 269, *270* (photo)
Williams, Esther, 168, *168* (footnote)
Williams, Henry Llewellyn, *131*
    (footnote)
Wilson, Volney, 229–230
Wilson, Woodrow, 191
Wiltse, Jeff, 206
Windle, Bob, *242* (footnote)
witchcraft, 39, 53–54
Womanhood magazine, on mixed sea
    bathing, 152–153
women
    arrests for violation of clothing
        ordinance, 154–156
    butterfly stroke introduced at
        Olympics, *231* (footnote)
    English Channel swimmers, 136

women (*continued*)
    mention in *The Compleat Swimmer*
      of teaching women to swim,
      73–74
    opinions on mixed sea bathing, 152
    pools for, 95
    restrictions on competitive
      swimming, 150–151
    swimming-meet culture, 153
    teaching women to swim, 27, 74,
      103
    witchcraft, 39, 53–54
    See also English Channel swimmers;
      swimwear
Wordsworth, William, 94
Works Progress Administration (WPA)
    construction of pools for
      masses, 194–195
Wrigley, William Jr., 119, *119* (footnote),
    121 (photo)

Wrigley Ocean Marathon, 119–122, *119*
    (footnote), *121* (photo), 154
Wylie, Mina, 153
Wyndham, William, 76
Wynman, Nicholas, 63–64, 74, 92

Xerxes, 28

Yale Water Carnival 1935, 178
Yeats, Jack B., 283
YMCA (Young Men's Christian
    Association), 189, 217–218
Yorzyk, William, 230–231
Yoshiyuki Tsuruta, 238
Young, George, 120–122

Zehntbauer, John, 174–175
Zeus, 24
Zhou Enlai, 236
Zorn, Zac, 243